about the author

Gwyn Topham has been travel editor of *Guardian Unlimited* for five years and recently worked as a news reporter for *The Sydney Morning Herald*. He wrote this book while in Sydney, watching the ships go by. He now lives in London.

Overboard

The stories cruise lines don't want told

Gwyn Topham

RANDOM HOUSE AUSTRALIA

Random House Australia Pty Ltd
20 Alfred Street, Milsons Point, NSW 2061
www.randomhouse.com.au

Sydney New York Toronto
London Auckland Johannesburg

First published by Random House Australia 2006

Copyright © Gwyn Topham 2006

All rights reserved. No part of this publication may be reproduced, stored in a retrieval system, or transmitted in any form or by any means, electronic, mechanical, photocopying, recording or otherwise, without the prior written permission of the publisher.

National Library of Australia
Cataloguing-in-Publication Entry

   Topham, Gwyn.
   Overboard: the stories cruise lines don't want told.

   ISBN 978 1 74166 515 4.
   ISBN 1 74166 515 9.
   1. Ocean travel – Guidebooks. 2. Travellers – Attitudes. I. Title.

   910.45

Original cover image: US Library of Congress, Prints & Photographs Division, LC-USZC4-766. Colour poster by Adolphe Edouard Mouron.
Cover design and illustration by saso content & design pty ltd
Typeset in Bembo 12/16.2pt by Midland Typesetters, Australia
Printed and bound by Griffin Press, South Australia

10 9 8 7 6 5 4 3 2 1

Contents

Preface		vii
Introduction		xi
1	The Missing	1
2	Now Wash Your Hands . . .	18
3	Oil on Troubled Waters	32
4	The Unwelcome Guests	41
5	Down Under and Dirty	52
6	*Fairstar* the Fuckship	61
7	Dianne Brimble	68
8	The Enemy Within	73
9	The Smugglers	86
10	Under Attack	90
11	Bigger and Better?	104
12	. . . Or Cheap and Cheerful?	110
13	Going Overboard	114
14	Not a Bang but a Whimper	119
15	What Lies Beneath	124
16	Love Boats	134
17	Mutiny!	144
18	Short and Sweet	152
19	Storms in the Ports	156
20	That's Entertainment	160
21	Captive State	167
22	Disaster! From Rogue Waves to Infernos	171
23	Diving In	182
24	The New Dawn	188
Acknowledgements		195
Notes		197
Index		223

Preface

I WAS WORKING as a reporter at *The Sydney Morning Herald* when the coroner's inquest into the death of Dianne Brimble opened. The details of the case would become gruesomely familiar to the Australian public: a woman drugged and left naked to die, a story all the more shocking for having taken place in the apparently safe and carefree setting of a cruise ship.

Before then, I had shared the general perception that cruises were a gentle activity best left to the rich and retired. Occasionally, watching enormous, stately liners sail out of Sydney Harbour, I would idly wonder what life was like on board. I had joined one small-scale cruise in my previous role as travel editor of *Guardian Unlimited*, a job that had also taken me to Caribbean ports where towering ships would suddenly, surreally, flood the streets with visitors. There was nothing to suggest that these passengers would enjoy anything more than a serene holiday. But I was not aware of other aspects of modern cruising life.

At the same time that the Australian inquest was starting to unravel a tale of debauchery on the *Pacific Sky*, astonishing scenes were occurring on the other side of the world. In Washington, the relatives of victims of cruise ship robbery, assault and death were calling for help from the United States government. A congressman was warning that holiday-makers' safety was in question. Passengers had vanished into thin air. What was going on?

From the offices of the *Herald*, you can see P&O's ships when they dock to disembark and pick up new passengers at King Street Wharf. My editor sent me down to investigate. The passengers and crew members at the port that day were not what I had imagined: many were young and set to party. Mothers waved their daughters off with misgivings. Just a few hours into its voyage, the boat would pull back to Sydney to hand over some of its passengers to the police.

When that first piece was published on the front page of the *Herald*, readers and acquaintances started telling me about their experiences, good and bad. In the United States, where cruising is one of the most popular types of holidays, passengers were swapping tales online. Newspaper archives and websites pointed to an astonishing litany of accidents, death and crime on board.

So I embarked on this book, speaking to people who had seen the best and worst of cruises. Crew members from ships around the world, entertainers, security officers, maritime experts, onboard lecturers, agents and representatives of cruise lines in Australia, the US and the UK – as well as whistleblowers, lawyers, environmentalists and activists who had seen the damage cruise ships could do. Passengers who loved to cruise, and would do so again and again – and some whose journeys had encompassed such astonishing events as mutiny, pirate attack and even watching their ship sink below the waves. And a group of committed individuals who were carrying the hardest burden of all: taking on the cruise lines and searching for answers after their relatives had simply disappeared while on a holiday at sea.

Cruising turned out be an industry of some controversy: paying pitiful wages to workers, polluting the seas, run by powerful companies and largely self-regulating. From 'fun ships' in Australia to the poshest of traditional lines in Britain, from Sydney to Southampton, many could be traced back to the same head offices in Miami – and gave out the same broad, standard answers to questions about their ships. Fuller responses proved harder to obtain. As a travel editor, commissioning stories of blissful holidays on the ocean waves, I had been wined and dined at the Ritz by cruise lines. Now, they stopped returning my emails.

In the months that I spent writing this book, more amazing ships were unveiled, more campaigns were fought, and more unexplained disappearances hit the headlines. Some major stories were still unfolding, not least the pursuit of justice for victims and new legislation to protect passengers.

And around the world, of course, millions of holiday-makers enjoyed trouble-free cruises. But you can read about the good times in any travel supplement. For now, here are the stories that cruise lines don't want told.

Introduction

IT WOULD BE, wrote Mark Twain, a picnic on a gigantic scale. A pleasure cruise was to set off from New York to Europe and the Holy Land in 1867: 'a brave conception; it was the offspring of a most ingenious brain'.

> They were to sail for months over the breezy Atlantic and the sunny Mediterranean; they were to scamper about the decks by day, filling the ship with shouts and laughter – or read novels and poetry in the shade of the smokestacks, or watch for the jelly-fish and the nautilus over the side, and the shark, the whale, and other strange monsters of the deep; and at night they were to dance in the open air, on the upper deck, in the midst of a ballroom that stretched from horizon to horizon, and was domed by the bending heavens and lighted by no meaner lamps than the stars and the magnificent moon – dance, and promenade, and smoke, and sing, and make love . . .

Fast forward nearly 140 years, to Australia, and a P&O security officer discussing life on board:

> If the nightclub is jumping, they'll keep the bar open to 5 am. By then, they're making love all over the place, not actually in front of

people, but in public places ... What can we do? Ask them politely to get dressed and do it in their cabins, not on the deck.

Some picnic. How did cruising, once synonymous with adventure, refinement and romance, come to this?

Not long after the great shipping lines, Cunard and Peninsular and Oriental, started taking transatlantic passengers in the 1840s, some decided to go along purely for the ride. By the late nineteenth century, the pleasure principle was taking off, particularly in Germany and in the USA, where the Caribbean was already being touted as a maritime playground, although P&O claims to have 'invented' modern cruising in 1904, when its first cruise voyage with shore excursions took place.

Most sea journeys were made through necessity rather than choice, but on ocean liners the opulence, dining and entertainment on the first-class decks were antecedents of cruise life to come.

Between the wars, cruise holidays grew in popularity – particularly in America, where offshore boat trips were an opportunity to enjoy a drink during Prohibition. In Australia, where the first white settlers had arrived by boat from across the world little more than a century before, the first cruise set sail just before Christmas 1932, on P&O's liner the *Strathaird*.

Widespread, affordable air travel signalled the beginning of the end for passenger liners as an essential mode of transport. During the 1960s, many ships, military transporters as well as civilian vessels, were becoming redundant.

But the lure of the ships would remain. Ocean liners created new schedules; navy ships were refitted for holiday-makers.

A cruise was a byword for luxury, the millionaire lifestyle. A holiday that offered the freedom of the seas, the chance to wake in exotic ports; officers in starched white uniforms would stroll the decks and liveried waiters would attend to passengers' every need; the formal elegance of tuxedos and cocktail dresses, champagne and fine food was the order of the day.

For most ordinary people, going on a cruise was in the realm of lottery-winning fantasies, or at the very least, the trip of a lifetime, frequently something to look forward to only in retirement.

While the stereotypes persist, and many ships do still cater for the retired and the super-rich, the reality is that more and more people of all ages and incomes are clambering aboard. The dream has become just another holiday possibility.

In 1970, just half a million people went on a cruise ship. By 2006, that number had swollen to 15 million annually.

Business is booming. Around 300 liners are currently plying the world's seas, with more on their way, ever larger and more sophisticated, towering over buildings in the ports they visit. America is at the forefront, with ships flooding out of Miami and Florida to the Caribbean and beyond. In Britain, more ships cruised into Southampton in one day in 2006 – including the famous *Queen Mary 2* and *Queen Elizabeth 2* – than any day in the last forty years. Australia is seeing bigger ships in Sydney and Brisbane than ever before.

Cruising has become an enormous, multi-billion dollar industry, concentrated in the hands of a few key players. Twelve major cruise lines, Cunard and P&O among them, are ultimately owned by the same giant entity, Carnival Corporation and plc, with space for 139,000 passengers on their ships – twice as many as nearest rival, Royal Caribbean.

In this global industry some differences emerge: broadly, British cruises are more traditional, formal, and occasionally educational, often including guest speakers on board. Americans boast the biggest ships, as well as the most exclusive; gaudy megaliners are a uniquely American dream. And the US lines' Caribbean cruises have often promised a somewhat wilder experience since Carnival unveiled its 'fun ship' philosophy in the 1970s, though perhaps not quite as wild as some in Australia, where cruise ships have long taken on all ages –

and all comers. Australian vessels' longer Asian voyages are relatively sedate affairs, but on many of the ships that head for the sunshine of the Pacific islands and Fiji, a partying crowd is on board, and almost anything goes.

Who could resist? As the Cruise Lines International Association states in its guide for first-time cruisers:

> It sounds too good to be true! Is it? The one complaint we hear time and again is that cruises end far too soon! Beyond that, it's hard to find any negatives . . .

And yet there have been moments when the idyllic veneer breaks down; when suddenly another side of the cruise experience is revealed. There is only the thickness of a ship's hull, the height of a railing, the conscience of a crew member, the vigilance of a fellow passenger, a few drops of a drugged drink between a safe, fabulous holiday and potential tragedy.

Out on the seas where the captain's word is law, ships fly the flags of barely functioning states, and thousands of people are all cooped up together from one distant port to another. Some cruises still have the aura of a genteel, upmarket retirement home; others, primed for nightlife, sail on alcohol and sex. Women out for good times; drunken packs of men on the prowl; people gambling for high sums in the casino. Crew members hired from the poorest countries in the world, stuck below deck for most of the year, serve customers who may have paid more for a night than they earn in a month.

It's little wonder that crime, disease and death have stalked the decks of cruise ships.

The cruise industry says that negatives – the downside to cruising – may be hard to find. But as the cases of the missing, sick, robbed and overworked people detailed in the following chapters show, they certainly exist. Lock the cabin door.

1

The Missing

IN 1975, DURING the last days of the Vietnam War, Hue Pham and his wife Hue Tran spent two weeks on a boat in the Pacific. With two thousand others they floated at sea on a cramped container ship, surviving on no food and very little water, before a US Navy plane found them and led them to the safe haven of Subic Bay. Mr Pham, a high-ranking officer in the South Vietnamese Army, and his family were fleeing their native country for their lives.

Thirty years later, having built a successful new life in the US, the couple, now aged 71 and 67, celebrated with a Caribbean cruise on the *Carnival Destiny*. This was a boat journey that they would not survive. They were reported missing off the coast of Mexico. The US Coast Guard mounted a search. No trace of their bodies was ever found. Their fate remains unknown.

☆☆☆

One day in 1999, Gregory Miller, an Australian man travelling on the *Norwegian Star* cruise liner, woke up facing a hangover and a puzzle. His partner of ten years, Mark Anthony Mazey, was no longer beside him in the cabin. The night – and much of the day before – had seen them consume a large amount of alcohol, cruising around the South

Pacific islands of Vanuatu. Mr Miller had retired to bed comparatively early, at 1 am, while his partner kept drinking. There were reports of an altercation, taunts from another passenger who called Mr Mazey a 'poofter'. A crew member escorted Mr Mazey away from the bar and back to his cabin at 3 am.

In the morning there was no sign of him. Mr Miller searched the ship for several hours while it was docked in Port Vila, then raised the alarm. It was too late. Mr Mazey was never found. Detectives told a coroner's inquest that they believed he may have jumped to his death in a fit of drunken depression.

☆☆☆

Late in 2004, on the last night of a nine-day cruise to the Mexican Riviera, heading back up the west coast of the USA, Annette Mizener was reported missing.

The thirty-seven-year-old from Wisconsin had won the cruise on the *Carnival Pride* in a competition, and took her parents and daughter on holiday with her.

On that final day, she had joined her daughter on a snorkelling treasure hunt; in the evening, the two of them went on stage for the karaoke, singing Britney Spears's '. . . Baby One More Time'. Less than an hour before her disappearance was registered, she was seen in the ship's casino talking to crew members and an elderly, tuxedo-wearing passenger. Her parents had arranged to meet her at the bingo – something Ms Mizener had already won twice and was eager to play again. But she never made it.

Her parents, Wally and Heidi Knerler, were immediately concerned when they did not see her at the bingo on time; more so when an announcement came over the tannoy that her purse had been found, and would she like to collect it. They rushed to find cruise staff. The damaged purse, missing a few beads, had been discovered near a railing on the lower deck.

The ship was searched, but there was no more sign of Ms Mizener; eventually the *Carnival Pride* turned around and trawled the seas for a woman overboard. The US Coast Guard led a search over more than 800 square kilometres of water well into the next day, but without success.

The FBI investigated but no explanation was ever forthcoming. A CCTV camera nearby had been obscured – covered up by a map of the ship. A judge declared Ms Mizener officially dead, but the family – who rule out suicide and suspect foul play – still have no answers.

☆☆☆

These are just a few of a string of unexplained disappearances and deaths on cruises that have occurred in recent years. Between 2003 and 2005 alone, twenty-four passengers and four crew members disappeared from cruise ships worldwide, and 178 passengers reported being sexually assaulted. These figures are those supplied by the cruise industry itself. An FBI director said that the true number of crimes on board could be much higher.

Disappearances reported by the International Council of Cruise Lines included twelve that they believed to be suicide, and one accident; five other people were 'recovered or found'. That left at least ten more people in two years 'missing for unknown reasons' – vanished into the deep blue sea, never to be discovered.

What detective could hope to piece together a murder case without even a corpse? The chances of ever finding a passenger dumped out of a ship into the ocean are slim indeed – even assuming that the victim was alive when he or she went overboard. And on a cruise ship, there is no detective on hand to seal off cabins, to keep all passengers and crew on board, to examine potential crime scenes.

For relatives of victims, the deaths leave a terrible, insoluble puzzle. The son of Hue Pham and Hue Tran, Son Michael Pham, said his parents had no reason to take their own lives. They were, in fact, excitedly planning to visit their native Vietnam for the first time since they had fled the country, looking forward to meeting relatives again after thirty years away. 'Two American citizens with no personal or financial problems, no serious health problems, living the happiest time of their lives, both vanished without a trace or witness,' he said. The seven-night cruise was a Mother's Day gift, and their daughter and granddaughter were on board with them.

Relatives of victims have complained that they or their loved ones were not sufficiently protected by the crew on board cruise liners – to the point where they persuaded US politicians to hold a congressional hearing. The Subcommittee on National Security, Emerging Threats and International Relations, no less, was convened – to hear of the perils that were facing civilians on their dream holidays.

Congressman Christopher Shays' opening statement to the hearings had an arresting impact:

> Ocean travel puts passengers and crew in a distant, isolated environment and subjects them to unique risks and vulnerabilities. Like small cities, cruise ships experience crimes – from petty to profoundly tragic. But city dwellers know the risks of urban life, and no one falls off a city never to be heard from again. Cruise passengers can be blinded to the very real perils of the sea by ship operators unwilling to interrupt the party for security warnings.

He warned that there was:

> ...a growing manifest of unexplained disappearances, unsolved crimes and brazen acts of lawlessness on the high seas. According to industry experts, a wide range of criminal activities, including drug smuggling, sexual assaults, piracy and terrorism, threaten the security of maritime travel and trade.

Mr Pham was one of those who appeared in Washington, urging Congress to impose federal regulations on the industry. He told them that four hours had elapsed between the crew on the *Carnival Destiny* being notified of his parents' disappearance and the coastguard being called – and that hours more passed before any search was under way.

Other witnesses told of cases of alleged sexual assault and robbery, being drugged, finding their possessions stolen. A common theme to their complaints was that the cruise lines with whom they travelled had not done enough to help them. Some witnesses claimed that the cruise lines obstructed efforts to find either truth or justice.

The committee also heard about the case of Lynsey O'Brien, a fifteen-year-old from Dublin who fell overboard while on a Costa cruise. Her parents had booked a week-long cruise down the coast of Mexico on the *Costa Magica*, reuniting with old friends and family. It should have been a trip to brush everyday cares aside. As her father, Paul, said in a TV interview on *Primetime* on the US television network, ABC, as far as he was concerned it was 'totally, totally safe'.

After dinner on the third night of the cruise, some of the older children in the O'Brien party left the others. When Lynsey didn't come back to meet them on time, her parents sent her older sister off to find her.

Lynsey was in one of the ship's bars, drinking cocktails. It was nearly midnight. The cruise charge card she carried showed that she was a minor; somehow, though, she had managed to sign for the alcohol. The bartender later said she had shown him fake ID; he had mixed up a vodka-laden Sex on the Beach cocktail and at least nine other drinks on her account.

Lynsey's parents were furious when they discovered their daughter almost too drunk to walk, and called a senior crew member to complain. Kelly took her younger sister back to her cabin. Her father Paul fetched her a glass of water; she'd be tending a sore head in the morning, he imagined. She wasn't allowed to drink, holiday or otherwise; there would be stiff words in the morning. But for now, he would just tuck his daughter safely into bed. 'I leaned over, I kissed her goodnight. I said, "I love you, pet, I'll talk to you tomorrow."' That was the last time he would see her.

A minute later, the panicked screams of the O'Briens' twelve-year-old daughter rang out. Lynsey, staggering out to the balcony, sick, had leaned over the edge, vomiting. And from her seventh-floor cabin, 140 feet or just over 40 metres above the sea, she had plunged overboard.

Mr O'Brien started to charge all over the ship, desperately seeking help, banging on walls, screaming, frantic with shock.

No help would arrive soon enough. On the boat, just one floor above the O'Brien family, were a couple well placed to witness the rescue effort. Kurt and Sharon Byrd were both veteran police officers with the Cincinnati Police Department. They rushed to the balcony on hearing the screams. Scouring the waves, they saw nothing. Sharon kept her eyes fixed on the churning waters, while her husband dashed to the phone to raise the emergency alarm. Something was very wrong; they needed to get someone up here, fast.

When at work in Cincinnati, Mr Byrd was the commander of an underwater search and rescue unit. He questioned what was going on – was the boat not going to slow down and turn? When the first life ring was thrown in the water, he called again. He told ABC *Primetime* 'I said unless this girl's an Olympic swimmer, she's not going to make it anywhere to these life rings. You're searching in the wrong area.'

But as the Mexican coastguards who were eventually enlisted in the search said, even the impact of landing on water from such a height could have been enough to kill someone.

The rescue effort was to no avail. Lynsey's body, like those of other passengers before her, has never been found.

For the family the response was not enough. 'Not one lifeboat was dropped down – nothing,' Mr O'Brien told an ABC journalist. 'There was no rescue effort whatsoever put in place. As far as I'm concerned, the ship has no procedure whatsoever for a person overboard. There's no procedure. Nothing.' A family friend, Brian Mulvaney, told the congressional hearings: 'What makes this utterly unbearable is that the cruise ships believe they have no accountability for their actions ... Paul O'Brien sought help from the FBI and was told that there is nothing they can do because Lynsey was not a US citizen.'

In an internal report, the cruise firm, Costa Cruises, claimed that Lynsey could not have fallen overboard by accident. The bartender, who was fired, said she had shown him ID that claimed she was older; she was clearly used to having a drink, he said. In his view, the teenager had been angry and committed suicide.

Costa Cruises said it had retrained crew in alcohol service and strengthened its policies against serving minors after Lynsey O'Brien's death. The cruise line pointed out that it has no legal obligation to enforce a minimum drinking age when in international waters, even though it has a company policy to make sure children are not served alcohol.

Her death was, the company said, due to 'underage drinking'.

Her father does not disagree on that point. 'If Lynsey had never been served alcohol on board the cruise ship, my daughter would still be alive.'

Back in his native Ireland, Mr O'Brien launched a campaign for justice and cruise ship safety, approaching leading politicians, apparently with some success – the Irish foreign affairs minister Dermot Ahern was moved, after another death through fire on the *Costa Magica*'s sister ship, to say he was 'concerned about safety at sea and particularly on cruise ships'. Mr O'Brien then took his campaign to the US, where he appeared on various TV shows to raise awareness of the events on the *Costa Magica*. He was eventually hospitalised with exhaustion, missing a scheduled appearance on *The Oprah Winfrey Show*.

Where the ultimate blame for Lynsey O'Brien's death lies may still be fought out in the courts. In June 2006, Mr O'Brien filed a suit for $50 million in compensation, having rejected an out-of-court settlement for $50,000, pledging to give any monies to charities.

O'Brien's lawyer, Brett Rivkind, had much experience in taking on the cruise industry. When he was hired by O'Brien, Rivkind was also representing a family in a case that was reported to Congress and that had, more than any before, brought the issue of missing passengers to public attention: the disappearance of a young, handsome, wealthy honeymooner, George Allen Smith IV.

Smith, a twenty-six-year-old from Connecticut, USA, was cruising in the Mediterranean with his new wife, Jennifer Hagel Smith. After a lavish wedding in Rhode Island, the couple flew to Europe, and in Barcelona boarded Royal Caribbean's *Brilliance of the Seas*, a large resort ship that caters for the younger and more active end of the market.

The Smiths' married life would last barely ten days.

On 5 July 2005, a week into their honeymoon cruise, Smith was discovered to be missing. A large bloodstain on a metal overhang 22 feet (6 metres) beneath his cabin was the first sign that would point to a terrible conclusion. Smith had gone overboard and was now presumed dead.

The night before had, witness accounts agreed, been a riotous one for the Smiths. After a day sightseeing on the Greek island of Mykonos, George, a large, athletic man who regularly pressed weights, and his similarly sporty wife spent much of the evening in the bar and gambling in the casino. They were drinking with new friends and acquaintances from the cruise: Josh Askin, a young man travelling with his parents, and three Russian-American men. Mr and Mrs Smith had both been drinking heavily. Some witnesses report the bride being flirtatious with other men in front of her new husband.

She herself later said:

> I remember being at the casino, I remember being around George. I remember very vaguely leaving the casino area to go to this revolving bar and then I remember nothing. We must have been drinking heavily. I don't remember anything.

At some point, Mrs Hagel Smith left the bar; according to some reports, after a drunken row, kicking her husband in the groin before storming out — an account of her actions that she denied. Mr Smith, already extremely drunk, continued to socialise with the other four men. Someone produced a bottle of absinthe, an extremely potent spirit, and the group started doing shots.

When the bar manager decided to turf out the last drinkers at around 3.30 am, Mr Smith was so intoxicated that the other men had to help him back to his cabin. His wife was not there.

What happened next remains shrouded in mystery. However, a man in the neighbouring cabin has since provided some details. Clete Hyman was a deputy police chief from California, with decades of service experience under his belt. He was woken by a noise, something that sounded like a drinking party in the room next door, men cheering. He called the ship security to complain about the disturbance and banged on the walls to let the men know they were keeping others awake. He would continue to be disturbed, by voices, by things being moved around. At one point he opened his cabin door to find three men talking in the corridor. He said he later heard sounds coming from the balcony, the scraping of furniture. And then, after a couple of minutes of silence, what he would describe as 'a horrific thud'.

Hours would elapse before this thud would be connected to the disappearance of George Smith. Jennifer Hagel Smith, meanwhile, was found, according to the cruise line, at 4.30 am, passed out drunk in a ship corridor. When a crew member helped her back to her cabin, she was its only occupant.

At 8.30 am, when the ship was berthed at the small Turkish port of Kusadasi, a teenage passenger in a cabin below the Smiths' noticed the bloodstain on the canopy and called security. By this time many passengers had already left the ship for a daytrip to the ancient site of Ephesus. Royal Caribbean says the crew immediately tried to establish the whereabouts of all the passengers — a task made easier by the computerised SeaPass security cards that automatically clock passengers onto and off the ship. Three passengers among those apparently still on board could not immediately be accounted for; one, unrelated to the incident, was later found, leaving just the Smiths. Jennifer was tracked down to the ship's spa, where she was having a massage. That just left George missing, gone without trace – bar one bloodstain.

Turkish forensic investigators were called in, and police interviewed Mrs Hagel Smith and took statements from passengers and crew. Mr Smith's sister and parents would later be highly critical of the authorities' reaction, claiming that too little was done to get to the bottom of the incident; a sea search was not started until the afternoon.

An FBI agent holidaying in the area was called in. Eventually, all the evidence was turned over to the FBI. By evening, the local investigators were satisfied they had done all they could on board.

With the captain apparently worried about the risks of rubber-necking passengers leaning over their balconies to see the evidence on the outside of the ship, the bloodstain was cleaned away and the ship continued on its voyage. If anyone had been responsible for Mr Smith's death, that person or persons would still be on the cruise. In the words of the dead man's sister, Bree Smith, who is convinced that foul play was to blame, 'the *Brilliance of the Seas* sailed off into the sunset with the murderers on board, therefore, jeopardizing the safety of all the other passengers'.

No charges have yet been laid; the FBI investigators have not come to any conclusion. Was it a tragic accident, suicide or foul play?

The three Russian-Americans would not make it to the end of the voyage: another incident involving a video camera and a young woman in the ship's jacuzzi led to an allegation of rape. They rejected the accusation, but were evicted from the cruise in Italy.

A year after his disappearance, the family of George Smith were still searching for answers. And they have pursued the case – and the cruise line – with considerable energy. Dr Henry Lee – a forensics expert who had been involved in such high-profile cases as the OJ Simpson trial and JonBenet Ramsey murder – was called in to visit the ship many months after the event. Royal Caribbean allowed him on board but baulked at his request to simulate a fall by throwing a mannequin off the balcony of the cabin, arguing that it would upset the passengers. Bree Smith has declared: 'We're going to continue until our dying day to make Royal Caribbean accountable and to make sure the perpetrators of the crime are brought to justice.' True to her word, the family was pivotal in bringing about the congressional hearings into the cruise industry in Washington and in establishing a campaigning group, International Cruise Victims, to make the many stories of the missing known. On the campaign website, the family states: 'George's life will not be taken in vain, as his death has already called attention to the dire need for reform in the under-regulated cruise industry.'

For its part, the cruise line strongly dismissed any allegations that it mishandled the case. Both the local police and the FBI were notified swiftly. Royal Caribbean eventually issued a statement entitled 'Top 10 Myths Regarding Royal Caribbean's Handling Of The Disappearance Of George Smith', to combat what it described as 'a lot of inaccurate and unfair speculation about our company's response to the incident'. The myths it denounced as false included: that Royal Caribbean engaged in a deliberate cover-up, which impeded the investigation; that the company destroyed evidence and compromised the crime scene before the forensic investigation was complete; that Turkish authorities had no jurisdiction over the ship; that crew ignored a blood trail and other signs of struggle in the cabin; and that guests observed crew cleaning the Smiths' stateroom in the days after Mr Smith's disappearance.

Captain Bill Wright, Royal Caribbean's senior vice-president of marine operations, said that while there were always lessons to be learned, in this instance he was very proud of the manner in which the officers and the captain responded under very difficult circumstances, and said they had followed company procedures.

In June 2006, a further twist came in the saga, one that would split Smith's blood relatives and the Hagels, the two families briefly united by marriage. The Smiths filed a lawsuit against the cruise line, alleging intentional infliction of emotional distress and invasion of privacy: 'The defendants' conduct constituted extreme and outrageous behaviour, which went beyond all possible bounds of decency so as to be regarded as shocking, atrocious, odious and utterly intolerable in a civilized community.' Just hours later – as the deadline for filing a suit for wrongful death approached – Royal Caribbean announced that the widow, Jennifer Hagel Smith, far from filing the separate lawsuit that the family had expected, had agreed to a settlement.

No details of the pay-off were revealed by the cruise line or Mrs Hagel Smith, who issued a long statement in which she said:

> As many great peace and spiritual teachers have said, through great suffering comes great awareness. Furthermore, we have come a long way to where we are today, on a journey seeking change, answers and closure . . .

She said she would continue to work with the FBI and set up a charitable foundation in her husband's name.

The furious family vowed to press on with the lawsuit and depose Mrs Hagel Smith on the stand, believing that she was not telling them the whole truth. The widow rejected their accusations entirely, saying she had taken an FBI polygraph test.

Royal Caribbean International's president, Adam Goldstein, meanwhile said of Mrs Hagel Smith: 'She has handled herself well under the most trying of circumstances and we applaud her constructive approach to resolving this matter.' She returned: 'I appreciate Royal Caribbean's cooperation, sincerity and efforts moving forward, which I believe will play a major role in helping all of us find closure.' The case remains open.

Perhaps the most shocking story of all told before the hearing had taken place on another Royal Caribbean–run cruise, this time in Alaska. A forty-year-old woman, Merrian Carver, had disappeared. Her father,

Kendall Carver, testified. There was no evidence of foul play; but then, there was precious little evidence at all. Royal Caribbean's Celebrity Cruise Line ship the *Mercury* set sail from Seattle. On the second day, the cabin steward realised that Ms Carver's room was no longer occupied. According to the steward, he cleaned and left a chocolate on the pillow, then reported her absence to his immediate boss, who told him he would deal with it. The steward would continue to place chocolates on the pillow of the missing woman each night. There would be no sign of this passenger ever again. And yet, when the ship docked at the end of the cruise in Vancouver, British Columbia, and all those on board disembarked, no-one thought to notify the police or Ms Carver's family. Her belongings were simply packed away and business continued as normal.

It would be a scarcely credible story, and one perhaps never known, were it not for the persistence of Merrian Carver's father Kendall, a former company CEO, who spent tens of thousands of dollars on private investigators and legal fees in an attempt to discover the truth. He himself was only alerted to his daughter's presumed death when his granddaughter called him to try to find out where her mother was. Weeks after he had filed a missing persons report, police found his daughter had bought a ticket to go on the cruise.

Mr Carver's legal efforts finally forced a statement from the cabin steward – that he had reported her disappearance after two days of the cruise but his immediate boss had told him the situation would be dealt with. His manager was later fired by Royal Caribbean, a fact that Mr Carver would only find out several months afterwards.

At the congressional hearings, Christopher Shays, the Republican congressman for Connecticut, whose constituents included George Smith's family – would lash out at the cruise line after they made an expression of regret for Merrian Carver's relatives. Shays said:

> It would be better if you cooperated with the family, and didn't make them have to seek this information the way they sought it – having

to spend literally tens of thousands of dollars. So your actions would speak more loudly than your statement, frankly, and your actions appear not to support your sorrow.

The circumstances of Carver's disappearance may never be known. Royal Caribbean said that it did not monitor the comings and goings of guests on ships; that it was not unusual for a guest to sleep in someone else's cabin, or to leave things behind. In a statement that further distressed the family, the cruise line concluded:

> The death of Merrian Carver is a horrible tragedy, but, regrettably, there is very little a cruise line, a resort or a hotel can do to prevent someone from committing suicide.

Mr Carver pointed out that the case was still open and Merrian Carver had not been declared dead by the family or the FBI. Later, the findings of private investigators and tip-offs from crew would strengthen the family's belief that suicide was neither the only nor most likely explanation.

Like the families of George Smith and Hue Tran and Hue Pham, Mr Carver has not let the matter rest, joining with them to run the International Cruise Victims campaign.

Son Michael Pham, who spent a year trying to get more information about his parents' disappearance from the cruise line without satisfaction, says:

> We don't want to go dealing with our tragic loss in public, we're not those kind of people. But we have had to go through the media because we have no other way.

As representatives from the cruise industry pointed out, statistically cruising is a very safe vacation: a disappearance toll of 24 passengers in two years from 2003 to 2005, with over 10 million passengers cruising annually with American lines in 2004 compares well with life on land. According to the FBI figures that Michael Crye, the president of the International Council of Cruise Lines (ICCL), presented to the hearings, one person out of every 2800 is reported missing in the USA every year. Tragedies that happen on board are just a terrible part of daily life. Disappearances are much more likely to occur on land than at sea – although, of course, to go missing on land does not carry the same presumption of death as disappearing from a ship in the ocean.

Those who have seen the sharp end of onboard disappearances say that cruising is relatively safe – but with qualifications.

Mr Pham argues that the 'millions of passengers' cited should be placed in context. The ICCL uses the FBI's statistics to compare the passengers on American cruise ships with the population of a big city, making the incidence of crime appear minuscule. But as Mr Pham points out, the comparison is only valid if each inhabitant of that hypothetical city has a lifespan of a week. It would be more meaningful to look at the total passenger capacity of US cruise ships at any one time, rather than the total number of passengers carried over a period of a few years. A medium-sized town of two to three hundred thousand people is in fact a far more accurate analogy than a big city – which means that twenty-four missing people starts to look a somewhat more chilling statistic.

Lawyer Charles R. Lipcon, of Florida law firm Lipcon, Margulies & Alsina, who are specialists in tackling cases involving cruise lines, says, 'As long as people take the right precautions, it's a safe holiday.'

Cruise lines have been beefing up security on board in recent years and installing CCTV. Some recent incidents have been treated with more openness and prompt referrals to the FBI. But Lipcon is sceptical about how much the industry has changed:

> I've been thirty years suing cruise lines. Recently they're putting a happy face on the whole thing and trying to act like they're cooperating when in fact they don't want to cooperate at all. Since

Senator Shays's congressional hearings the cruise lines have been much more cooperative. When the hearings are over the cruise lines will go back to business as usual.

A similar thing happened ten years ago; the industry was in front of Congress, and they did the right PR moves, and when it was over it was back to business. They'll do whatever is in their best interest – they don't have much regard for the niceties of what should be done.

Son Michael Pham says:

We live in the United States and we thought we had rights. When we started dealing with the cruise lines, we realised that as a foreign registered company in international waters they don't have to do anything – very easily you get bounced around from the Bahamas [the flag state on many ships] to Panama [where some cruise lines are registered as corporations] and if there was a crime committed by a passenger with a foreign passport then you have another jurisdiction that you have to deal with.

He points to the case of Lynsey O'Brien to highlight the difficulties:

What happened when she was served drinks, was that they fired the bar tender and he went back to his own country. Many crew members come from places like Indonesia and the Philippines – how can you prosecute them there?

As a memorandum for the hearings committee noted:

Primarily, American passengers should be aware that even though they board a ship in a US port it does not necessarily mean they are fully protected by the US justice system.

Liability is in any case limited for these victims. The legislation often referred to in America is the Death on the High Seas Act or 'DOHSA'.

It dates back to early in the twentieth century when the US Congress enacted a law to protect widows of sailors by making companies provide them with a salary in the event of their spouse's death.

Now, though, according to Mr Pham, this law means that any case involving death at sea limits corporate responsibility to pecuniary losses – that is, the salaries that the deceased person would have earned – rather than punitive damages. While victims' families say that money is not their motivation, the huge costs involved in running a lawsuit with no likelihood of retrieving damages inhibit any attempt at legal action. And, says Mr Pham, DOHSA gives shipping companies little incentive to make corrections and address their practices.

Thomas Dickerson, a US judge and expert on travel law, has put it bluntly: 'Maritime law protects cruise lines; it does not protect consumers.'

But as maritime lawyer Brett Rivkind told the hearings, legal action has occasionally pushed the cruise industry to state its position clearly. In a memorandum of law filed in court in response to Kendall Carver's pursuit of the truth about his daughter's disappearance, the cruise line said it had 'no duty to investigate'. That meant, according to Rivkind, that the industry was not currently accountable to anyone.

In May 2006, following the hearings, a twenty-one-year-old man, Daniel DiPiero, who had been drinking heavily, fell over the rail of the *Mariner of the Seas* on the way to the Bahamas. Weeks later, Micki Kanesaki, fifty-two, was reported missing from the *Island Escape* in the Mediterranean in June; her body later washed up in Calabria, Italy. And at least two more unidentified crew members have fallen overboard from cruise ships since. Ships' searches never found the victims or told how and why they vanished; the number of the missing continues to grow.

2

Now Wash Your Hands . . .

SAILING DOWN FROM the UK port of Southampton into the warm waters of the Mediterranean, a passenger on the P&O superliner, the *Aurora*, noticed a lurch. It was coming from his stomach.

In the autumn of 2003, the British public might not have been familiar with the Norwalk virus and its related strains, collectively known as noroviruses. Yet *norovirus* would soon become a name – and for the passengers, an unpleasant taste – on everyone's lips. Highly contagious, spread from person to person, the symptoms of a norovirus are hard to miss: diarrhoea, stomach cramps and violent, projectile vomiting. Trouble at both ends. These viruses are transmitted, as doctors delicately express it, through the faecal-oral route. Someone on the *Aurora* hadn't washed their hands, and now the bug was out and about, rampaging through a closed space. Ships' crews are well versed in trying to control outbreaks of disease, but no amount of precautions would stop this one spreading to what the managing director of P&O called an 'unprecedented' degree.

Notices were delivered to the cabins early in the cruise, warning passengers of the norovirus. The self-service buffet was closed down. Passengers, who were issued with disinfectant wipes, took to pushing lift buttons with their elbows, and protecting themselves from such danger zones as doorknobs by holding tissues as they twisted them. A no-touch policy was enforced. The casino's gambling chips were disinfected.

'We suspected there was going to be a problem,' a passenger related to the *Telegraph*, 'because of the notices delivered to our cabin. And then people started going down like flies. Then we were avoiding people, avoiding places, until you inevitably went down with it.'

Standard cruise protocol is to confine passengers to their cabin once symptoms are reported. They were dark days – not least for those sharing one of the inside, windowless rooms, waiting for their vomiting and diarrhoea to pass. Outside the cabins, teams of cleaners in protective clothing were spraying down the doors. One afflicted mother said of the debugging teams, 'They looked like the blokes from *ET*, which was frightening for the kids.'

Disinfectant was spread through every deck. The crew were fighting a losing battle: more than 500 of the 1800 passengers would soon feel that telltale tug in their guts, its sudden onset surprising some.

Andrew Williams from South Wales took six days to succumb. He had got off the boat for a shore excursion in Sicily. 'I felt perfectly well. Suddenly I was vomiting in the street.'

Perhaps the spectacle of apparently genteel cruise visitors projectile vomiting in ancient beauty spots sounded the alarm for other ports around the Mediterranean. By the time the *Aurora* had made its way around Italy, north to Venice, local medical officers were refusing to allow sick passengers to disembark. Many of the sick were, in any case, all too happy to stay in the vicinity of a flush toilet and their bed.

In the next port, Dubrovnik, on Croatia's Adriatic coast, health inspectors again insisted that all sick travellers remained in their cabins.

But the Norwalk virus, like other noroviruses, is not an easy one to contain. While each passenger might typically only suffer the runs and throw up for twenty-four hours or so per bout, the incubation period can be several days, and medics are still uncertain just how long the virus can survive on surfaces and elsewhere. (Some unfortunates on the *Aurora* managed to pick up a second dose on their way around the Mediterranean.) The line between the sick and the healthy was a fragile one, impossible to ascertain in such an enclosed environment. The norovirus can also be spread by minute airborne particles of vomit – and some passengers were not always making it out of the dining room before their dinner returned to haunt them.

As the ship sailed down past Albania, fears on land were growing. The *Aurora* approached Athens for the next scheduled stop. At the port of Piraeus, the Greeks were eyeing the $500 million liner like a biological Trojan Horse. Representatives from the *Aurora* argued their case for five hours in a meeting with health and marine officials. Eventually the Greek health minister himself, Costas Stephanis, made the ruling. Not one passenger from the sick ship would be touching Greek soil. Just, as he put it, 'to be on the safe side', the authorities forced the *Aurora* to anchor six miles offshore.

By now, the plight of those on the ship was making headlines around Europe. 'Left adrift on ship from hell,' read one. A man on board was photographed from afar, plaintively holding up a sign reading, simply, 'Help'. Two British medics were flown out to join the six doctors and nurses already on the beleaguered ship, along with five crates of medical supplies.

The passengers, meanwhile, were forming into two camps: the noisily desperate and the more traditional cruisers – posh, elderly, with an upper lip that would remain stiff, no matter what gut-related indignities it witnessed. The first group issued demands for compensation, having paid between £1500 and £5500 each for the sixteen-day cruise, while the second group claimed it was a lot of fuss over nothing.

Then passengers started dying. One man was reported dead, followed by another. It would emerge that neither death was caused by the virus – both were elderly men with heart conditions – but that would prove little comfort to some. 'Like a mortuary' on board, one woman told the press.

Left out at sea by the Greeks, the *Aurora* set sail for Gibraltar, the British enclave bordering the southern tip of Spain, hoping for a more sympathetic welcome. After four days without touching the shore, the passengers were finally allowed to disembark, on condition that they surrendered their passports.

Such was the reputation of the *Aurora* by now that even this precaution did not prove enough for the neighbouring Spanish. In a move that was announced as protecting the general health of their people, the Spanish government closed the border with Gibraltar – the first time in eighteen years.

It sparked a furious response, with the British foreign secretary, Jack Straw, denouncing the closure as 'unnecessary and disproportionate'. But the border remained closed until the liner left.

By the time the ship returned to Southampton, nearly all of the surviving passengers had recovered to full health and the *Aurora* was the most famous ship in town. Public recriminations saw some passengers blame others for their poor personal hygiene. Others, including a couple who had recently featured on television in a wife-swapping program, threatened to sue the cruise line for kidnap.

The man with the sign saying 'Help' told reporters that it had been 'an absolute holiday from hell'.

He might have been surprised to learn that his experience was in no way unique – simply more widespread and more public than usual. Outbreaks of stomach upsets plague the cruise industry. While ships claim to have very high standards of hygiene – and are regularly inspected, especially in American ports – any confined community risks rapid contamination if one person goes down ill.

All outbreaks of sickness on American cruise ships calling at US ports are logged by law – a requirement that means their epidemics are perhaps more visible than those at nursing homes, hospitals or schools, which, as the cruise industry repeatedly claims, are just as likely as ships to suffer from norovirus outbreaks. (Although, of course, a day off school or work with a sickie is more of a bonus than being locked in a cabin during an expensive holiday.)

Unfortunately for much of the cruising clientele, noroviruses hit the elderly and very young the hardest. And there is another reason why noroviruses can become maritime incidents: outbreaks are often linked to eating contaminated raw shellfish, especially oysters and clams. One source of such contamination? Sewage, dumped into the sea by boats.

Beyond the grim physical experience of such viruses, some people can develop longer term complications. These are thought to include chronic fatigue, irritable bowel syndrome and kidney damage. Class action lawsuits have occurred.

The incidence of norovirus outbreaks has ballooned. Only 319 norovirus cases were recorded in Britain in 1986; by 2002, cases topped 3000. Some observers have pointed out that norovirus symptoms are nearly identical to those of salmonella and other types of food poisoning. Laboratory tests might be needed to prove one or the other. And while a salmonella outbreak might leave a cruise line open to litigation, for having served ill-prepared food, it would be comparatively blameless in the case of a norovirus, potentially brought in by any passenger. Any company might understandably prefer to find noroviruses responsible for widespread illness among its passengers.

The *Regal Princess*, cruising from Copenhagen to New York, was another ship that suffered a mass outbreak. An elderly passenger described the scene to the UK *Daily Telegraph*: 'There was sick everywhere. There were people throwing up in the bathrooms, the lifts, the dining rooms. It was horrible.' Another passenger, a British man, said:

> I ended up being as sick as a dog for a large chunk of it. I don't want to go into details but suffice to say I had a season ticket for the loo.

More than 300 people were hit by the norovirus on that trip. Another 200 were struck down with the bug on the *Aurora*'s sister ship, the *Oceana*, on a seventeen-night Mediterranean cruise in 2005.

On another, Princess Cruises abandoned the entire voyage to curb an outbreak. Occasionally, cruises have been cancelled before they have started, in a bid to rid the ship of lingering viruses – also giving any afflicted crew, some of whom might be unwittingly carrying the virus, time to lose any trace or contagion instead of reinfecting a new boatload of passengers. Almost all crew who report sick on cruises are those in the front line of customer care, mixing with the passengers – allowing the cruise lines to point the finger of blame squarely at the dirty habits of their guests.

But just how clean are the ships? One Nile cruise ship, the *Karim Palace*, was – perhaps unsurprisingly – exposed by an undercover microbiologist as having high levels of bacteria in the pool, cabins and buffet. He even found that the thick dirt on his cabin's phone had bacteria that a lab would confirm as of 'fecal origin'. His investigations on behalf of the UK television program *Holidays Undercover* were hampered when he himself fell foul of the inevitable stomach bugs.

For those unable to go to such elaborate lengths, the easiest way to check a cruise ship's cleanliness – at least for those stopping at US ports – is to read the reports made publicly available by the Centers for Disease Control (CDC) Vessel Sanitisation Program. CDC inspectors now perform regular checks on every ship that docks in the US. A perfect score is rare – and even those that do get the full 100 on the card usually receive a report that has a host of warnings about possible concerns.

It doesn't necessarily follow that the grander the ship, the cleaner. As recently as 2000, Cunard's *Queen Elizabeth 2*, a regular choice of the regal and famous, scored a mere 79/100 in a CDC Vessel Sanitisation Report – a score that falls short of the minimum score of 85 that the American health inspectors deem satisfactory. While every year several ships do manage to hit 100, the *QE2* has never been one of them.

Even in 2006, scoring a respectable 92 from the CDC, the ship was warned about a range of violations, including problems with food storage and handling, the water in the spa pools and cracked tiles on deck.

More unpleasant were some of the unhygienic parts of ships revealed by the British consumer watchdog magazine *Which?* and later reported in the *Daily Mail*. The magazine had obtained port health authority reports on cruise ships belonging to various lines that turned up such nasties as an infestation of cockroaches, a larder where flies were tucking into the food, and a leg of veal found defrosting some ten months after its use-by date had passed.

P&O said it had since acted on the reports – its *Aurora* was host to the ageing meat, while sister ship *Oceana* had the flies – while Cunard maintains that the cockroaches found on its vessel *Caronia* had long vanished before it was sold off to Saga, where it was rebranded the *Ruby*. Health inspectors also reported that they had 'little confidence' in the food safety standards on board Thomson's ship, the *Celebration*. It turned out to be a ship that could ill afford passengers to succumb to stomach upsets: on a cruise soon afterwards, the *Celebration* had to send its passengers home from Spain after an alarming mass toilet failure flummoxed engineers. The ship, caught short, turned for home after five days.

While ships can justifiably claim to be defenceless against the unhygienic practices of their passengers, it is worth noting that a report in an American scientific journal showed a definite correlation between large-scale diarrhoea outbreaks on cruise ships and the scores that they had achieved on mandatory sanitation inspections carried out by health authorities. When cruise lines cleaned up their act in the 1990s, far fewer of their passengers got sick.

It seems, though, that a clean ship is no guarantee. Travelscope, the British tour operator that booked passengers on to the MV *Van Gogh*, which failed to leave Harwich for a cruise in 2006 after a huge attack of the norovirus, likewise reported that 'the bug was probably brought on board by a passenger on the previous trip', according to *The Guardian*. So many of the crew had been struck down by what was now being called 'winter vomiting disease' that the ship was held in port, the coastguard deeming that the crew would not be able to cope in an emergency.

The ship's previous cruise around Norway had seen 70 of 500 passengers fall seriously sick. Two elderly passengers were carried off the ship on stretchers and taken to hospital. With so many struck down by diarrhoea, it was perhaps unfortunate that a coastguard should observe that cruising people were not normally in 'the first flush of health'.

Carnival's Princess cruise line was another that had to offer 30 per cent cash refunds and vouchers for future holidays as compensation to passengers in the Mediterranean in June 2006. The *Sea Princess* laid more than 200 of its passengers low with the familiar norovirus, and cancelled a planned stop in Lisbon to return to Southampton a day early for thorough disinfection. Irate passengers had been given a letter on the first day of the cruise warning them of widespread 'norovirus activity'. There had been a small outbreak on the previous voyage, but Princess Cruises said it didn't believe that the two outbreaks were linked, an explanation that some passengers found hard to accept. One told the BBC that they were 'up in arms', holding Princess responsible for the sanitation of the ship.

Another, David Cordon, from Wakefield, Yorkshire, related how his new father-in-law had barely made it to his daughter's onboard wedding. Cordon said that his bride's father had just about tottered uncomfortably down the aisle to give her away, when nature called. 'Then he had to go straight away.' The captain prudently refused to shake hands with the happy couple.

They weren't the only couple to suffer marital difficulties aboard. *Holidays Undercover* reporters spoke to Paul and Fran Hughes, who had been looking forward to a special wedding conducted by a captain in full regalia on the *Sea Princess*. On day two of the cruise, Mr Hughes was struck down by the norovirus and confined to his room for a forty-eight-hour quarantine period – due to end just as the wedding would take place. A ship's doctor cleared him fit an hour before the ceremony. Standing but weakened, the groom pledged to love his bride in sickness and in health – which was just as well, because before the day was out the new Mrs Hughes had also succumbed to the spreading virus. She took to her cabin sick before the wedding night and remained there in quarantine for the rest of the cruise. It was, Mr Hughes admitted: 'A bit of a passion killer to say the least.'

The mother of Joshua Woodcock, twelve, appeared on the same program, and related how her son had been struck down by a severe attack. Despite the small size of the cabin, she said: 'He couldn't even make it to the toilet – a matter of feet – before the diarrhoea came.'

While P&O told the quarantined passengers that room service would be available, the virus's spread was such that some found it took several hours for their calls to be answered and any meals delivered.

The *Sea Princess* had only come into service in the Mediterranean the previous year, having formerly been operating as the *Adonia*. Hollywood actress Goldie Hawn had been flown over to perform the ritual rechristening of the ship in Southampton but, instead of swinging the champagne bottle, stayed confined to her hotel room – with a stomach bug.

In most cases, including even the worst outbreaks on the *Regal Princess*, the *Aurora*, and countless others, the cruise lines have been able to announce that the bug was brought on board by a passenger; nothing to do with the actual ship. Sometimes, though, it might *look* as though the ship is to blame, and it appears no amount of cleaning can save them. To have an illness strike at the very guts of one boatload of passengers is unfortunate, but some ships in the US and Britain recently achieved particular distinction by having mass outbreaks of a norovirus on consecutive cruises.

It's not known whether Celebrity Cruises named their ship the *Mercury* after the ingredient rising in the ship's doctors' thermometers.

But what is on the record is that hundreds fell ill sailing on this ship from San Diego to Mexico in early 2006: over 200 experiencing severe vomiting and diarrhoea on the first jaunt and over 100 laid low on the next. The American medical assessment team for cruise ships said such events were 'very rare'. David Forney, chief of the Vessel Sanitation Program for the Centers for Disease Control and Prevention in Atlanta, told *The San Diego Union-Tribune* that the cruise company had an excellent protocol for dealing with such outbreaks. Unfortunately, he said, the staff 'were not real successful in implementing some of their own protocols'. One of the first things they were supposed to do was let passengers know there was something going on, so that if they saw someone vomiting, they could report it to the ship's medical centre. But, he said, they were cleaning hard. 'I understand the ship smells like chlorine.'

Royal Caribbean Cruises, who own Celebrity, give sick passengers incentives to stay in their cabins, such as vouchers for future holidays for those who might wish to repeat the experience.

Only a few months later, in June 2006, *The Seattle Times* reported that the same ship was undergoing another deep clean, after pulling in to the US port with 121 more sick passengers. It's little wonder that the ship's captain had apparently already turned to drink, being pulled off the ship in mid-May after coastguards caught the smell of alcohol on his breath.

The *Mercury*'s woes were matched across the Atlantic that summer by what was popularly described as the 'curse of the *Black Prince*' – a relatively small vessel operating out of Leith, near Edinburgh, Scotland, for Fred. Olsen Cruise Lines. *The Times* reported that in late May, a twelve-night Baltic cruise saw twenty passengers out of 393 struck down with vomiting and diarrhoea; a subsequent cruise, taking in the Norwegian fiords, would see 136 people – one third of the *Black Prince*'s guests – heading urgently for the bathroom. Despite deep cleaning, the bug would strike again in massive numbers: in July, 114 passengers who sailed on the cruise to Iceland and Greenland shared their pain. Lawyers started looking into claims on behalf of passengers, claiming that the operators were risking clients' health by swift turnarounds in port with infected boats. The staff of Fred. Olsen Cruise Lines said they were bemused; arguing that it was invariably a passenger who brought the bug on board. However, they promised to rip up the carpets and hold the ship for two days of steam cleaning and antiviral treatments before the next cruise. Edinburgh council officials said they would carry out an investigation.

According to the CDC's statistics, over 100 cruises in the last five years have seen major outbreaks of sickness on board – primarily, when any cause has been diagnosed, due to a norovirus. Shake hands with the captain? It's enough to make anyone prefer a quick salute.

Yet even this comprehensive data compiled by the American authorities only touches on cruises that stop at US ports. It is left to websites like the excellent cruisejunkie.com to try to record the sickness elsewhere: for example, the case in which several hundred passengers and crew fell sick with the Norwalk virus on a cruise from Osaka early in 2006 – a more extreme outbreak of something that had, crew claimed, been occurring for over a month.

In any case, experts believe that the problem may be under-reported. The CDC's David Forney told a medical inquest that a typical scenario was one in which sick passengers would refuse to report their symptoms to a ship's medical facility, saying that if they did: 'They're going to tell me I have to stay in my cabin. I've paid for this cruise. I'm going to go out and have a good time as best I can.'

It is not just gastros that can afflict the guests. The Public Health Agency of Canada issued a report pointing to the potential incidence of STIs, with 5–9 per cent of travellers having casual sex. The report noted that cruise ships were largely staffed by crew members who came from places where AIDS and hepatitis B were a growing problem.

The authors were concerned too by the possibility of exposure to tuberculosis and by the threat posed to ageing travellers by influenza outbreaks on board.

The agency also warned of a rare syndrome that follows a sea voyage: *mal de debarquement* (MDD), or disembarkation sickness. The symptoms, including sensations of rocking, swaying and imbalance, can persist for up to several years – enough to drive a sufferer back on a gastro-ridden boat. (On a brighter note: classic seasickness is now comparatively rare, on American cruises if not yet in Australia, thanks to stabilisers deployed on large modern ships. For those who do succumb, cruise nurses will often offer drugs, at a price; injections are usually preferred as those who take pills tend to have trouble keeping them down.)

Rubella outbreaks have also been known to take hold among largely unvaccinated foreign crew, putting passengers at risk.

In 2005 a report was issued by the CDC to raise medical awareness of the potential for contracting legionnaire's disease on a cruise ship: in a six-month period, two people (one of them a woman only forty-five years old) died of the respiratory illness following Caribbean cruises.

The problem was not a new one: back in 1994, the Celebrity Cruises ship, *Horizon*, had been the scene of an outbreak of legionnaire's, with six passengers contracting the disease and one dying. US state health authorities attributed responsibility for this outbreak to the ship. Carnival claimed the event cost the cruise line millions in lost custom, and eventually won an enormous lawsuit victory in 2006, when a jury awarded it $194 million in compensation from Essef Corp, a company that supplied allegedly defective filters for the ship's whirlpool.

With such an array of infectious diseases stalking the waves, it is little wonder that in Australia, the New South Wales government has started to worry about cruise ship passengers spreading diseases. Medical researchers found that in the seven years to early 2006, twenty-four outbreaks of disease occurred on ships that docked in Sydney, affecting

2300 travellers – and listing influenza and respiratory infections alongside the norovirus.

By June 2006 they could add another outbreak, as the norovirus and flu combined to leave dozens of passengers laid low over the course of a twelve-day cruise on the *Pacific Sun*. Most guests on board still reported having a good time and praised the swift reaction of the crew in limiting the spread of the outbreak, through constant spraying of the ship and quarantining any passengers showing symptoms of the rampaging bug.

One passenger, a certain Mr Wanless, was notably less happy: locked in his cabin after crew adjudged that his sickness was clearly caused by the norovirus. At the end of the voyage he launched a compensation claim, angrily protesting that he had simply had too much to drink.

Even typhoid was once brought back to Australia by passengers on the *Fair Princess*, who exposed the 900 people on board to the deadly fever they had contracted on a shore excursion, the Kokoda Trail trek in Papua New Guinea, probably by consuming contaminated food or water against the advice of the crew. The Australian government issued urgent health alerts after three people ended up in hospital.

The *Fair Princess*'s successor at P&O, the *Pacific Sky*, was involved in another urgent health alert when an outbreak of meningococcal disease killed one man and left another in intensive care soon after he had disembarked in Australia.

Early in 2006, with spectres such as bird flu rearing their heads worldwide, the New South Wales Minister for Health, John Hatzistergos, was moved to demand a national cruise ship health surveillance program: 'The threat of serious infectious diseases to our population cannot be ignored.'

Ultimately, though, it is a norovirus that is most likely to burst the dream-like bubble of a carefree cruise. There is, however, a silver lining to this dark and noxious cloud. Cruise lore has it that the average passenger, flocking gannet-like to the ship's restaurants for up to seven ample meals a day (excluding cookery demonstrations and room service) will pile on up to a kilo in weight for every day on the boat; that is, potentially six kilos or more over a week's holiday. The US Coast Guard has become so conscious of Americans' increasing obesity that it has ordered a review of all ship safety regulations based on standard passenger sizes. A good bout of the runs – be it brought on by a norovirus, Shigella, E. coli or any other gastrointestinal affliction recently recorded on cruises – is perhaps nature's way of keeping a ship's ballooning cargo in check.

3

Oil on Troubled Waters

EVEN ON THE cruises where there is no hint of a norovirus, several thousand passengers and crew generate an awful lot of sewage. In a single week, a typical cruise ship will rack up a good 210,000 gallons of the stuff. Add to that one million gallons of 'grey water' – the water flushed through sinks, showers, galleys and laundries – and 35,000 more gallons of bilge, or oil-contaminated water. Where does this waste go? It's mostly pumped – treated or otherwise – straight into the deep blue sea.

As cruise ships take passengers to some of the most idyllic islands and pristine seascapes on the planet, many are, critics say, leaving behind a dirty trail – polluting waters, affecting marine life and pumping toxic smoke into the air.

An international maritime treaty, the MARPOL Convention for the prevention of marine pollution from ships, bans the dumping of any sewage within four miles of land, and completely prohibits the disposal of plastics and the most poisonous of chemical wastes (such as those from onboard photo laboratories) anywhere in the seas. But there have been breaches – and the biggest cruising corporations have all been fined for both breaking the law and then attempting to cover up their practices.

A US government report into cruise ship pollution showed that sixty-nine cruise ships belonging to forty-two different companies were regularly involved in illegal dumping and falsifying records, or did not account for where their waste had gone.

In the 1990s, Royal Caribbean launched a campaign called 'Save the Waves', showing films on board and making the staff wear badges to raise passengers' awareness of environmental issues. Unfortunately, this overt commitment to saving the waves was not quite matched by the reality of the company's practices. In July 1999, it was fined a record $18 million after pleading guilty to a number of counts of pollution. US Attorney General Janet Reno was moved to say: 'Royal Caribbean used our nation's waters as a dumping ground, even as it promoted itself as an environmentally green company.' The company routinely falsified the ships' logs, she said – so much so that its employees referred to the logs with a Norwegian term meaning fairy book.

In a plea agreement, Royal Caribbean admitted that it routinely dumped waste oil from its fleet of cruise ships – even in areas as environmentally sensitive as the Inside Passage of Alaska. The cruise line also pleaded guilty to the unprecedented charge that it deliberately dumped into harbours and coastal areas a variety of toxic pollutants, including hazardous chemicals from photo-processing equipment, dry-cleaning shops and printing presses. 'This case,' promised Reno, 'will sound like a foghorn throughout the entire maritime industry.'

In 2002, this would be underlined when the other big cruise lines again stood in the dock – and Carnival was hit with a fine to match Royal Caribbean's. An investigation carried out by various US government agencies, including the Coast Guard and the Environmental Protection Agency, found that ship engineers had been again falsifying records of how they dumped waste products. One method was to flush clean water past meters which were supposed to measure the oil content of the dirty bilge water, in order to produce a respectable reading, while the unfiltered bilge was sent straight into the sea. Carnival was also given a community service order and put on five years' probation.

Later that year, Norwegian Cruise Line was also fined $1 million after admitting both discharging oily water and lying about it in the log. Tom Sansonetti, Assistant Attorney General for the Department of Justice, said the cruise line deserved credit for owning up, but said:

> ... the sad fact remains that the practice of dumping waste oil and maintaining false log books has proved to be commonplace in the maritime and cruise ship industry.

While cruise ships had access to the technology to separate oil and water, buying the proper filters could be costly. Dumping substances could save the companies up to US$10,000 per cruise, according to Sansonetti.

In the wake of the convictions, US coastguards have been provided with infra-red cameras to search for oil sheen in the water around cruise ships at night.

Despite the large fines the US government imposed on companies for dumping in its waters, it has yet to ratify all parts of the MARPOL agreement, and still allows cruise ships to pump out wastewater along much of the US coast.

Individual states have passed laws of their own. Even Arnold Schwarzenegger, not previously known as an ardent environmentalist, signed in tougher laws as governor of California after local outrage at the discovery that a Crystal cruise ship had pumped 36,000 gallons of sewage and bilge water into the Monterey Bay National Marine Sanctuary. In the state of Alaska, tight regulations have been in place for several years and stringent monitoring is carried out by the state government environmental protection agency. Ships sail very close to land in the Inside Passage – a beautiful, pristine wilderness, home to wildlife such as polar bears – and are obliged by law to have an advanced wastewater treatment facility.

Elsewhere, the lines often operate simply according to 'memorandums of understanding', or voluntary agreements, with states. There was, then, no law flouted when the Norwegian Cruise Line's *Pride of Aloha* sent 70 tons of treated effluent into Honolulu Harbor in 2005. According to the cruise line and Hawaii's Department of Health, it would not prove harmful. It was the second discharge in six months. As the state government admitted, it relied on cruise ships to report such incidents: 'We just have very limited resources relative to the number of facilities and operations.' The memorandums set out 'understandings' only in the word's most sympathetic and lenient sense – the agreements between states and cruise lines generally contain nothing that allows enforcement or penalties for breaches.

Ships have reported many leaks themselves. Even the most regal and refined have owned up to dirty discharges. The *Queen Elizabeth 2* itself came under investigation in 2006 after it reported dumping some 3000 litres of what it described as 'paper pulp' in the seas around Cape Breton, Canada. Essentially, Canadian transport police believed, they were looking at a lot of used toilet paper.

A somewhat less refined ship was prosecuted under the MARPOL Convention in Australia. Luggage labels washed up in the garbage on Evans Head Beach in New South Wales late 1995 showed just where the assorted plastic and other debris was coming from – P&O's very own *Fairstar* the Funship – but it took forensic evidence, CSIRO computer modelling of currents and wind direction, and the work of the Australian Federal Police and government agencies to secure a conviction in 1998.

Although the dumping was thought to have occurred beyond the immediate coastal waters of New South Wales, throwing plastic into the sea is illegal anywhere at sea – just hard to detect and enforce in international waters. On this occasion, New South Wales Police were on hand to meet the *Fairstar* next time it returned to Sydney Harbour. The *Fairstar* – or more accurately, the Fairstar Shipping Corporation of Liberia, where the boat was registered – was fined just $10,000.

Most of the ways in which ships can pollute are less obvious. One recent focus for attention has been the discharge of ballast water: the large volumes of sea water sucked into the depths of a ship to stabilise it. This practice transports species thousands of miles from their native habitats, sometimes wiping out fragile ecosystems. One such effect, of particular interest to pizza-loving cruise passengers, was the near-extinction of the Black Sea's anchovy fisheries. This marine trauma was believed to have occurred after a particularly voracious jellyfish hitched a ride over in the ballast water of a ship from North America. Feeding on the Black Sea's rich plankton, the comb jelly *Mnemiopsis leidyi* spread rapidly – in the process, wolfing down zooplankton that included the larval anchovies. The embattled anchovies were apparently rescued by the accidental introduction of a further alien species, whose own favoured snack was the comb jellyfish. Marine researchers said ballast water was also probably responsible for the spread of giant Asian whelks that have knocked out oyster populations in waters far from their original home.

Air pollution is another big concern of environmentalists, who point out that cheap bunker fuel – the fuel burned by ships – contains far more sulphur than the diesel used by vehicles on land. According to estimates from the Port of San Francisco, about 90 tons of pollutants in the form of soot and nitrogen oxide were dropped on the city's waterfront by cruise ships in 2004, and the development of a new terminal would push it even higher. A recent Californian health report had linked carcinogenic pollution from diesel fumes to thousands of premature deaths.

The cruise industry says the good news is that cruise ships are slowly cleaning up their act – and environmentalists agree, if guardedly. Certainly, the question has been firmly addressed by all the major cruise lines, with environmental statements and general commitments prominent on all their websites.

According to Oceana, an international ocean conservation organisation that runs campaigns to protect the world's oceans, Royal

Caribbean is leading the way, at least in installing water treatment systems. In 2003, the cruise line was targeted by Oceana, because, said anti-pollution campaign director, Jackie Savitz, 'More than any others they were touting their green credentials. We flew light planes around the ships carrying banners saying "Got sewage?" and "Royal Caribbean dumps daily".'

Now, the cruise line says it is installing advanced wastewater purification systems on all its ships, although only three out of twenty (including the new *Freedom of the Seas*) had had them installed by early 2006. There is also an environmental officer assigned to every ship.

Such officers are also assigned on every Carnival ship. Still on probation after its 2002 convictions, the corporation maintains a hotline for any member of the public or crew to report any environmental concerns.

Some of the details of actual measures taken remain obscure. The Carnival Cruise Line has installed a high-tech grey water filtration system on at least one of its twenty-one ships and another Carnival brand, Princess Cruise lines, has trialled new UV treatment solutions for ballast water. In Carnival's most recent publicly available environmental report, the corporation declared it was:

> ...conducting an intensive multi-phase investigative study of the various AWWPSs [advanced waste water processing systems] currently available in the marketplace. The systems studied include purification plants currently installed on some [of] Carnival's ships.

There have been other positive signs of environmental stewardship, from protecting marine life to plans to reduce air pollution. Holland America Line launched a computer-based training program that taught its own crew and others how to avoid hitting whales – in vain, for one endangered humpback skewered on the bow of the Celebrity *Summit* in August 2006. Another, pregnant, humpback whale was a victim of a cruise ship strike in 2001, while the *QE2* rammed a 60-foot whale in

1996. *The Daily Telegraph* reported that the captain had described the accident as 'sad', but 'one of those things, like running over a cat'.

Carnival recently endorsed a new project in San Francisco to set up a dockside power system to supply electricity to cruise ships, cutting emissions from the ships' own diesel-fuel generators. Seattle and the port of Juneau in Alaska already supply shore side power for cruise ships. Campaigners such as the Bluewater Network have applauded it as a positive step to be replicated elsewhere, but also want to see ships use cleaner fuel in general. Royal Caribbean has installed gas turbines on the four 'Radiance class' ships in its fleet, which it claims will reduce emissions enormously.

In these respects, as in others, the cruise lines say they have made great efforts to limit their impact on the environment. Ships have reduced the amount of plastic on board, eliminating much of the kind of packaging and disposable toiletries found in hotels on land. Carnival also points to a recycling program that 'achieves a recycling rate of nearly 65 percent, which is higher than most communities'. Leftover food goes through grinders on most big cruise liners, and ships have state-of-the-art disposal equipment on board to separate and treat waste.

As industry executives baldly state, they started in a maritime culture that barely considered whether jettisoning garbage was of any significance at all. In his book *Selling the Seas*, Bob Dickinson, Carnival CEO, recalls a time when even sewage flushed straight into the sea was thought to be good for the fish. An Australian crew member recalled how waste was dealt with on one ship in the early 1990s:

> All the garbage was stacked on the crew deck. Everything went overboard at night when the disco was finished and all the passengers were too pissed to notice. It was disgusting.

These days, up to five crew may be employed on board larger ships as full-time waste disposal men. According to Teri Shore of Bluewater, 'The cruise industry is definitely more aware of environmental concerns and we hope that is trickling down from managers to people on board ship.'

Even if the cruise industry is, as it claims, now at the forefront of environmentally conscious shipping practices, it may not be enough to pre-empt further legislation and possible sanctions.

In the US, a Californian congressman and an Illinois senator have sponsored a bill to place tougher measures on the cruise industry. The new laws would require advanced waste systems on ships, prohibit discharges of sewage within 12 miles of shore and in the Great Lakes, and potentially expand the reach of the US Coast Guard and Environmental Protection Agency beyond that limit, as well as stepping up inspections, sampling and monitoring, and allowing citizens to sue any cruise line which flouts laws on dumping.

Interviewed on ABC Radio's *Background Briefing*, Michael Crye of ICCL described it as 'over the top':

> It's singling out an industry that has already taken the steps to minimise, if not eliminate, its impact on coastal waters, and saying, 'Oh, well you've done the right thing; how about going this next step?'

The cruise industry claims that local municipalities cause most of the problems in coastal waters. It is, said the ICCL, 'ironic' that such laws should be enacted when the cruise industry is doing so much to clean up.

But campaigners say the laws are still necessary. Teri Shore said: 'The problem is there's no enforcement, no monitoring.' Environmentalists are loath to trust the industry after the history of crew falsifying reports. Jackie Savitz said: 'It's like the fox guarding the henhouse.'

The small number of ships which feature the most advanced sewage treatment systems generally operate in Alaska, where monitoring of discharges is carried out by the Environmental Protection Agency. According to Royal Caribbean's senior vice-president of marine operations, Bill Wright, these systems pump out water that looks and smells like Evian.

The standard marine sanitation devices mainly used elsewhere are outdated and ineffective, Savitz says. 'There is nothing illegal – they are well within their rights to use this equipment and dump at sea. Unfortunately it doesn't stop pollution.'

While the US government debates bringing in new laws, regulation is less stringent on other nations' coastlines, and extremely difficult to enforce in international waters, where any environmental requirements amount to little more than a voluntary code.

The process of improvement is ongoing, and as better waste management systems are built into newer ships, some observers believe that the cruise industry will one day reach a position of 'zero discharge', dumping nothing into the sea.

The cruise industry continues to make public statements of commitment, saying that:

> ICCL member lines and their employees are firmly committed to eliminating all forms of pollution through improved environmental policies, procedures, and technology. These measures are not only intended to ensure compliance with the stringent domestic and international laws that govern shipboard operations; they are vital to preserving the waters on which we sail.

Campaigners are watching. Savitz says: 'We still have the banners.'

4
~

The Unwelcome Guests

EVEN WHEN THEY are not pumping out noxious fumes or sewage, cruise ships may not always have a positive effect on the areas they visit, critics claim: not due to negligence or any flouting of environmental legislation, but simply through offloading boatloads of tourists.

The logic of cruising sits ill with the dream. Iconic brochure shots show ships passing deserted island beaches, but should a liner actually decide to drop anchor there, that beach would soon be shared with hundreds, if not thousands, of fellow passengers, battling for a spot on the sand. Ports and coastlines have been reconstructed to accommodate ships that can dwarf the towns that they visit, especially in remote Pacific islands.

In Belize, one of the fastest growing tourist ports in the Caribbean, locals have begun to question how they can maintain a reputation as a laid-back ecotourist destination while providing a short stop for daytripping cruise passengers. The tourist board says that 800,000 visitors stopped here in 2005 – nearly three times Belize's population. Unfortunately for those who want to see the wildlife, shoals of fish and flocks of birds are giving way to herds of tourists.

A local tour director told the *LA Times* of his shock at one day finding the reef where he took small groups of visitors had been overrun:

'There must have been 600 people in the water, and the boats were lined up like cars. We didn't see a single ray or shark.' Having watched the tourists trample the coral, he concluded: 'We are destroying the very things that people are coming to see.'

At least some cruise lines claim their ships are now taking more care with their anchors, which have played their part in the destruction of swathes of coral reefs around the globe. Holland America was fined $300,000 by the Virgin Islands for one such offence, and later made a hasty donation to the Cayman Islands after one of its ships dragged its anchor through another reef in a popular scuba and snorkelling area.

Cruise ships are able to reach some of the otherwise most inaccessible, pristine parts of the planet, from Alaska to Antarctica. Conservation groups claim that the natural wilderness of Antarctica is threatened by mass tourism, and that wildlife colonies, particularly those of penguins and other seabirds, are being overwhelmed by the growing number of visitors. The Antarctic and Southern Ocean Coalition's figures show that fewer than 5000 tourists visited during Antarctica's 1990–91 summer; they calculated that the number would top 30,000 in 2006. While a self-regulatory code of conduct limits the number of passengers disembarking at any site and requests that tourists remain at least 15 feet (around 5 metres) from seabirds, some have questioned its efficacy. Some operators have found that you can no more catch the wind than a flock of determined tourists with camcorders; one visitor recounted seeing other people clambering over colonies of chinstrap penguins to get a photograph, without the guides reacting. Other conservationists worry about the size of some cruise ships visiting the Antarctic, citing a higher potential for marine pollution.

Such fears took on a whole new dimension when it was announced that the *Golden Princess*, carrying 3800 passengers and crew – ten times the size of the average expedition cruise ships – would sail to Antarctica in early 2007. Delegates to an international Antarctic conference in 2006, who lobbied in vain to keep cruise liners away, said any accident risked an 'unthinkable disaster'. Princess Cruises denied the liner's new itinerary would place passengers or the environment in danger.

In Australia, the little-touched Kimberley region has been identified by tourism experts as an area where the impact of cruise visits should be monitored: a local version of Alaska, whose pristine and inaccessible nature is making it an appealing destination for global tourists looking for virgin territory to explore.

It is an issue of particular concern now in those islands most famously untouched by human development, the Galápagos. In May 2006 the *Discovery* visited the tropical archipelago off Ecuador. With 650 berths, this cruise ship was extremely large by the standards of tourist boats that normally visit the islands — carrying, in fact, five times as many passengers as the next largest vessel. According to conservationists, it set a worrying precedent.

Graham Watkins, the director of the Charles Darwin Foundation, told *The Guardian* that large ships would push out small, local operators, and increase the toll that tourism takes on the environment. Arrivals have more than doubled in the last couple of decades, drawing in more tourism workers from Ecuador's mainland and placing a great demand on natural resources.

Some in the Galápagos have already reported that the islands, once prohibitively expensive and inaccessible for all but the most committed visitor, are now seeing tourists who ignore basic regulations intended to preserve the unique ecosystem, straying from the paths and lobbing rocks at the unsuspecting fauna.

Tourism turns over about $200 million annually in the islands, but — despite the donations of some guests on small expedition boats such as those operated by Lindblad — barely any of the proceeds go into conservation. Watkins told *The Guardian* that conservation can only work if the Galápagos's biodiversity 'is owned in the hearts and minds of those that live there'. Cruise ships, by contrast, always have other ports to sail to.

Many cruise ship passengers are no more sensitive to local practices than they are to Belize's fragile coral reef or to Ecuador's ancient island species. The cruise lines themselves have in the past tried to address this. In 1933, P&O distributed a letter to its passengers visiting Papua on the very first designated Australian cruise ship, the *Strathaird*. In the letter, the Lieutenant-Governor of Papua thanked P&O for visiting the island's shores, but also suggested cautioning visitors not to indulge locals who were already starting to engage in the tourist industry's greatest practice: fleecing the unwary by demanding 'ridiculously exorbitant prices for insignificant services'. The letter ended:

> The Lieutenant-Governor ventures to suggest that you should call the attention of tourists to the dangers of this thoughtless liberality, and to ask them to join with the Government, the missionaries and the older men among the natives themselves, in helping to keep the character of these people unspoiled by such practices as indicated.

Such delicate sentiments would not necessarily permeate through the generations. Journalist Ian Verrender used to live on the Pacific island of American Samoa, where the locals were intensely religious, usually belonging to the more radical sects of Christianity – including the Seventh Day Adventists, Mormons and Jehovah's Witnesses. Verrender noted that 'even girls who had been brought up in Hawaii and sent back home for some "cultural realignment" tended to observe the rules – in public at least – about modesty'. The women would wear lava-lava, a wrap-around skirt like a sarong, at all times, even when swimming. The contrast with the passengers arriving on the *Fairstar* cruise ship couldn't have been greater:

> They would just stumble off drunk. I remember once seeing an Australian woman wearing nothing but a G-string bikini and high heels standing next to a policeman in the middle of the town directing traffic.

Hotpants and swimsuits were common among the daytrippers:

> The place is hot and humid. It's one of the wettest places on earth and closely resembles a sauna, so the attire was appropriate from an Australian viewpoint. But culturally, it was completely insensitive.

In parts of the Pacific, the islanders have resisted the influx. In 2003, campaigners persuaded the cruise industry to drop plans to start calling at one of the most rural and untouched Hawaiian islands, Molokai. Locals said that they had not been consulted before the itineraries were announced – that the ships were not coming at their invitation, and they feared for the cleanliness of their seas, where many fished for a living.

Another Hawaiian island, Maui, attracts cruise ships once a week but the cruise companies' plans for more visits encountered some local resistance. An inhabitant put it like this:

> Hotels have to go through years of permitting, mitigate their effects, contribute to parks and road improvements but if you build a hotel and float it on our waters (incidentally dumping all its trash and sewage in our ocean), you get the Maui taxpayers to pay for your dock, your terminal, your security screening and you don't have to contribute a thing to Maui's roads, beaches and parks which are overrun with thousands of cruise ship passengers every day.

Despite such concerns, other places are aggressively courting the cruise ship market. Cruise ship passengers coming ashore are seen as potential cash cows, buying souvenirs, duty-free goods, and taking taxis or daytrips. Ross Klein notes in *Cruise Ship Blues* that in recent years, Central American ports in Panama and Colombia have offered to undercut fees charged to cruise ships by competing stopover destinations, and even pay ships to land passengers at their shores.

Development of new terminals is continuing worldwide. Kochi

in India is investing US$22.7 billion to become a global hub. Even Hartlepool, a north-eastern British port whose inhabitants are legendary for having once hanged a monkey in the belief that he was a French spy, has recently planned to attract international visitors by developing a cruise terminal.

In Australia, Queensland premier, Peter Beattie, has declared that he wants to make his state 'the cruise mecca of the South Pacific'. A new international cruise ship terminal opened in August 2006 in the Brisbane suburb of Hamilton, in a development to be surrounded by exclusive waterfront flats. The developers, Multiplex Living, encouraged upwardly mobile Queenslanders to move into the new Portside Wharf in advertisements saying – presumably without irony: 'Spend time in a cruise ship port and you'll see more of the world than you will ever see travelling.' The wharf would be, they said, a place of 'Mediterranean millionaires . . . multilingual conversations in coffee shops, the experiences of the well-travelled exchanged over river views'. Like the shops that line cruise jetties in the Caribbean, selling American brands such as Tommy Hilfiger and Calvin Klein while blocking out the local businesses, the Queensland that cruise passengers first encounter appears to be a projection of the world they have supposedly travelled away from.

A sustained campaign of protest helped prevent another planned cruise terminal from being constructed nearby – threatening to destroy the actual Australian lifestyle that locals enjoy: surfing, swimming, walking on the beach and exploring marine life. The proposed new Gold Coast terminal was to be built on Southport Spit, virtually the last piece of undeveloped ocean-front land in the area. After local opposition groups mobilised thousands of people to join protests and sign petitions opposing the terminal, the state government finally announced it was shelving the scheme for environmental reasons.

While the state government moots the economic benefits of such projects, its own studies do not seem to promise a flow of riches from cruise trippers' pockets. Tourism Queensland research found that cruise passengers to Australia spent an average of just $80 per person during stopovers in Brisbane.

As local communities from Anchorage, Alaska, to Australia's Gold Coast have become very much aware, virtually all of cruise passengers' spending takes place on the ship – the place where they eat and sleep, which accounts for most travellers' expenses. Even daytrips are usually arranged directly through the ship, leaving ground handlers with a smaller cut. In parts of Alaska, Hawaii and elsewhere, cruise lines have bought out local tour operators and businesses, channelling even more of the revenue to the parent corporation. As cruise fares become ever cheaper, the passengers are generally less affluent, and therefore likely to have less cash to spend on daytrips ashore.

In Alaska, groups claiming to seek to protect the local economy have recently clashed with others seeking to protect the local environment from cruise ship tourism. Stringent laws on pollution are already in effect, but years of concern about how cruising may be affecting the natural habitat has led to further action. Locals cite the annoyance of helicopter tours, of visitors swamping small ports such as Juneau. A citizens group's campaign to toughen up regulations on ships visiting the state culminated in a referendum being held in August 2006. In a close-run ballot – held just three days after a Celebrity cruise ship entered the port of Anchorage with an endangered whale skewered on its bow – the public decided to introduce a new $50 per passenger tax and a further tax on the ships' gambling proceeds, as well as requiring ships to obtain pollution permits and carry a state-appointed environmental ranger when in Alaskan waters. The supporters of the proposed new measures, a group called Responsible Cruising in Alaska, claimed:

> The cruise lines are 'selling' Alaska – while impacting our docks, roads, public facilities, wildlife, and the quality of our lives. This initiative will do nothing to turn visitors away; it will help keep our tourism industry sustainable while protecting the needs of all Alaskans.

The measures had been vigorously opposed by the cruise industry; it emerged that a group campaigning against the taxes called Alaskans Protecting Our Economy was virtually entirely funded by a trade association from beyond the state, the North West CruiseShip Association, based in Canada.

The freedom to turn away or discourage cruise ships is, however, a luxury. In some places, where locals might earn just a few dollars a day, economies have become beholden to the cruise ship visitors, low-spend or not. One man who eked out a living diving for and hawking starfish and conch shells in Nassau, the Bahamas, told a *Florida Today* reporter that he didn't 'even want to think about' life without the ships.

Nevertheless, cruise ships provide only an insecure source of livelihood, and can be affected by factors beyond local control; in the aftermath of Hurricane Katrina, Belize found its cruise income down by over 20 per cent – partly because Carnival's *Elation*, a regular visitor, was commandeered to house aid workers in New Orleans.

As Polly Pattullo, author of *Last Resorts: the cost of tourism in the Caribbean*, points out:

> Nobody in the Caribbean owns a cruise ship. It's not a home-grown industry. And it is so fragile and opportunistic. If something isn't exactly to the cruise company's liking, they just cut an island out of their itinerary.

This, Ross Klein recounts in *Cruise Ship Blues*, was the fate of Grenada. Over several years in the 1980s, Caribbean islands attempted to raise passenger taxes and port fees to increase revenue. The rises were resisted by the cruise industry and rescinded in the early 1990s, but in 1998 Carnival did agree to pay an extra $1.50 per passenger earmarked for a new waste management scheme for Grenada, supported by the World Bank. In late 1999 it reversed its decision and announced it was boycotting Grenada over what it claimed was an unfair tax. A spokesman told the *Los Angeles Times* that while it was only $1.50, the company couldn't start just paying out, as the reason that Carnival made the kind of money it did was that it paid great, great attention to controlling its costs.

The cruise companies' ability to change itineraries to suit themselves increased when they came up with a whole new concept in ports of call: the private island. This meant their schedules, costs and convenience were no longer encumbered by the real world outside the ship. According to Ross Klein, Norwegian Cruise Lines was the first to dream up the idea in the early 1990s. Sold to the passengers as an exclusive destination, a private island essentially allows a cruise line to retain all profits from food and drinks, activities and tours:

> There is no competition, so all money spent on the island contributes to [a company's] revenue and profit, and as an added benefit, passengers tend to enjoy the experience.

While cruise lines point to their enormous contribution to both local and national economies in terms of jobs and spending, taxes paid by the giant corporations are negligible. For example, because Carnival is incorporated for tax purposes in Panama, and can claim that its operations are on the high seas, it coughed up a mere $3 million in income tax on a pre-tax income of $1.9 billion in 2004. As Robert S. McIntyre of Citizens for Tax Justice told *The Washington Post*, 'That's not even a tip.' The 25 per cent tax that US companies typically pay could have left an equivalent company with a $475 million tax bill. Royal Caribbean reported a profit of $475 million the same year, but said it was exempt from corporate income tax, and paid only negligible tax on income relating to its subsidiaries.

In the aftermath of Hurricane Katrina, three Carnival Cruise Lines ships were chartered to provide emergency accommodation for the homeless of New Orleans – at a cost of US$236 million. Politicians from both major US parties denounced the contract. Republican senator Tom Coburn pointed out that at the price taxpayers were paying to house people on a stationary ship, 'The federal government would actually save millions of dollars by forgoing the status quo and actually sending evacuees on a luxurious six-month cruise.' But while Carnival said that they 'would make no additional money on this deal versus what we would have made by keeping these ships in service', they did have one major concern. Would having these boats moored so long in American waters jeopardise their tax status? *The Washington Post* reported that Carnival's CEO wrote to the United States Treasury to appeal for a waiver of US taxes: 'We do not want to jeopardize our tax exemption, nor do we want to interrupt our relief efforts for failure to secure this assurance from the Treasury Department.'

For all the double-edged effects of cruise ships sailing into ports, their presence is never so controversial as at the end of their working lives. Environmental problems do not end when a ship stops sailing; instead, in some of the world's poorest countries, they are often just beginning. Decommissioned ships often head for the shores of India, Pakistan and Bangladesh, to be broken up manually by workers for scrap.

When it was launched into the seas by the wife of General de Gaulle in 1960, the SS *France* was the latest of the great ocean liners, set to cross the Atlantic between Europe and New York: too long even to fit into the locks of the Panama Canal, and marked by an avant-garde design, luxurious trappings and winding staircases. In the course of an illustrious decade, Salvador Dali and his pet leopards would sail on the SS *France*, and its cargo would include the *Mona Lisa*, on her way to be exhibited in the United States. Taken out of transatlantic service in the 1970s, the ship became the SS *Norway*, a Caribbean cruise ship, before an explosion in the boiler room killed seven people and ended that career. It passed into the service of a Malaysian cruise company, and was renamed the *Blue Lady*. By 2006, it had faded, and was finally set for the scrapheap.

The ship was sent first to Bangladesh's shipbreakers, before environmentalists persuaded the government there that the dangers were too great. The huge vessel contained tons of toxic substances, including asbestos and carcinogens such as polychlorinated biphenyl and heavy metals. The cost of proper asbestos decontamination exceeded the ship's scrap value. Rejected by Bangladesh, the ship was instead towed to Alang in India for dismantling.

Greenpeace said that breaking up the SS *France* would further endanger the health of nearly 10,000 workers at the Alang yards; men and women who often use basic tools in primitive working conditions.

Some workers at Alang have resented the actions of environmentalists. One man who was still trying to make a living at Alang, despite having lost one hand in an accident, asked a Reuters journalist: 'Do we stop living as there is always a fear of dying?' But Greenpeace activists in India and beyond are demanding that all shipping industries take more responsibility for the fate of their vessels; as one told *The Observer*, 'the shipping industry will have to pay to get rid of toxic ships, instead of workers paying with their health and their life'. The Basel Convention, which aims to stop developed countries sending toxic waste to poorer countries for disposal, was invoked to stop such ships ending up in the breakers' yards. Such appeals failed, and the cruise liner's end was set for September 2006 in the dumping ground of Alang: a place that was once itself, before the ships came, an unspoilt beach.

5

Down Under and Dirty

BLAME CAPTAIN COOK. Most non-Indigenous Australians can trace their ancestry back to migrants who made long arduous journeys by ship from the other side of the planet – many of whom were forcibly transported. No society with a history like this could ever entirely regard a boat journey as a genteel activity. And yet Australians have made cruising their own, though the activity bears as much resemblance to the traditional concept of cruising as Aussie Rules does to football. It's not so much blue rinse as blue movie.

All the old elements are there, just a little modified: stroll on deck, sip a cocktail, meet new friends and wake up to a new horizon. Or to be precise, as a recent cruise showed: get on board at Sydney's King Street Wharf, drink heavily, have a punch-up and be under arrest in a police station under the Harbour Bridge by dawn.

Something of a record was set in spring of 2006 when just over four hours of a cruise had elapsed before Sydney's maritime police had to be called in. P&O's *Pacific Sun* was barely 30 miles out to sea at the time. A twenty-nine-year-old Victorian man, who had been restrained by crew after assaulting both a female crew member and a security guard, was handed over to police, ending up with a $400 fine. Two other men were also escorted off the vessel for breaching the peace.

But peace was always going to be a rare commodity on the *Pacific Sun*, known by many as a 'party ship'. And this fully booked 'Runaway to Sea' cruise promised nothing so boring as stops at a foreign port or tropical island. The allure? Three nights simply to party in duty-free waters.

A P&O spokeswoman claimed that they don't do booze cruises – a statement that might have surprised many of the 1896 passengers booked on the Runaway to Sea. 'Three days on the piss,' had said one man, waiting to board the ship at King Street Wharf at the beginning of the cruise. 'Just a grogfest, isn't it?' said another, a forty-year-old with his wife, racing along the wharf with his suitcases. 'Like a floating RSL,' reckoned a third.

Forget exclusivity. Berths on the *Pacific Sun*'s trip could be bought for as little as $650, including all food and entertainment. Low fares and 'mates' rates' (special deals allowing passengers to squeeze in an extra friend for a few dollars more) have opened the seas to a new generation, who might have preferred Bali before bombs took the sheen off its party scene.

At nineteen, Stephanie was already a serial cruiser. At a bar on the wharf in the afternoon before the ship set sail, she explained the appeal. 'All my work pay goes on saving for the next cruise. I'm going on for three days, and not going to sleep, so it feels like six days.' Several of her friends had travelled on the *Pacific Sky* and *Sun* before. 'Awesome,' they said. They loved the food, the entertainment, the escapism, but above all 'the party atmosphere'. They went to party – not necessarily looking for sex – although one admitted to having had more than one partner on her last cruise. 'You know, you have a couple of drinks and then . . .'

Kirsty, twenty-four, arrived at the last minute by taxi, rushing to get on the boat. Before boarding, she said, dryly: 'We plan on not being drugged and raped.' She was meeting a lot of other female friends, who would all look out for each other, she said. Her friend Jessica had been on a cruise before: 'Lots of pashing.' And there would be more this time, the two women said.

Outside on dock, relatives were waving goodbye to the cruisers. Passengers included several couples who were leaving the children with their grandparents. As they boarded, their families watched from the dockside. 'We're going to let our hair down,' one couple in their forties said. The husband added: 'In fact, I already have.' They had been on the cocktails in a nearby bar for several hours before the scheduled departure time.

On the dock, a mother was looking apprehensive. She was waiting to wave her two daughters off on their first cruise. At twenty-four and twenty-one, having travelled to Europe, they should be okay, she said, and yet she was nervous. She had told them drink spiking was a risk: 'Only cans and screw-top drinks. That's my main concern.'

Tony, a middle-aged, bearded vet who had travelled from interstate, looked slightly incongruous. What was he expecting on board? 'Christ only knows.' He felt a three-day cruise was a good way to test the waters. He'd heard the stories from the *Pacific Sky*, but said he wasn't too worried. 'Things go on everywhere, don't they?'

At the gates to the port, four men eyed up passing women with whom they would be spending three nights in a confined space. One had been on a cruise before – and he 'couldn't get enough of them'. 'Chicks,' he said, banging his fist into his palm. 'All the girls are up for it. Lot of oldies – but they go hard.' Sometimes, he reckoned, 'all drugged out, easy'.

Judging by comments made on an internet talk board, other past Australian cruisers concur with his opinions. One, a veteran of P&O's *Pacific Sun*, said: 'Alcohol is the best thing about the cruise, closely followed by the women.' Another man agreed: 'If you can't pick up on a cruise there is something wrong.'

Advice for other young men considering a P&O cruise was candid and considered. Should one of them visit the Pacific, and which island? One counselled:

What I didn't know in 2002 that I found out in 2003 is that you can get your hands on some EXTREMELY cheap weed in Noumea. That made the day go by a lot better.

Another pointed out that the island itinerary doesn't really matter. 'The most fun is had on the boat anyway. Cheap drinks, loose women. What more could you ask for?' It's one point of view.

Sydneysider Mary Anne Thompson said she and her family, passengers on the curtailed *Runaway to Sea*, weren't perturbed by the unscheduled return to Sydney Harbour: 'It didn't really matter because the cruise didn't have a destination anyway.' She vowed never to get on board again, jaded by the huge queues in the dining room for breakfast, and the similar lines to reclaim unspent credit that passengers had put on their cruise cards, the only method of payment at the bars on board. But they hadn't been disturbed by any shenanigans.

On other voyages, not all passengers had been so lucky. On these ships, joy or despair could largely be a question of where guests were sleeping. On the upper decks, the cabins or staterooms tend to be priced to attract a slightly wealthier, and often older clientele. The cheaper areas downstairs, sleeping four to a cabin, can prove particularly attractive to two very different types of passenger: parents with children, or young, partying groups on mates' rates. Unfortunately, as a one-time-only passenger travelling on the *Pacific Sun* with her family found when billeted in the next cabin to the partying and loudly fornicating, there is nowhere to move on a fully booked cruise.

Perhaps Australian cruise operators are just ahead of the game. In Britain and Europe of late, the travel industry has started marketing the concept of cruising at a younger generation – the kind of thirty-something who might be attracted by a branded coffee, a trendy onboard gym, or the promise of visiting the Mediterranean's hipper cities.

Australian companies have not messed around by targeting consumers who themselves only have a few decades left. Another of their innovations has been a huge commercial success: the school leavers' cruises or 'schoolies'. The passenger list on a schoolies cruise will consist entirely of those yet to do a day's work in their lives – a stark contrast to the retirees who usually populate cruise ships.

In the words of one schoolies cruise veteran, the itinerary is simple. 'Lots of drinking and pashing lots of boys.' And, of course, no teachers around to keep matters in check. In the words of one ex-crew member who would have to entertain them: 'They were a fucking nightmare. Horrendous. In every way.' A musician, he would be unable to leave the stage on schoolies cruises:

> We couldn't take a break, because if we did some fuckwit would decide he was going to play drums, with two schooners of beer in his hand. And then vomit in a corner.

One former crew member from the *Fair Princess* gave a more positive perspective: 'Schoolies cruises were well known as being the one time when crew could always get laid if they wanted to.'

At least one P&O schoolies cruise has arrived back at Sydney to be met by police. At other times, the law has tried to head off trouble in advance: in November 2004, a team of nineteen marine police with sniffer dogs boarded one ship before it set off on a schoolies cruise to New Caledonia, and seized a stash of marijuana. Police said there was also a noticeable quantity of white powder in the harbour car park near the boat, which they assumed had been jettisoned. 'Obviously someone saw us doing the rounds,' an inspector told a reporter from *The Sydney Morning Herald*.

The *Herald* had also reported on another particularly notorious trip which had taken place a year earlier, in December 2003. Five men were taken off the *Pacific Sky* by police after what the cruise firm would only describe as a number of 'incidents' – incidents serious enough to see the men held in the brig – the ship's jail cell – for two days, on orders of the captain, for 'anti-social behaviour'. P&O said the captain believed the behaviour of these men was 'a threat to the safety of the passengers'. All 1500 of them.

Nine other young passengers had already been expelled from the ship en route through the South Seas, at the ports of Noumea, Port Vila and Mystery Island. And the voyage had been further disrupted by a hoax man-overboard alarm; an eighteen-year-old was questioned by security staff and police, having left the ship circling for seven and a half hours on a vain search, at a cost of $20,000 in fuel and $3000 in deck furniture thrown overboard to mark the spot.

Boys will be boys. But then, the five arrested on disembarking the *Pacific Sky* weren't exactly boys, or even school-leavers for that matter, but a group of men in their early twenties – a gang of what any school-age girl on board would instantly have recognised as a whole other sub-species of Australian cruisers: the Toolies – a wonderfully descriptive abbreviation for the 'too-old-for-schoolies'.

If there's one thing worse than a shipload of rampant schoolies, it's the unwanted, menacing presence of the toolies. Drawn like hyenas to the floating meat markets, with sex on the brain – and the money to pay for the drinks – they are every parent's nightmare.

Former crew member Daina Brampton worked on many schoolies trips, and recalls that in the midst of the general unpleasantness ('the worst, really horrible kids'):

> . . . you'd have the nasty old men. We'd see them there, perving, some of them well over forty, deliberately booked on to be with these eighteen-year-old girls. We'd be like: you creepy old buggers . . .

According to passengers on board the particularly anarchic 2003 cruise, much of what occurred could be laid squarely on the shoulders of marauding toolies. One female passenger told Sydney's *Daily Telegraph*:

> They would come up to girls in the hallways or on the dance floor and rub their breasts or grab them on the bum even if they were

walking with a boyfriend. One guy took his shirt off and started rubbing up against me. I would yell at them to go away, but security did not seem to care.

One friend of mine was trying to get into her room when four guys grabbed her. They were touching her and said they wouldn't let her go until she put her hand down their pants.

Another eighteen-year-old girl was able to tell just why the first seven men to be put ashore for misbehaviour were kicked off the ship. They were trying to break down the door that she had locked to keep them outside her cabin.

On board ship, the passengers were locked in together at close quarters, booze was flowing, and feats of drinking were feted: one man guzzled down two bottles of white wine in a row at the dining room table, to general acclaim. Girls complained of physical intimidation and indecent assault. Boys reported fight after fight.

P&O denied that there had been excessive drinking on board, and pointed out that security was far higher on schoolies cruises than on other voyages, with three times as many officers present. Nevertheless, after this particular series of events, the cruise firm did crack down on the toolies, making it a policy to restrict schoolies cruises to those aged between sixteen and nineteen, with approved escorts. A spokesman said: 'If you're going to have them on board, it's better to have them all on board. We've had experiences in the past when our normal passenger profile is mixed with schoolies – and that's not going to be a good outcome for either party.'

But problems persisted, and despite the cruises remaining extremely popular with the kids, P&O decided that the class of 2006 would be the last on their ships – refunding thousands who had already booked for December 2007.

Still, as one security guard told *The Sydney Morning Herald*, there are some situations that leave them flummoxed – even on the adult cruises. With alcohol flowing, and the nightclub jumping, men and women can be found wandering the ship naked. By 5 am, he said, 'they're making love all over the place, not actually in front of people, but in public places ... What can we do? Ask them politely to get dressed and do it in their cabins, not on the deck.'

Another security manager on the *Pacific Sky* estimated seeing an average of fifteen to twenty naked passengers every night. But then, not all security guards themselves appear to have been exactly keeping things calm: a *Sunday Telegraph* journalist on the *Pacific Sun* reported how one female guard in uniform got down on all fours on the dance floor, while a male colleague behind her simulated sex to the sound of the music.

One particularly lecherous man was escorted out by security; his ignominious exit made more notable by the fact that he was himself a member of the ship's entertainment staff. A musician in the band, he had pulled down his pyjama waistband, offering to 'swap' garments with the journalist.

Over the course of her eleven-day South Pacific cruise, she reported one man left on a drip after binge drinking, another group of men starting a brawl on the dance floor and a young Sydney woman ending up spending three days in a medical centre after an attempt to slide her across a soapy bar counter in Vanuatu badly misfired.

Some cruise staff might not necessarily want passengers to order fewer drinks. Jeff Dobjeckie, a former security manager on the *Pacific Sky*, told a reporter from *The Daily Telegraph* that the bar staff would need plenty of takings at the boat's watering holes, the Legends Bar and the Starlight Disco, to claim a decent commission. Enough, he said, to depend on everyone 'getting blind drunk'.

Alas, such days of unbridled alcoholism, exhibitionism and free love appear to be numbered: back on land, an embarrassed P&O Australia was pledging to crack down on excessive behaviour. Bars, it announced, would no longer stay open twenty-four hours, having instead a brief breakfast moratorium from 4 am till 10 am. The cruise line went so far as to announce publicly that they were changing their onboard regulations to make public nudity and sex a disembarkable offence.

Even the government felt obliged to get involved. The New South Wales Minister for Gaming and Racing, Grant McBride, said the government would provide cruise ship operators with workshops on the responsible service of alcohol, to tackle what he described as an obvious lack of safeguards on the ships. Something, the minister said, needed to be done to protect Australians on cruises. (P&O said that it would welcome the opportunity to bolster its own extensive staff training in serving alcohol responsibly.)

Yet where did this debauchery start? In the family tree of Australian cruising, one ship stands out as the daddy, or at least as a somewhat dissolute uncle: the TSS *Fairstar*.

6

Fairstar the Fuckship

IT WAS A grand beginning for a liner: born to serve the Royal Navy of Queen Elizabeth. The *Fairstar* started life in 1955 as the HMT *Oxfordshire*, a British troop ship commissioned to transport soldiers out to distant colonial outposts such as Hong Kong. However, the end of empire was imminent, and the need for such ships diminishing. The *Oxfordshire* only saw five years of active service as a troop ship.

Refitted as a passenger liner, it was bought up by an Italian shipping firm, Società Italiana Trasporti Marittimi, and renamed the *Fairstar*. Operating at first between Europe and Sydney, it brought many new migrants out to Australia, on seven-week voyages that traversed such spectacular and exotic waters as the Suez Canal. But as the popularity of cruising grew, its role as a pure pleasure ship came to the fore.

With ornate public lounges, a nightclub, a swimming pool and even a 'Bavarian Beer Hall' with a huge timber bar, early passengers recall it as an exciting and modern ship for the times. Maritime historian Reuben Goossens, who sailed from Melbourne via Sydney to Naples on the *Fairstar*'s second voyage from Australia in 1964, has fond memories of being 'one of the young set, listening to Eric Burdon and the Animals' great hit "The House of the Rising Sun" in the ship's Jungle Room'. Goossens says it was 'a teenager's delight':

On the port side there was the milk bar, a jukebox with a dance floor. On starboard side were a number of poles with two seats attached and a shelf for drinks, leaves sprouting from the top of the poles . . . [it was] a unique room, perfect for those so full of 'puppy love'.

By 1974, the *Fairstar* was permanently based in Sydney, and becoming known as a place to party. The owners rebranded it '*Fairstar* the funship'. It was a name that betrayed a certain amount of tender anthropomorphism, but the *Fairstar*'s name would suffer the indignity of distortion as the industry sailed into a less gentle era, in which cruising would no longer be associated with pursuits as innocent as puppy love: the age of *Fairstar* the Fuckship.

Music, alcohol, and the promise of much, much more: the boat would soon grab a special place in Australian hearts. Almost one million passengers would sail on it in its time based in Sydney Harbour. An ex-cruiser recalled his maiden voyage: 'The first chick I talked to said to me, "Did you know they call this the P&O Fuckship?" My jaw dropped. As they say, the rest is history.' A couple who returned to the seas in 2006 on the *Pacific Sun* reminisced that it was also called 'the Floating Orgy' and said, 'It used to go up and down, and not from the waves.'

Did the ship deserve that reputation? Sandy, an ex-stewardess who went on to work for Norwegian Cruises in the US, said: 'Orgy ships? Well, they were definitely that.' Drinking, she said, was very much encouraged by the bartenders – the more drinks they sold, the more money they made.

The ship's Sharp End bar had the wildest reputation, with cruise staff and passengers involved in many drinking games, Sandy said. 'I even remember lying on the bar so the guys could drink shots from our bellybuttons. It was wild, but lots of fun.'

Murray Ferguson was a musician on the *Fairstar* for seven years, from 1990 until its final voyage. He played bass and sang in the Aquarius Lounge. It was, he said, 'loud, smoky and full of drunks'. He said he must have seen Port Vila and Noumea four hundred times – ports of call that 'lose their appeal pretty quickly'. Perhaps that is one reason why P&O started the forerunner of their Runaway jaunts. 'Occasionally we'd do a Cruise to Nowhere. Passengers would come on pissed on the Friday and drink right through to the Monday morning.' Even crew would drink on duty, forbidden as it officially was. It was, Ferguson said, an Australian institution.

A *Sydney Morning Herald* journalist took a cruise in the early 1990s on the *Fairstar*, concluding with admirable understatement that 'this cruise is not a holiday for thinkers'. But she reported that passengers left the ship with tears in their eyes after days on board enjoying such highlights as the sleazy lines of the maître d, a cruise director crooning the theme to *Love Boat*, single girls brandishing streamers in the Starlight disco with condoms tied to the end and tug-of-war competitions between teams called the Anzac Wallies, Wogs Without Women, the Penetrators and the Nutcrackers.

For the Pacific islands on the *Fairstar*'s itinerary, a visit from the holidaying Australians was an event indeed. Ian Verrender, a former resident of Pago Pago in American Samoa, recalled the ship's visits as 'a real eye-opener': 'The really odd thing about the whole experience was looking at Australians and Aussie culture as an outsider.'

Pago Pago was a quiet little town, he says, 'with an enormous fish factory that stank to high heaven and serviced a fleet of Korean trawlers and purseiners'. But every month when the *Fairstar* hit port, the place just went crazy:

> They would just stumble off drunk. I don't know why the ships stopped anywhere, because most of the passengers would just head straight to the bar. It was clearly just a total pissup. Thousands of young pissed Aussie yobbos, looking for the closest bar, usually Sadie Thompson's at the Rainmaker. And girls wearing next to nothing.

Any overnight stopping place in the Pacific islands, such as New Caledonia's capital, Noumea, would take the full brunt of both passengers' and crew's party urges. Stops in Sydney were too short and busy for crew to relax, usually a frantic day of disembarkment and reloading. An ex-crew member relates:

> You'd never get much time in Oz so we would do our partying overseas. There was one guy who'd be the one to see about drugs. The stopovers would usually involve having a pill and then hitting the nightclubs – a place that was apparently the gay club most of the time but whenever the ship was in the Australians would flood the place.

These idyllic forays through the South Pacific islands could not last forever. Sadly, the ship was growing as corroded as its passengers' livers. And the *Fairstar* was earning another reputation: it was becoming known for always breaking down.

Most of the time, says Murray Ferguson, the passengers wouldn't tend to notice:

> You could just float for hours. Once we got stuck on a sandbar on a Pacific island, on a night when the captain was sick and the staff captain had taken over. We had to get tugs to pull the ship off, but all the passengers were in the disco and never knew anything about it.

Occasionally, though, it became all too obvious: Ferguson remembers playing gigs when the boat lost all power, when the lights, sound and air conditioning all disappeared.

Losing the air conditioning was not as trivial as it sounds, another former crew member says: 'There's no way of getting any air down through most of the boat otherwise. It would have been horrible.' Not least on the occasion of the *Fairstar*'s most notorious breakdown, in 1991, which occurred in the comparatively lawless waters off Vietnam. In baking tropical heat, the ship drifted helplessly for five days without power. The *Fairstar*'s longer Asian cruises were generally populated by a much older clientele, barely inclined to have to rough it in such conditions. Tempers flared and fights even broke out. While some passengers were shown to their darkened cabins by torchlight, many found themselves driven up to sleep on the deck by the sweltering conditions below. One member of the crew died of a burst peptic ulcer. Others complained of rashes breaking out, suspecting that some of the supposedly fresh water on board was becoming contaminated.

Eventually the *Fairstar* was rescued by Vietnamese tugboats that took its passengers into port, many of them drenched by monsoonal rain in the transfer. A crew member recalls: 'We were taken to this police centre with military police shoving machine guns in our faces.' For some, the experience was particularly nerveracking. On return, one former US soldier from San Francisco told *The Sydney Morning Herald* that he began to fear for his safety under questioning by Vietnamese officials in Ho Chi Minh City. 'Because of my nationality, I could have been in danger. I mean I am an ex-serviceman of the US Army.' Another Sydney passenger's comments seemed to sum it up for many: 'That ship should be scrapped.' One of the crew later said: 'We should never have sailed. It wasn't fit to go.'

P&O said that the *Fairstar* had been 'very thoroughly' checked by Lloyd's shipping inspectors and the crew. But even with reissued safety certificates and multi-million dollar refits, more breakdowns would occur.

The *Fairstar*'s days were numbered. A new ship was ordered by P&O. Ferguson remembers passing the substitute, a liner that would become the *Fair Princess*, on its way down to Sydney. 'We couldn't believe it when we saw it. This rust-bucket that no-one wanted in the Northern Hemisphere anymore.' It was, Australians soon realised, a new ship only in the sense that it was new to them.

Whether or not they had the *Fair Princess* in mind, in America, Carnival executives were buoyantly proud of their own advances, and the concurrent 'repositioning' of old, uninspiring ships outside their own market – dumped on the Aussies. (It is, to some extent, a trend that has continued. Of all the ships assessed by the latest edition of the independent cruising bible, the Berlitz *Complete Guide to Cruising & Cruise Ships 2006*, P&O's Australian ships could barely have ranked any lower. Out of a table of 114 large cruise ships carrying over 1000 passengers, the *Pacific Sun* and the *Pacific Sky* came in 108th and 111th place. Even the latest addition to the fleet, the superliner *Pacific Dawn*, which P&O has heralded as the Australian industry's 'coming of age', will have been operating elsewhere under a different name for sixteen years before making her maiden voyage from Sydney in 2007.)

While the crew hoped they would make a go of the new ship, there was something about the *Fair Princess* that they felt was all wrong. 'It was just no fun – it just didn't have that energy,' said Daina Brampton. 'The *Fairstar* had this welcoming feel, great atmosphere – something that has never been recreated.' The *Princess* would break down more seriously and often than the *Fairstar*. Its maiden cruise was marked by flooded cabins and restaurants, an electrical fire and missed ports of call, culminating in a rebate given to all the 1070 passengers on board by P&O. Taken out of service barely three years later, the *Princess* was the last such passenger liner to grace Australia, before the new generation of purpose-built cruise ships was launched.

The *Fairstar*'s last cruise was, fittingly, described as a 'raucous affair' by *The Daily Telegraph*; passengers danced the night away at pyjama parties, some doing backflips from the bar. Even the piano player managed to break an arm. A red-eyed passenger told the paper: 'I can sum up this trip in two words: bloody fantastic.' The ship sailed in through the heads of Sydney Harbour, flying a white 91-metre pennant that extended the length of the ship – traditional for a vessel being decommissioned – and a giant 'Goodbye Oz' banner, signed by a number of the 1200-plus passengers.

For all the bad press about sickness, breakdowns, and the occasional excessive debauchery, crew such as Katie Arnold remember it fondly:

'It was a really nice ship, something special. You had a lot of people who would come again and again, familiar faces – it was like a family.'

Around 1000 people had taken at least twenty cruises on a ship that had become a national icon. One passenger had been away with the *Fairstar* a record seventy-seven times.

With the commemorations done, the ship would eventually slip quietly out to sea to be broken up in Alang in India, leaving just a few items of memorabilia to go on display in the Maritime Museum in Sydney's Darling Harbour. The *Fairstar* may now just be so much recycled scrap metal on a distant shore, but its memory and spirit – to the eternal dismay of many Australian parents with children of cruising age – are very much alive.

7

Dianne Brimble

MUCH OF THE dream of the cruise is about throwing off the shackles of everyday life, being carefree. The sea beckons with adventure; the cruise ship promises escape, romance. For by far the majority of the many Australian passengers who have sailed off on cruises over the last decades, the reality would more or less meet their expectations – not perhaps the airbrushed serenity of an ocean liner, but certainly a giggle, a mildly anarchic holiday-camp-on-sea, the kind of fun and release that can be hard to find in the throes of everyday life.

How do different people interpret that licence to party? Unfortunately, no-one can choose all their fellow passengers; but can only hope that at sea, away from police and hospitals, some level of human decency will prevail. But innocent illusions are hard to maintain in the light of one Australian cruise: the events of one night in September 2002 would take several years to come out, and were shocking in the detail. In 2006, witnesses at a coronial inquiry would testify that by the end of the first night of a cruise on P&O's *Pacific Sky*, one woman lay naked, drugged and dying on the floor of a cabin, ignored and ridiculed by the men who had left her there.

It has become commonplace to describe a cruise as a 'trip of a lifetime' even in an era when for many it is just another holiday. But for Dianne

Brimble, a separated mother of three, a cruise was a once-in-a-lifetime luxury. With her sister Alma Wood, she had saved hard for this holiday for two years, both women wanting to take their young daughters away.

Yet, for all the anticipation, there was anxiety too: in the week before the trip, Mrs Brimble talked of a dream, a premonition of something bad to come on the cruise. The ship set sail from Brisbane; photos show Mrs Brimble waving excitedly setting off on her holiday. In another photo, taken by someone unknown to her, she is seen outside the port terminal, in the background of a group photo of eight men who were also about to board.

Out at sea, after the evening meal on that first night, Mrs Brimble's sister decided to take the kids to bed and turn in for the night. But Dianne loved to dance; according to her mother, of all the six siblings, she was the one who came into the world dancing. In the cabin, she changed her shoes and put on some make-up, and headed back out to the ship's nightclub.

She danced with a few people that night: with a friend, with a crew entertainer, and eventually with three men from Adelaide, part of a group of eight who had already made their presence felt on board; the officer in charge of hotel security had made a note to keep an eye on them. At 4 am, a security guard saw her leaving the nightclub with them, apparently in good spirits. She went back to one of their cabins, D182 on Dolphin deck.

The next morning, her sister Alma was paged urgently to come to the nurses' room. When she got there, the ship's doctor gave her the stark news: 'Dianne's dead.'

A toxicology report would show that she had died of an overdose of gamma-hydroxybutyrate, a party drug also known as GHB, GBH fantasy, or liquid ecstasy, and often described as a date-rape drug. Mrs Brimble, her family said, didn't even like to take Panadol. Someone, they said, had put that drug in her drink without her knowledge.

How Mrs Brimble came to have the drugs in her system that night has not been proven. Photos from a digital camera and the eventual testimony of witnesses at an inquest would reveal that before her death at least one man had sex with her, and took photographs of her even when she was passed out naked on the floor.

Australian police were called in: they flew to Noumea and boarded the ship two days later while it was in port, but somehow the investigation was terribly flawed. The cabin had not been sealed off as a crime scene. The men who would become 'persons of interest' in the eventual investigation and coronial inquests had been allowed back into the cabin by staff to collect their belongings (including bottles of unspecified liquids) and then moved to new quarters – even while Mrs Brimble's bereaved family were kept locked out of their own cabin, in which she had never slept. The digital chip from the camera that would provide crucial evidence of the night's events was discovered on the ship by a seven-year-old boy. Police did not search the cabins being used by the eight men. Key witnesses were not interviewed for days, and at least one of the police officers ended up dancing in the disco.

It would take nearly three and a half years before some of the truth of what happened to Dianne Brimble would be established publicly, at the coroner's court in Glebe, Sydney. The family said they just wanted the truth to be told, grim and harrowing though it would prove.

Much of what was revealed came from women in a nearby cabin who the three men pursued that night even as Mrs Brimble lay unconscious, near death. The women, two sisters and their friend, had likewise been drinking all night and day, ever since boarding; but they declined the offer of GHB.

One of the men was running up and down the corridors, naked except for a life jacket. His friends said he had just 'fucked a fat chick', and the women said they were shown pictures to prove it. Another member of the group passed out; the others stripped him, and started to play with his genitals, photographing him for posterity.

At one point, the man in the life jacket, who had been in and out of the women's cabin, told the others that Mrs Brimble was out cold and he couldn't bring her round; one woman went over to look but did nothing to help her, presuming that she was drunk and asleep.

Asleep in the cabin D182 was another of the men from Adelaide. In a police interview he said he had taken three sleeping pills, woken up to find Mrs Brimble in bed with him, and pushed her out. 'She just rolled over, hit the floor, it was like, yeah, goodnight, stay there.' He said he later awoke, tried to carry her to the shower to resuscitate her, and dressed her and called the ship's doctor. Cruise staff told him, he said, that they were fifteen minutes too late to save her.

Later in the inquest, one of the ship's entertainment crew, the magician who had danced with Mrs Brimble on the first night, would testify that he had been threatened by one of the Adelaide group later in the cruise. He also testified that he was told to keep his mouth shut by security officials and the cruise director on the three occasions that he attempted to voice suspicions about the death, after he heard the news from a friend of Mrs Brimble. A lawyer for P&O suggested that the magician was silenced because he had been drinking excessively and raised his voice.

Families in neighbouring cabins on board the ship were also apprehensive about the men, who burst into the room where their teenage daughters were staying. One of the girls said she was disgusted, offended and 'a little bit scared' by the men's sexual advances. The families asked the ship staff to move them, without success.

But then, such goings-on were not uncommon, Ann Taylor, the security manager on the *Pacific Sky*, told the inquest. She had once come across a passenger spiking another passenger's drink, and had dealt with a number of complaints of rape.

Whatever the exact truth or the eventual outcome proves to be, the case has massively shifted perceptions of cruising in the eyes of the Australian public. In the wake of Mrs Brimble's death, P&O moved to improve security on ships, with increased checks including sniffer dogs for drugs, and plans to install CCTV on board. By the time of the inquest, P&O announced it would be stopping twenty-four-hour drinking and emphasising the responsible service of alcohol. A spokesman said that the cruise line accepted that in the past its responses to certain excesses had occasionally been inadequate.

P&O also tightened up the branding of their ships – apologising for an advertisement that appeared in 2003 showing bikini-clad women under the legend 'Seamen Wanted'. On the reverse of the promotional postcard was the slogan: 'More girl. More sun. More fun. There's nothing else a guy needs to know,' next to a photograph of the *Pacific Sky*.

The advertisement was submitted as evidence at the inquest, despite the objections of P&O's lawyer at such material being placed before the court. The coroner, Jacqueline Milledge, said that all details about the cruise culture were relevant; that Mrs Brimble did not die in a vacuum.

The cruise line said that the advertisements were 'unacceptable and are not the way we represent our company today. They are insensitive and do not represent our values.'

The *Pacific Sky* – now linked to four different deaths – was sold off to a Spanish cruising firm, making its last voyage under that name for P&O in May 2006.

In July 2006, P&O said that Mrs Brimble's family would receive a full refund for her cruise ticket and her family's, with interest. Travel insurance claims had been rejected because of the drugs found in her system.

Mark Brimble, Dianne's ex-husband and the father of her two sons, became the Australian spokesman for the International Cruise Victims association and has said publicly, 'We need to do everything we can do to prevent other people or families having to endure what we have already experienced.'

8

The Enemy Within

'Is GOING ON a cruise the perfect way to commit the perfect crime?' This was the question posed, not by some isolated conspiracy theorist who had watched too much daytime TV, but a congressman from the US Republican party.

Christopher Shays, who served on the congressional committee hearings into the cruise industry, believes that the crimes committed at sea that make it into the public domain back on land are just the tip of the iceberg. An assistant director of the FBI has backed him up, testifying that while the FBI had opened 305 crime cases on the high seas in the last five years, he was sure that many crimes on board were not being reported.

Shays added that he thought some cruise companies were doing their level best to make sure as few crimes as possible would be reported. 'There's a huge incentive to downplay any incident, to sail on,' he said.

It was something that Sydney woman Natalie W found to her cost, when a rape case she hoped to bring against a crew member from a Pacific cruise broke down because a key witness – an employee of the cruise line involved – repeatedly failed to appear in court.

Natalie, a secretary barely out of her teens, had spent a comparatively quiet day on the cruise: pizza for lunch, an afternoon passed in company, and in bed asleep before midnight in the twin cabin she shared with a friend. She woke to find a crew member sexually assaulting her. Her cabin mate came round from a deep sleep to see him leaving her friend's bunk, pulling on his trousers.

The traumatised Natalie was taken to the ship's hospital and the young women's belongings were transferred to a luxury cabin. It was a move that would block future investigations; with the girls gone, the crime scene was not preserved but cleaned up – destroying any evidence.

Natalie was sedated, barely leaving the security of her new quarters before the cruise line sailed into Sydney days later – to be met by police. On the basis of evidence submitted to the ship's security officer, a crew member was arrested and committed for trial.

Many sexual assault cases go unresolved, so the arrest was promising; however, the police had not reckoned on the disappearance of a witness – and not just any witness, but the security officer charged with the safety of all the passengers sailing on that ship. Still working for the same cruise line months later, he simply never got on the plane from the Bahamas to give evidence at the trial. Police claimed that the security officer had received a written statement that was crucial to their case – and without his cooperation, they were helpless. An interview with Interpol gave some indication of the officer's motives – apparently he believed he would lose his salary of US$4000 a month if he turned up to give evidence of the alleged rape in court.

The trial was adjourned, and reconvened a month later, but the security officer failed to appear once more, ignoring a subpoena.

The judge ruled that the trial could not go ahead. The accused walked out without having to face the charges and returned to the Philippines a free man.

The cruise line said it had not prevented the officer from giving his testimony, and said: 'Our legal position at the time was that [he] was under no obligation to attend.'

The Director of Public Prosecutions in New South Wales believed that the cruise line had 'obstructed' the attendance of the key witness.

Bringing a prosecution for crimes at sea is difficult. Charles R. Lipcon, a lawyer specialising in cruise ship suits, says that legal situations passengers find themselves in are frequently murky:

> It's complicated. At any given time there could be more than one law. If it's in international waters, first of all it's the laws of the flag state. If the crime happens to, say, an American citizen and the vessel ends at a port in the US, the American federal government would have jurisdiction.

Other claims to jurisdiction could arise depending on where the vessel sails from; though normally if a boat is in the territorial waters of any country, matters would be tackled under the laws of that country. With boats travelling from place to place, Lipcon says the potential for dispute is heightened:

> Sometimes people don't know what time the crime happened, and sometimes you could have two or more possible countries' laws coming into play. What I've seen over the years is that it's a hot potato for everyone, and nothing much gets done.

His firm does not normally take on cases that do not have a clear jurisdiction.

The industry body, the International Council of Cruise Lines, sees the situation differently, and says: 'Cruise lines operate within a very strict legal framework that gives both federal and state authorities the right to investigate crimes on board cruise ships.' In cases involving Americans, it says the FBI has the authority to investigate and prosecute alleged crimes in international waters.

While most of the 200 to 400 cases that Lipcon's firm may be addressing at any given time are related to accidents involving negligence or unseaworthiness, common among passenger complaints are alleged sexual assaults. Convictions are rare. Lipcon says he has never seen anyone successfully prosecuted for sexual assault: 'I've heard of about one case in thirty years.'

Instead, passengers resort to civil suits. As another maritime law specialist, Brett Rivkind, explained to the congressional hearings, the threat of civil liability does not necessarily act in everyone's best interests:

> If this remains the sole means to police the security on board the ships, the cruise lines will continue not to have an incentive to thoroughly investigate a crime on board its vessel in fear of establishing civil liability on its part.

Investigations are instead, he claimed, geared towards limiting any blame that could be attached to the company, rather than solving a crime.

The industry body, the International Council of Cruise Lines, insists: 'The cruise industry places the highest priority on the safety and security of its passengers and crew.' A cruise ship is, they say, comparable to a secure building with a twenty-four-hour security guard. 'Since a vessel operates in a controlled environment, access can be strictly enforced.'

Suits have generally been settled out of court, and few settlements allow the plaintiffs to talk about their experiences. One mother, however, refused to sign such a document after Carnival settled a damages claim for the rape of her young daughter. April Smith (not her real name) was twelve years old, on a Caribbean cruise with her family, when a crew member offered to take her to a place on the ship where she could see dolphins playing. She followed him trustingly to a secluded, employees-only area, where he raped her. He warned her never to speak of it, or he would find her and kill her. The girl did reveal the crime to staff on board but lost her nerve when asked to identify the rapist, feeling that she was not believed; she was never examined.

She was almost eighteen before she told her mother what happened and the family filed a lawsuit against the cruise line. While the settlement was undisclosed, her mother was adamant that other passengers needed to hear about the crime and know that their safety was not assured.

Janet Kelly, a forty-nine-year-old estate agent and mother of two from a small town in Arizona, was another victim of cruise crime who testified before the congressional hearings. A bartender with whom she had exchanged a few words served her a drink on the last night of the cruise, as the ship returned from Mexico to Los Angeles. That fruit cocktail contained a little more than fruit and a shot of alcohol. As she felt her legs give way, and her brain fuzz over, the barman took her to a bathroom that only employees were allowed to use and, before she passed out completely, he raped her.

It was only after flying home that she went to a hospital for tests. The FBI was called in, but it was weeks before the barman was interviewed. He claimed it had been consensual sex. The detectives decided not to proceed with a criminal case – at which point, Janet Kelly sued the cruise line.

The company sacked the barman for misconduct, as company policy officially forbids sex with passengers, even consensual sex. Kelly reached a settlement with the company. The barman, she later learned, was rehired by another cruise company – but then sacked again, for falsifying his employment records.

Rehiring is not uncommon, according to industry insiders. Randy Jaques, from Nevada, USA, who has been the chief security officer on many ships, recounted how on his very first day on board a new ship, he saw a familiar face. It was a crew member he had personally fired ten years before, considering him a threat to passengers.

As Jaques said, a genuine firing was quite a rare event; a staff member who a passenger complained about might receive a warning, or possibly be fired, but quite often he or she would just be transferred to another ship. In the busy shipping lanes plied by North American cruise liners, he said, 'It's very easy for them just to be put on another boat, especially if you're in Miami or St Thomas, say, but even in Alaska it's quite possible.'

Sydney maritime consultant Peter Burge agrees: 'If a crew member is complained about, many cruise lines wouldn't worry about it all. If there's no publicity about it, who's going to know?'

The ICCL says that it has a 'zero tolerance' policy towards crime: 'In the rare instance crimes occur on board, cruise lines report and cooperate with the appropriate law enforcement authorities.' This policy does not appear to have been applied on every ship. Jaques believes that the extent of crime as reported to US Congress and the FBI does not reflect what really goes on at sea. 'The cruise companies just want it to go away.' Hundreds of women have signed Jane Doe agreements, he says, settling with the cruise lines with a confidentiality clause. He claims he has personally dealt with over fifty sexual assaults at sea.

A British security officer, Geoff Furlong, who spent ten years working on cruises, had similar experiences, claiming to have dealt with hundreds of cases of alleged crime. 'Hardly a week went by' without something happening, he said in an interview with ITV's *Holidays Undercover*. 'Many times I would take statements, take forensic evidence, file reports but I never got anywhere.' When passengers did try to report assaults, the hotel department would offer them free champagne, dinner or holidays – anything to placate them, he said. Even rape victims, he claimed, were bought off with champagne.

The procedure for a ship's security officer is to report crimes to the company's home office. To call the FBI direct, said Jaques, was 'above my pay grade'. In fact, he explained, he often did not even have the authority to make the call to the home office – a responsibility left to the ship's captain. 'You're under the thumb, restricted. He has total control.' And from there, 'It's up to the home office to decide whether to report it or not to the FBI.' Often, Jaques would be left not knowing the outcome:

The captain may or may not tell me, but then by that time the voyage is coming to an end and the passenger is walking off the ship. Every voyage, passengers are asking, how is this going to be taken care of? And I'm not able to give them an answer. Basically you give them a business card and that card has a guest relations phone number on it, and that's all . . . That's the problem – they go off down the gangway and we load up with another two to three thousand passengers, and crew on some ships, and we sail again.

For foreign passengers on US boats it could be even worse, he said, as companies are more fearful of litigious Americans who may live in the heart of their biggest cruising markets. Complaints from passengers resident elsewhere are less likely to be taken seriously, Jaques claimed. 'I've seen captains be downright rude to passengers who complain, and say, especially if it's a charter, "Well, it's only a boatload of Mexicans."' Jaques said he had 'seen felonies of all types', but sexual offences were among the most common complaints. He believed the incidence of assaults committed by passengers has grown, with groups of men coming on a ship and specifically targeting women using drugs or alcohol. 'They watch to see who wins the drinking games.'

Charles Lipcon agreed:

There's a lot of use of date rape drugs now – it's becoming an epidemic. It used to be the crew members raping passengers and now it's passengers raping passengers. I think the word is out that if you rape someone on the high seas, no one does anything about it, so any perverts out there are just getting on board.

I got information out of one cruise line on a case we were handling of 174 sexual assaults. Out of 174 over three to four years, none was prosecuted. What message does that send out? They don't get arrested. It's just out of hand and it's getting worse by the day.

Of course, investigating crimes is not what security guards are hired for. Speaking with *The Daily Telegraph*, Jeff Dobjeckie, a former security specialist on Australian cruise ships, said he was told on more than one occasion by his bosses on board that he was security, not a policeman – he wasn't paid to think.

Jaques has set up an investigations agency, Maritime Investigations International, to help victims at sea, and is working with the International Cruise Victims group. He explained that even though he has both a police and military background, like any security officer needing to investigate a possible crime at sea, he faced many difficulties:

> Security officers generally have crime scene investigation experience but the problem is we don't have the crime scene tools. It's very difficult when you're by yourself. You just can't fathom being out there with no one to help you. You're in the middle of the ocean – it's very, very difficult. The equipment that we have is outdated – but even if you had newer equipment, you don't have the assistance that you need. A crime scene takes several individuals to process and it can take hours. But in our case it's done by the seat of your pants.

That's if crime scenes are preserved at all. As noted in the previous chapter, four men on the *Pacific Sky* were allowed to reclaim their possessions from the cabin in which Dianne Brimble died. Former security officers on Australian cruise ships recount similar experiences. After one incident of violent assault on a ship, between a husband and wife, the security officers entered to find the woman had been choked and the man slashed with a broken bottle, both needing medical attention. While the officers believed it should be left as a crime scene, they were ordered to clean up the cabin, the couple returned, and nothing was done.

The International Cruise Victims group, which says it wants to work with the cruise industries to improve passenger safety at sea, advocates full-time independent police on board ships. ICV spokesman Son Michael Pham, whose parents disappeared at sea, said that while he totally agreed with the cruise lines' argument that crime of all kinds can happen anywhere, on land more than on sea:

> What happens afterwards? If a crime happens, after that time there is a criminal on that ship. What stops a criminal going on board to get away with murder?
>
> If you look at the crime stats that [the cruise industry] finally gave to Congress, you have less than 10% of all crimes prosecuted. With the missing there is no prosecution, period.

He says that the stories of loss and sexual assaults on the ICV website are a small portion of all the case studies they have on their database; many more people had contacted them but did not want – or were not permitted by settlements – to make their stories known.

On a large ship, the security officer would typically have around ten crew members working for him. As far as their crime scene experience goes, Jaques says it is virtually non-existent: 'They're used to breaking up fights in the disco.'

On *Holidays Undercover*, Geoff Furlong put it bluntly: 'They are employing security staff that you and I would not employ on a building site.'

Even breaking up fights is sometimes further than staff go. David, a young Canadian working as a security officer on a large American liner, said non-intervention could be the best policy: a colleague on another ship had, he said, watched as 'a thirty-strong fight broke out … the security guards thought it best to let the guests punch themselves out.'

Another marine expert, consultant Peter Burge, gives a flat answer when questioned about standard levels of passenger security on many ships:

Security only becomes an important issue when something becomes obviously dangerous. Generally they make sure people aren't going to fall overboard in rough weather, and give them warnings, because they are required to by international law. However, in terms of personal safety, there are no laws. They leave them entirely up to the shipping company that operates the ships or the laws of the country they are operating in. In international waters they will defer to the laws of the country under which flag they sail. Out there, there are no police. No one can charge you with anything. Is an offence committed in international waters likely to be prosecuted in NSW?

David, the young Canadian security officer quoted above, agrees. He admits that he is effectively the police force on board during worldwide voyages. His background *is* in security – but more the nightclub type. He says: 'There's limits on what we can do. If it's an extraordinarily bad offence, the captain can order them confined to their cabin. But that has to be really bad.' The captain, he says, is judge and jury.

And while Randy Jaques warns that the shipping industry is rife with 'sexual deviants', there is little chance of hearing one testify against another. Burge confirms: 'There is a code of silence amongst the crew, if not amongst the officers.'

Rivkind says many crew members are worried that they could lose their job if they do not help the company by keeping any crime allegations quiet. It was a fear aired at an inquest in Australia by an entertainer on the *Pacific Sky*, who did not go to police with his (unfounded) suspicions about a passenger he believed to have been involved in the death of Dianne Brimble.

How can passengers be better protected? In the USA, Christopher Shays, the congressman who held the hearings into the cruise industry in late 2005, has introduced legislation that would require cruise lines to report to the US government all crimes committed aboard any ship calling at US ports: the Cruise Line Accurate Safety Statistics (CLASS) Act. Its statutes would force cruise ships to report any crime, person overboard or missing person incident to the Department of Homeland Security within four hours; to submit quarterly reports to be made publicly available on the internet, and to refer all customers to that information; and to submit to inspections of its security equipment and personnel. Ships could be denied entry to the US port or their owners fined $250,000 for failing to comply.

And the ten-point plan that the International Cruise Victims association presented to Congress, urging new legislation to increase security and accountability, has been taken up in Australia by Mark Brimble, the former husband of Dianne Brimble, who became an Australian spokesman for the group during the inquest into her death.

The ICV has drawn up a wide-ranging blueprint. It demands that:

1. Background checks should be run on all crew members and officers. A single database must be created to maintain records of anyone fired from a ship, to ensure they are not rehired by another cruise line. Reliable staff should be stationed on all decks, all the time.
2. An international police force should be established at the expense of the cruise lines, connected to Interpol, to be present on cruise ships but not affiliated with the cruise line or its crew. As demanded in the proposed CLASS Act, reporting crimes should be mandatory.
3. Certified security training and procedures should be put in place for sealing off possible crime scenes, taking witness statements and following up properly.
4. Ships should be structurally enhanced to make it more difficult for passengers to go overboard.
5. Cruise lines should upgrade video surveillance systems and increase the number of cameras in all areas that passengers may frequent.
6. Companies should issue access or security bracelets to all passengers just before they board a ship, to be worn throughout

the entire cruise, on shore and off shore. These would be designed to include microchips bearing the name of the ship and identifying the individual passenger – allowing them to be detected if they go missing or fall overboard.
7. Ships should install rail alarms to signal any individual falling overboard and station lifeguards on each side of the ship's decks. Any ship should stop immediately and search when a passenger is reported missing or overboard.
8. 'Rape kits' containing medical examination equipment such as swabs and containers to preserve potential evidence of sexual assault should be available on all ships, as should licensed doctors, and no request for an examination should be refused or taken lightly.
9. Cruise lines should be held accountable for the safety of passengers who purchase shore excursions through them.
10. Finally, new legislation should be passed, clearly and stringently holding cruise lines accountable for the safety of the citizens of any nation on board, so that crimes will not be fogged under international maritime law.

Some of these measures are already in place to greater or lesser degrees on many cruise lines and ships – although the many cases where things have gone wrong show that the practice does not always meet the theory. Increased security and modifications could be expensive and perhaps infringe on the carefree environment that passengers enjoy. Cruise ship passengers might well have to bear added costs, both in terms of higher fares and loss of privacy; and it seems unlikely that well-heeled passengers on more upmarket ships would care to wear a tag. Is it a price worth paying? Victims' families certainly think so.

In Australia, P&O responded promptly to the plan. Managing director Gavin Smith said: 'We take Mr Brimble's suggestions seriously.' Nevertheless, he claimed that, on P&O cruises at least, there was no need to legislate to clear up jurisdictional uncertainty, as Australian citizens would be covered by the Commonwealth *Crimes at Sea Act 2000*.

Whether or not the proposals that the ICV have set out are adopted or passed into law, the awareness that the group has generated means that passengers are likely to be much more vigilant for their own welfare in future.

Concerns about crime and personal security on cruises have become shared by the most seasoned travellers. Even Arthur Frommer, the man behind the global tourism guidebooks, has now issued warnings to readers thinking of taking a cruise. He told the *Los Angeles Times* that passengers should take precautions – and specifically, he said, never go out alone at night on an open deck.

9

The Smugglers

ASSAULTS AGAINST THE person are not the only category of cruise ship crime. Some illegal activities are undertaken as part of broad, profitable operations that seek to exploit the routes covered by the ships: namely, smuggling.

Given the exotic itineraries of many cruise ships – plying the Caribbean, or taking in such places as Colombia, Panama and Rio de Janeiro – it is unsurprising that serious drug smuggling has been carried out. Although security has been greatly tightened for embarking passengers in recent years, shipping remains a relatively easy method of transporting illicit goods.

According to a Brisbane customs officer, compared to airports, at which potential smugglers face close scrutiny, a coastal port represents an appealingly insecure barrier.

Likewise, most of the drugs smuggled into Florida come via sea. The US Department of Justice says cruise ships frequently carry drug couriers, who typically conceal cocaine either on their person or in their baggage. They can slip through the net of customs officials on disembarkation by either storing cocaine on the ship to retrieve after it has docked or passing the drugs on to a corrupt crew member.

In 2005, a joint two-year investigation by US customs authorities and the Drug Enforcement Administration (DEA) led to ten people being charged with conspiracy to import hundreds of kilos of cocaine and heroin into the United States on cruise ships over a period of six years – a conspiracy that included both employees and guests on cruise ships.

In the course of the investigation, drugs were seized on seven occasions from a variety of ships, including two Norwegian Cruise Line ships, the *Majesty* and the *Sea*, Celebrity's *Summit* and the *Zenith* – and even the Disney Cruise Line ship, the *Disney Magic*. It's a long way from Mickey's kids' club.

Charges extended to smuggling offences on at least twenty other cruises, including those aboard Celebrity's *Horizon* and *Millennium*, Royal Caribbean's *Enchantment of the Seas* and *Nordic Empress*, and others. Drug mules strapped cocaine, heroin and crack to their bodies, boarding ships around the Caribbean and Panama.

Another trafficking organisation using cruise lines was exposed in September 2000 by US customs authorities and the DEA. Drug couriers – mainly workers on Carnival cruise ships – had been smuggling cocaine and heroin into the USA, hiding the drugs – often in the form of small 'bullets' of heroin – in secret compartments in the bottom of their shoes. Early in their investigation, codenamed Operation Creole, officers arrested two individuals carrying 2.7 kilograms of heroin on board a Carnival ship. Their information led to the arrest of several other workers smuggling drugs on Carnival cruises, and eventually the head of the trafficking ring, based on the island of Aruba.

In the mid-Atlantic island of Bermuda, a popular port of call with mid-sized ships, drug trafficking has apparently reached a point where local police automatically suspect cruise ships' crew and passengers and searches are common: many have been caught with drugs. One recent seizure of cocaine was valued at over US$4 million.

Others have transported cocaine much further on a cruise ship. Three passengers on board the Cunard liner *Caronia* were found to have something worth a little more than an Armani jacket in the suit liners they were carrying in their luggage when they disembarked at the British port of Southampton. Customs officers found no less than $3.1 million worth of cocaine in their bags.

It's enough to make one fear for the members of Cocaine Anonymous, the drug users' self-help organisation, which was planning to celebrate its twenty-fifth anniversary next year with a group cruise from LA to Mexico.

Of course, many drugs are taken on board simply for passengers' own recreational purposes. As the Dianne Brimble case so gruesomely demonstrated, party drugs have been widespread on ships in Australia and beyond – to the point where P&O even felt moved to state on its website for the benefit of customers ahead of embarkation that 'P&O Cruises does not condone the taking of prohibited substances onboard *Pacific Sky* or *Pacific Sun*.' And presumably not on their sister ships either, but perhaps the more mature clientele on those cruises did not require the warning.

The appearance of sniffer dogs at some ports has made it more difficult and riskier for anyone to take drugs onto a ship, although the drug that killed Mrs Brimble, GHB, has long been marketed to clubbers by dealers as a substance that the dogs cannot detect. Some passengers have reported purchasing softer drugs such as cannabis on the Pacific islands on cruise stopovers, despite ships having the power to instantly put ashore anyone found using them – a potentially expensive sanction for the expelled.

Police searches of cruise ship passengers are comparatively rare, so when police did turn up to check those boarding the Carnival *Celebration* at the Ed Austin terminal in Jacksonville, there was reportedly some consternation in the boarding queue – with those far enough back to do so making a dash for the toilets or the nearest rubbish bins. Detectives had been alerted to the possibility of planned rampant drug-taking on the cruise by some expert sleuthing: reading passengers' posts in an internet chat room. In all, eleven would-be holiday-makers found themselves hauled down to the station, for possession of ecstasy, cocaine, marijuana and even heroin.

People smugglers have also been known to use cruise ships, especially those entering the US from the Caribbean. In the 1990s, it was comparatively simple to slip onto ships that did not provide sophisticated electronic passes for passengers: anyone disembarking was only issued with a re-entry pass that corrupt crew or officials could easily duplicate. Border patrols found that crime gangs in the USA were bringing in members from the Bahamas, slipping in via Florida on day cruises.

The Caribbean has been similarly fertile territory for animal smuggling. Two cruise crew members – Dwayne Cunningham, a comedian, and Robert Lawracy, a dive instructor – were sentenced to between one and two years in prison for smuggling iguanas and tortoises. Some of the reptiles included species of rock iguanas only found in certain islands in the Bahamas, before the two men brought them into the US via the cruise ships on which they were employed.

Such smuggling has also been exposed in less likely places. A World Wildlife Fund investigation into how foreign species – dead or alive – were making their way into the UK found that one of the major channels was via cruise ships calling in Scotland. Over five years in the unlikely port of Greenock, near Glasgow, customs officials seized some rare booty from cruise ships: five tiger claws and an astonishing grand total of thirty-three stuffed crocodiles.

10

Under Attack

FOR THE DILIGENT who have washed their hands, locked the cabin door, avoided fraternising with the dodgy blokes down the corridor, kept their drink in full view, and not walked too close to the deck rail in high winds, what more could there possibly be to worry about? The threat of terrorism, and now in particular, al-Qaeda.

In October 2000, a US Navy warship, the USS *Cole*, was in harbour in the Yemeni port of Aden, when a speedboat carrying two suicide bombers rammed into its port side. Seventeen soldiers were killed. This was no cruise; but the fatal attack demonstrated that large ships – even military ones – were vulnerable to a fast approach from a small vessel.

In April 2006, crews on ships around the world received updated briefings, after a specific security threat was made against one of the most famous ships of all: the *Queen Elizabeth 2*. It was sailing off Egypt, a country where lethal attacks on tourists have become commonplace.

'We believe there is no cause for alarm,' said Cunard. However, the ship was placed on a higher level of alert. Boats escorted the *QE2* on its journey through the Suez Canal and extra police were positioned on guard around the quay when the ship docked in the north Egyptian port of Alexandria.

Security personnel on ships are clear where their priority lies. For all the crime that can – and does – occur on board, the chief threat is external. 'Our main function is counterterrorism and anti-piracy,' stated a security officer on a Carnival superliner.

The 2006 alert was not the first time that the *QE2* had feared the worst. In 1972, Britain even sent RAF bomb disposal experts parachuting into the Atlantic Ocean to deal with a feared terror attack on the liner. That time, the supposed bomb turned out to be a hoax.

More false alarms have hit ships in recent years: in June 2006, the *Sea Diamond*, a medium-sized ship just acquired by Louis Cruise Lines in Greece, had to evacuate more than 1000 passengers before the start of its three-day voyage from Piraeus, after a telephone call from someone claiming to represent a Turkish terror group who said there was a bomb on board. Nothing was found.

Perhaps the least successful of cruise ship bomb hoaxes was perpetrated in 2003 on a large American liner by one of the ship's own passengers. The fake bomber was, it emerged, sufficiently unhappy with being stuck on the glitzy Royal Caribbean resort ship *Legend of the Seas* that she penned two handwritten notes to crew threatening to 'kill all Americans abord [sic]' – around 2000 of them – if the ship continued on its voyage from Mexico to any US port.

The *Legend*, on its way to Hawaii, was diverted from the state's main port to anchor off a smaller island, where it was greeted by 120 members of an armed anti-terrorism task force, complete with forty sniffer dogs. The ship was searched for explosives and chemical or biological weapons but none were found. When passengers were interviewed, the culprit confessed: Kelley Marie Ferguson, a twenty-year-old woman from California who had been dragged on the cruise by her parents, but wanted to be at home with her boyfriend – and who thought she could get home quickly if the cruise was cancelled and the ship returned to Ensenada. The holiday, planned as a family-bonding exercise by Mr Ferguson, ended with his daughter being sentenced to two years in prison under the Bush administration's new Patriot Act.

Despite such hoaxes and false alarms, since an infamous episode in the Mediterranean in the early autumn of 1985, no-one has taken threats against cruise ships lightly.

Alexandria again played a part in the story. The Egyptian city had been the last port of call for an Italian ship, the *Achille Lauro* – a pre-war liner loved by shipping enthusiasts, which had been restored with a distinctive blue livery and was now carrying around 680 passengers on a twelve-night Mediterranean cruise. On the morning of 7 October, it was relatively quiet on board: most of the guests had disembarked for an excursion to the Pyramids, to rejoin the ship when it reached Port Said. As the ship sailed up the coast, a crew member stumbled in on an unlikely scene. In a cabin, with guns on view, was a group of four men who had declined the daytrip: armed members of the Palestinian Liberation Front.

The PLF men went into action. An emergency radio message from the ship's captain alerted the world that hijackers had taken control of the ship. The next day, the hijackers confirmed the news and issued their demands. If fifty Palestinians held in prison in Israel were not released, they would start to kill their hostages on board – and if anyone approached the ship, the *Achille Lauro* would be blown up.

It sparked a stand-off that would dominate the world's news and bring the presidents of several countries directly into the fray. An Italian cruise ship had gone missing just off Egypt, and the terrorists warned that American passengers would be the first to die.

Around sixty to eighty passengers were believed still to be on board, including a dozen Americans. The hijackers made the crew set sail for Tartus in Syria, but the cruise liner was refused permission to dock. During negotiations with Syrian port authorities, an alarming message came from the PLF: that they would kill a second hostage. It was the first indication that the hijackers had already carried out their threat to execute the passengers. In fact, an elderly, disabled American, Leon Klinghoffer, a retired appliance manufacturer from New York on holiday with his wife, had been shot twice. A waiter was forced to throw his body and wheelchair overboard.

The US drew up plans for a possible military assault on the boat; the Italians made their own contingency plans to take the ship back by force. Meanwhile the hijackers made the *Achille Lauro* turn back to Egypt. After two days of negotiations with Egyptian officials, the hijackers – guaranteed safe passage – freed the ship, its passengers and crew. But when the murder of Leon Klinghoffer was confirmed, American determination to capture the hijackers increased. An EgyptAir flight carrying the PLF men was intercepted by US military aircraft and forced to land in Sicily. Most of the hijackers were prosecuted and imprisoned in Italy, although the suspected ringleader, Abu Abbas, was allowed to make his way out of the country.

Abbas, who was finally captured by American forces in Iraq in 2003 and died in US custody, claimed that the men had not intended to hijack the ship, but had been on their way to the Israeli port of Ashdod, the next stop on the cruise itinerary, and only acted after being discovered.

Despite its notoriety, the *Achille Lauro* continued to sail as a cruise liner for nearly another decade until 1994, when it made a suitably dramatic disappearance from the seas (see chapter 22 on disasters).

The events of October 1985 were since brought to the stage in a 1991 opera, *The Death of Klinghoffer*, that proved too controversial to be performed in some cities. The opera – and protests against it – would be revived after the attacks on New York on 11 September 2001.

While the 9/11 attacks had nothing to do with the sea, they rekindled fears of terrorist acts occurring anywhere, and cruise ships were perceived as presenting large, easy, prestigious Western targets. Passenger bookings dropped sharply in the immediate aftermath (although the numbers have since more than recovered). Terrorism was back as the overarching fear: a television remake of *The Poseidon Adventure* saw the stricken SS *Poseidon* turned upside down not by a tidal wave but a bomb. At the time of writing, no such attack has yet brought down a ship, but the authorities would say it was not for want of effort on the part of terrorist groups.

In August 2005, an alleged al-Qaeda militant, Louai al-Sakka, was arrested in Diyarbakir, south-east Turkey, accused of plotting to blow up an Israeli cruise ship when it docked in the Mediterranean resort of Antalya.

Fears have grown to the extent that even the Queen cannot feel entirely safe cruising around the remotest of the British Isles. A cruise sailing up the west coast of Scotland was organised for her eightieth birthday celebrations, with family including Anne, Charles and Camilla and even (breaking the ship's no-animals rule by special dispensation) the pet corgis in the party. The jaunt required unprecedented security activity in the region.

In the ten years that had elapsed since the last such royal cruise, suicide bombings had become a reality. The special forces were placed on high alert – believing that terrorists could potentially whizz out in a speedboat raid from the hundreds of small harbours and inlets that dot the coast. It seemed unlikely in the isolated Western Isles. But now the luxury *Hebridean Princess* liner was subject to a strict exclusion zone: any boat foolish or unfortunate enough to come too close would face a missile attack. Royal Marine units were based on board, other special services units were on helicopter stand-by, and air patrols monitored the seas, hoping for no other explosions than the sound of clay pigeon shooting from the *Hebridean Princess*'s Skye Deck.

Even for cruises carrying less distinguished guests, security at ports has been tightened enormously. Any visitors, including friends or relatives, are barred from the ships on all but the most exceptional occasions. Invitations sent out for official functions such as media previews on board ships will routinely ask for passport identification to be sent well in advance, allowing security checks on those attending.

Passengers are screened by security officials, have to carry photo ID, pass through metal detectors at every port of call, and have any shopping from shore visits X-rayed. Some American cruise lines check all passenger lists against immigration and FBI records for any suspect guests on board. Customs officers X-ray baggage on departure. Sniffer dogs are now a common sight at ports – scenting out both explosives and drugs. Carnival says bomb searches are conducted before and after sailing, and shipboard provisions are inspected for explosives. Crew are frisked, and divers are sent to check the hull of the ship at every port, twice.

Still, a report from a US Department of State conference held in April 2006 said that there was growing concern that terrorists might switch focus to vulnerable targets either at sea and in ports, possibly using small high-speed boats as in the USS *Cole* attack. Not least was the worry that terrorists might 'directly target a cruise liner or passenger ferry to cause mass casualties'. The report also said that there was 'considerable apprehension' that terrorists could hijack a cruise liner, possibly bringing chemical, biological, radiological, and nuclear materials on board, to use as a 'floating bomb' near a port city.

To take over a cruise ship sounds a tall order, but the defence analysts' report said any such hijacking would simply be a case of terrorists starting to 'mimic pirate tactics'. Pirates, today? In fact, far from being an anachronism, marine experts warn, piracy is growing more sophisticated and its reach is spreading further than ever.

Just ask the passengers of one of the world's most luxurious cruise ships, the *Seabourn Spirit*. On their 2005 trip from Alexandria in northern Egypt to Mombasa in Kenya, they might have expected to take in many fascinating sights: perhaps a shore excursion to the ancient Pyramids to begin, and ending up with a lion or two on safari.

But it's a good bet that Charles Supple, an American doctor enjoying his retirement by splashing out on a top-end cruise, did not expect what he saw when he peered out of the stateroom window early one morning with his camera at the ready. On a nearby vessel was a creature that most westerners might have thought long extinct: a pirate. Yet this was no hook-handed villain with a cutlass, but someone far more immediately dangerous. Aimed squarely at the ship was a very modern rocket-launcher. Dr Supple dived for cover. The pirate fired.

In an email to his family, later published in *The Newcastle Herald*, Dr Supple recounted: 'What a flash! I dove to the other side and the rocket hit two decks up and two staterooms forward.'

The ship was cruising down the east coast of Africa, just past the Horn, in a stretch of water that passed the lawless, war-torn failed state of Somalia – a place that hardy aid workers had been forced to flee, from which even a US Army landing force had been driven out by the rampant anarchy on the streets.

The *Spirit* was a good 100 miles clear of the Somali coast, but the International Maritime Bureau had been warning for months of pirate attacks, urging ships to stay at least 150 miles out to sea. Some ships were able to avoid the area entirely, but any vessel travelling from the Mediterranean to Asia or Africa had to pass through.

It was around 5.30 am when the first grenade blasted through into one of the *Seabourn Spirit*'s suites; the occupants, still lying down in bed, escaped injury. Over the public address system the captain made the unlikely announcement: 'This is not a drill. This is not an exercise. We have been attacked by pirates.' Passengers were to stay in their staterooms and await further instructions, he said.

One British woman who had been on board recounted:

> Your immediate reaction is that it could not possibly be true. You don't know what to do. Naturally I got dressed in a fully coordinated outfit, in case I should have to appear in public. Then I heard what sounded like a machine gun. I asked my husband, what was that? But he insisted it was just the sound of the ship manoeuvring – he's very kind like that.

That British couple were on the safe side of the ship — away from the machine gun–toting assailants. Up on the bridge, the captain was alone, still in his towelling dressing gown, as he contemplated his next move. Two small pirate craft were menacing his boat, but there was obviously another larger boat out there somewhere. A little earlier, he had received a call from a ship claiming to be in distress, under attack from pirates, but the story hadn't seemed to add up. He had suspected someone was attempting to lure the *Spirit* into a trap and that now seemed to be confirmed. The pirates couldn't have come that far without assistance — a mother ship must be nearby.

For now though, the battle lines were drawn. On one hand, two small boatloads of pirates with machine guns and at least one rocket-launcher; on the other, a half-dressed captain and a young crew manning a substantially bigger ship. What to do? Ram them.

And so an unlikely sea battle commenced. The *Seabourn Spirit* — a much more mobile ship than many other modern cruise liners — tried to knock the two boats out of the water. Then it unleashed its secret weapon, a sonic blaster developed for the US Navy, the long-range acoustic device or 'LRAD'. This dish-shaped device fires focused, shrill blasts of sound up to 300 metres away, in a concentrated beam that doesn't affect the user but reaches the target at up to 150 decibels — enough to make sure you are heard when you want to clear an area, or when ratchetted up enough, to shatter glass — or even to burst the eardrums of oncoming pirates.

Passengers were sent to the dining room in the middle of the ship to await further instructions. All made their way down — with guests on the higher decks having to crawl to keep their heads below the parapet. People were terrified, but remained exceptionally calm, recalled one passenger. She said that the couple whose cabin had been shredded by a grenade had more trouble than most: 'The woman was in tremendous shock. She kept saying she had glass in her hair. She really wasn't there.'

Most, though, kept their decorum while under siege: when the ship's staff brought black coffee in cups for the guests, several requested saucers before they would drink it.

Some had taken refuge under the tables, while others stood. One of the ship's security men – believed to be ex-SAS – encouraged some to stand. 'He said you should always be standing up in this sort of scenario in case you need to run,' one recipient of his advice said. This man had also hidden table knives on top of the picture frames in the dining room in case they needed help in tackling any boarding pirates later. 'He'd rushed in and done this, which I thought was tremendously thoughtful.'

Forty minutes later, the captain appeared. The *Spirit* had given the cutthroats the slip, he announced, to loud applause. In the skirmish, only one member of the crew had been injured, caught by shrapnel from the blast. However, the captain was taking no chances: instead of the scheduled stops, they were going straight out to sea at a tremendous rate of knots, and would head for the Seychelles.

By 8.30 am the guests were having breakfast outside on the terrace, a little shaky but with service restored to normal, saucers and all. The captain and crew had been, all agreed, superb.

As one passenger, Mike Rogers of Vancouver, told CNN: 'We're always looking for adventure, but this is probably a little more than we would normally look for.' Australians Gayle and Bob Meagher, from Sydney, told Channel 7 television:

> It was a frightening experience to see the flash of a rocket launcher, and you just wonder what's about to happen to you in the next couple of minutes. A little bit more exciting than we planned for.

Another Australian passenger, Paul McGhee, who saw four of the pirates fire a grenade too close for comfort, said: 'I have never contemplated death before. That was the first time, and I don't really want to feel it again in a hurry.'

For cruise security officials on ships that must run through the wild waves of lesser charted international waters, only the spectre of al-Qaeda looms larger than the pirate. 'They would love to take a cruise ship,' a Carnival officer said. A small ship would be a difficult but not impossible target for pirates, even though it would involve scaling a much bigger vessel with many more crew than their own craft. It has become apparent that pirates have the weaponry: while simple long-bladed knives are still common in attacks on smaller boats in Bangladesh, others are carried out with machine guns, grenades and the kind of rocket-launcher aimed at the swiftly evasive Dr Supple. And the haul from robbing cruise ship passengers – especially wealthy travellers such as those on the *Seabourn Spirit* – could be rich indeed.

According to the International Maritime Bureau (IMB), piracy is still on the increase worldwide, despite the success of several governments in tackling certain piracy hotspots. Indonesian efforts are starting to curb an epidemic in the notorious Malacca Strait – the seas between Malaysia and the Indonesian island of Sumatra, which accounted for a large proportion of the 469 pirate attacks recorded in the year 2000 – but the area remains far from under control, as demonstrated by three attacks in swift succession on a Japanese cargo ship and two UN-chartered boats in July 2006. Other current piracy hotspots include parts of South-East Asia, the southern Red Sea and waters off the coast of Peru.

Security experts fear that further piracy could grow from the lawless state of Somalia, where heavily armed militias roam the streets and there is a market for goods of any provenance. In late 2005, the IMB issued an appeal for naval ships from the US and other countries to offer assistance to ships under attack. Soon after the incident with the *Seabourn Spirit*, the director of the IMB, Captain Pottengal Mukundan, asked that at the very least naval ships could stop hijackers from taking ships into Somali waters. 'Once the vessels have entered these waters the chances of any law enforcement is negligible.'

The cold truth is that most seafarers out there are on their own. In 2005, over 200 people were taken hostage; a dozen are still missing. Attacks have become increasingly violent. Many captains and crew have been bound, gagged, threatened with dismemberment, and sometimes killed. In some instances great loads of cargo have been seized along with ships themselves, apparently stolen to order by sophisticated gangs operating with the latest equipment; at other times the attackers will simply leave the vessels after taking any cash and jewellery they have found.

Essentially, say marine experts, pirates go where the money is, and it seems they have realised now that cruise ships are perfect for looting. Mark Dickinson of NUMAST, the British maritime workers' union, told the *Daily Express* that the attack on the *Seabourn Spirit* was 'eyeopening, because it showed that ships of any size are vulnerable'.

Luxury yachts are becoming a frequent lure for pirates, who have become such a threat that Rear Admiral Chris Parry, a former Royal Navy assault ship captain, warned a military conference in June 2006 that: 'At some time in the next 10 years it may not be safe to sail a yacht between Gibraltar and Malta.' Forget the pirates of the Caribbean; the new, well-heeled variety are moving in on the Mediterranean.

One British MP, Louise Ellman, said in April 2006 that it was 'only a matter of time' before a British ship was targeted. She spoke out after the House of Commons Transport Committee was told by Gavin Simmonds of the Chamber of Shipping that there was 'a new intensity and scale of violence' in pirate attacks, perpetrated by pirates using sophisticated paramilitary techniques.

Cruise companies will not give many details away about ship security, possibly not wanting to reveal their precise contingency plans ahead of attack. All ships are required to conform at least to the provisions of the International Convention for the Safety of Life at Sea, better known as the SOLAS Convention. According to Llew Russell, a security specialist and CEO of Shipping Australia, this means that ships have to train crew in maritime security measures, and – under recent amendments to the convention – that every vessel must have a ship alert system with two secret triggers that can be used to set off an alarm in the cruise line's global head office, issuing the ship's position and demanding an immediate response at any time.

Carnival claims that beyond these measures, it has a number of additional anti-terrorism initiatives up its sleeve, but that these are 'inappropriate to be disclosed'.

Cunard, the company operating the *QM2* and *QE2* from Britain, has teams of ex-Gurkhas among its ships' crew. Up to twelve security officers on the liners are drawn from the British Army's renowned Nepalese contingent, a tradition dating back to the early 1970s. (P&O also has some such soldiers aboard.) The Gurkhas are part of all aspects of the security operation, a Cunard spokesman said, but are particularly vigilant at port. Perhaps due to Britain's long history of coming under terrorist attacks, the cruise line claims not to have needed to tighten security in recent years.

Rumoured among some cruise passengers is the presence of undercover 'guests' on board certain ships – that the retired Colonel Blimp in the corner is not so much a doddery old gent on the G&T as a James Bond–style trained killer, ready to leap into action.

Security personnel are licensed to carry arms but won't officially reveal whether they do or not. An armed man stalking the deck poolside may be comforting to some but may not be the most reassuring image to include in the brochure, as a croupier who worked on an Israeli ship cruising the Mediterranean could testify:

> The security guys started carrying revolvers around one day. It was quite shocking – you're supposed to be on a relaxed cruise and then suddenly there they are, carrying guns.

Security experts also admit that ship crew, living at close quarters, can have volatile relationships; arguments are not uncommon – one crewman on the *QM2* killed another in a fight during a 2006 cruise – and guns on board are more of a risk to life than a protection.

Peter Chalk, a security analyst for the RAND Corporation and former lecturer in international relations at the University of Queensland, says while crew should be trained in basic anti-piracy measures, calls to arm ships would almost certainly prove counterproductive by encouraging pirates to resort to greater violence.

He recommends repelling boarders with fire hoses. Another measure taken by ships to avoid unwelcome intruders might be translated into lay terms as getting the hell out of there as soon as possible. In such known risk areas as the Malacca Strait, ships generally go at full speed ahead, according to Llew Russell. 'It's very difficult to board a fast-moving ship. You would need high-speed vessels that do at least 50 knots to stand any chance of catching it.'

However, plenty of high-tech devices are available to ships. As well as the LRAD deployed by the *Seabourn Spirit*, other defensive gadgetry recommended by the anti-piracy organisations includes the Inventus UAV and Secure-Ship. The Inventus UAV (unmanned aerial vehicle) is essentially a large flying camera that can circle for miles around a ship and relay its surveillance straight back to its crew, giving early warning of anything suspicious coming their way, while the Secure-Ship is an electric fence specially adapted for use at sea. Any unwanted intruders trying to board a ship fitted with one of these fences by any means other than the front door will find themselves on the wrong end of a 9000-volt pulse – not enough to kill, but certainly enough to deter – and will also set off floodlights and a very loud siren. The UK's *Daily Express* reports that maritime unions believe more such measures may be needed: the seas have become, they say, increasingly dangerous for everyone, even holiday-makers.

A stark example of just how important security has become to the cruise industry came in June 2006 when Royal Caribbean headhunted a man who was number three at the FBI, the bureau's executive assistant director, Gary Bald. He was appointed to a newly created position of vice president, global security and given broad responsibilities for 'assessing, managing and continuously improving companywide security'.

It was a coup that led some in the media to bewail the brain drain from the FBI – but at the same time, it highlighted how seriously cruise firms were taking security issues. To some extent, it would help reassure the public after Royal Caribbean had faced scrutiny over the disappearances of passengers such as George Smith. But Bald's recent background was firmly in countering more external threats: in his final post at the FBI, after nearly twenty-nine years with the bureau, Bald was in charge of global counterterrorism and intelligence programs, responsible for 19,000 employees. His move to Royal Caribbean underlined the magnitude of the cruise corporations; as the cruise line's CEO Richard Fain said:

> Thanks to Gary's leadership, our country is much better prepared in terms of security, and I am fully confident, given his résumé and resolve, that he will lead our company to even greater advances in our preparedness and security systems.

That 'preparedness' may yet prove crucial as the stakes escalate: in the context of a global 'war on terror' that shows little sign of abating, cruise ships, as the next chapter shows, will provide ever-larger, more prestigious targets.

11

Bigger and Better?

WHETHER FOR GENERATING column inches in newspapers or for fitting in an extra couple of tables in the casino, for many in the world of cruising, bigger can only mean better. And be it a psychological hangover from the Cold War or just a practical consideration for all that luggage, American customers in particular are irresistibly drawn to the most enormous ships.

While Europeans and Australians can only gawp, the giants of the ocean are rolling off for American markets. The biggest cruise ship ever seen in Sydney, towering over the Opera House at Circular Quay, pulled into the harbour for the first time in January 2006: the Japanese-built *Diamond Princess*, carrying around 2700 passengers – not to mention an enormous casino that included 260 slot machines. In April it set sail for San Francisco, with many passengers having flown out from the US with the express purpose of sailing straight back.

And yet it was about to become a mere slip of a thing, at only 116,000 tons. The cruise industry's new biggie, Royal Caribbean's *Freedom of the Seas*, started sailing in May 2006 from Miami, with a volume of 158,000 tons: 8000 more than the last record-holder, Cunard's *Queen Mary 2*. This monster was designed to carry a normal load of

3634 passengers — and could handle a maximum of 4370 — plus 1360 crew to tend to their increasingly diverse needs.

The ship was the latest in an ongoing trend for bigger and bigger vessels, offering more and more facilities. Casinos? Done that. Spas? Par for the course. On board the *Freedom of the Seas* are, among many features that the genteel elderly cruisers of yesteryear would never have dreamt of needing at sea, a surf park, a full-size boxing ring, and cantilevered whirlpools suspended 112 feet (almost 35 metres) above the ocean. But then, the scale is such that you need hardly know you were at sea at all. Inside, the ship's centrepiece is a 400-foot-long shopping mall, six storeys high. Every night a Disney-style parade makes its way past the shops. There are ten restaurants and sixteen bars. The biggest suite has fourteen beds. A 1300-seat theatre — bigger than many found in the great cities of the world — puts on Broadway shows. Elsewhere, there are such diversions as a climbing wall, a miniature golf course and an ice rink.

It comes with an impressive array of statistics. How many crew does it take to change the light bulbs? Well, there are an astonishing 750,000 bulbs on the ship. It will need to produce 713,000 gallons of fresh water every day — and 78,000 lbs of ice. And 350,000 separate pieces of steel were used to construct the enormous hull.

It is, enthused a reporter who had a preview as it left Hamburg before going into active service, 'not so much a ship as a small nation with an engine'. On its way from its Finnish shipyard to its eventual sailing ground, the Caribbean, it squeezed under Denmark's Great Belt Bridge with just nine feet — 2.75 metres — to spare.

A sister ship, *Liberty of the Seas*, comes into service in May 2007 with the same dazzling specifications, but even these twin ships will soon be tiddlers, thanks to another enormous work in progress in Akers Yard shipbuilders in Finland. Under construction is a ship that will dwarf all the current liners and carry half as many passengers again as the *Freedom of the Seas*.

This new, mammoth ship, ordered by Royal Caribbean, goes under the modest title of Project *Genesis*. It will cost the cruise company around US$900 million. Its chairman, Richard Fain, said it was about 'bold design, daring innovation and technological advancements'. It is also about economies of scale – having more passengers on board drives down costs.

More than 1500 workers will be involved in the construction of the 220,000-ton *Genesis*, which should take three years. At 73 metres high and 360 metres long, it will have the proportions of an old Soviet housing estate, if more aesthetic appeal.

With some predicting that the next generation could carry up to 12,000 passengers, the real limit to ships' size in future is likely to be ports and cruise terminals that struggle to accommodate these behemoths; not to mention the small islands and towns that would have to cope with 12,000 daytrippers searching for souvenirs and Starbucks. The Panamanian government recently announced a national referendum to decide whether to go ahead with a US$5.3 billion project to widen their canal to allow this new generation of ships to pass.

Meanwhile, some of the existing ships, the giants of an earlier time, are filtering down to other markets. P&O Australia have announced that the region's first superliner will join their fleet in 2007: the *Pacific Dawn*, currently known as the *Regal Princess* and sailing out of the USA as part of the Princess Cruises fleet. The 70,000-ton ship will be the biggest to be based in Australia – and too big to squeeze under the Sydney Harbour Bridge to the King Street Wharf where P&O's ships dock now. Another ship will be redeployed to Brisbane, meaning more passengers will be able to cruise from there too.

While not every ship can be the biggest, all are searching for a unique selling point in an increasingly crowded market. In July 2006, the Costa *Concordia* was launched: the biggest European ship, able to carry 3800 passengers. Christened by supermodel Eva Herzigova, the new flagship of Italian-based Costa Cruises (a Carnival subsidiary) would, said Costa, 'symbolise peace and harmony between European nations'. But more to the point, it would also hold the biggest health spa anywhere on the world's seas, covering two decks and 1900 square metres of the ship.

As if a week of dossing on board a cruise ship was not enough, passengers can hang around in its Turkish bath or solarium, and submit to Indian-inspired holistic treatments or thalassotherapy massages using air jets and 'hot ionised seawater'. Passengers can even stay in cabins opening directly onto the spa. Costa says that the giant spa will be a place where people can seek 'spiritual enlightenment and rejuvenation'; perhaps the two things cruise passengers require more than anything else.

In its search for more firsts, Costa pointed out too that the *Concordia* was the first ship with two swimming pools that can be covered by a shifting crystal roof – and what they bill as the first and only grand prix driving simulator on a cruise ship, allowing guests to learn how to race like the pros.

Does bigger necessarily mean better? The most exclusive and traditional of cruise lines would argue not. Cunard is bucking the trend in ordering a new liner that will not be the biggest in its fleet. Nevertheless, Cunard still claims that the *Queen Victoria*, to be delivered at the end of 2007, does achieve many seafaring firsts: the first private boxes in its theatre; the first floating museum, housing cruise memorabilia; and the first two-storey library at sea. It is fair to say that few cruise lines were battling to be first in those particular races.

In the battle of the American giants, where Vegas-style entertainment and ostentatious decor are prized, there is definite kudos in owning the biggest ships, but the megacruisers may bring their owners more problems than solutions, some believe. The risks of crime and contagion grow as populations sprawl. Moreover, not all ports will have adequate baggage handling facilities for 5000-plus passengers – and the reconstruction of ports and shipping canals will have environmental consequences. Many airports that serve incoming cruise guests would equally struggle with the baggage – and passengers who pick a cruise knowing that they will not have to pack or unpack during the holiday but may well dine in the same restaurants every night have little tendency to travel light.

Another alarming prospect has been raised: in a genuine emergency, could 5000 or more passengers be evacuated in time? While evacuations are a rare occurrence — the last complete evacuation of passengers from a cruise ship sailing from American waters took place back in 1995 — few can be 100 per cent sure what to expect when a ship is forced to disembark the population of a small town. Even though the fire that broke out on the *Star Princess* in 2006 was brought under control without the need for full evacuation, it took more than three hours to account for the passengers on board. A retired marine manager for shipping underwriters Lloyds Register told *The Seattle Times*: 'No one knows because it never happens. There are drills and people are trained, but how it will work out no one knows.'

Cruise ship passengers are run through general safety drills when they board. But full-scale evacuation drills where lifeboats are lowered only involve crew and never passengers — largely because even the drills themselves have proved hazardous, with many seafarers injured and even dying in what should have been a practice for a worst-case scenario. While aeroplanes have demonstrated that all their passengers can get clear to safety in a certain time, ships have yet to do so.

Maurizio Cergol, chief designer for Italian shipbuilders Fincantieri, told the *LA Times* that such safety issues are a matter of design rather than size. But he also pointed to difficulties in maintaining the flexibility of ships — and their appeal — as they get ever bigger. Not only will increased size make it difficult for boats to dock at some ports, reducing the number of places they can visit, but they could also spoil the view — not just for the people who have giant ships docking alongside them, but for the passengers themselves: the number of keenly sought-after cabins with balconies would be limited on very wide ships. Not to mention the chance of lounging around by the pool on the deckchair: bigger ships do not have proportionally more space up on the deck. Designers would need to find a way of combating the squeeze, and stopping the often fraught deckchair hunt from getting even worse.

Commercial considerations have deterred some of the cruise lines. Carnival president Bob Dickinson told a Seatrade conference that his company had had to reject some proposed megacruiser designs because they did not give 'the returns on invested capital we are used to'.

Despite this, other lines firmly hold that bigger is better. In September 2006, Norwegian Cruise Line placed an order for two ships that will each carry 4900 passengers. For Royal Caribbean, who are leading the way with the new monsters of the seas, the reasoning is simple; in *The Times*, Adam Goldstein, CEO, stated: 'The reason why big is better is because we can put more features in. We have some incredible options.' The bar is being set ever higher. 'We like to offer the unexpected to our guests,' Goldstein explained, 'so we knew that we had to come up with something fabulous at every turn for *Freedom of the Seas*.' Norwegian's CEO Colin Veitch likewise noted: 'There's just a lot more that you can put on a big ship.'

The ultimate reason for any eventual turn in the trend for bigger ships is likely to be passenger demand: holiday-makers may decide that they would rather, after all, escape the crowds than feel part of a population of 6000 others trawling the same route on the same ship. But if the popularity of Royal Caribbean's new ship — fully booked out at premium prices in its first year — is any indication, there will be plenty of takers yet for the monsters of the sea.

12
~

...Or Cheap and Cheerful?

QUEEN MARY MIGHT well have felt – and England's Queen Elizabeth may still feel – that the enormous, stately vessels parading proudly through the oceans are fitting tributes to their majesty. It is hard to imagine quite which monarch would be willing to put his or her name to a recent addition to the fleet of cruise ships: a bright orange hulk chugging around the Mediterranean, bearing passengers paying such unprincely sums as £20 a night.

The responsibility for this ship lies with tycoon Stelios Haji-Ioannou (or simply 'Stelios' as he prefers to be known), the Greek founder of easyJet, a budget airline flying between the UK and Europe. The same 'no-frills' philosophy inspired the launch of his cruise liner, the *easyCruiseOne*, in 2005, a ship that holds such unexpected features as no pool and tiny, windowless cabins of ten square metres, whose beds have orange headboards carrying the easycruise website address, as if to be memorised by the sleeping.

To get the lowest rates, passengers are expected to clean their own room. Some churlish commentators have pointed out that the boat has more the specifications of a ferry than a liner. In sum, say critics, it's neither easy nor a cruise.

It is, though, extremely cheap. It's one of the few ships that makes a virtue of the fact that its paying guests would rather be elsewhere: the concept of easyCruise, the cruise line says, is 'to allow its passengers to spend the maximum time ashore'.

Unlike a traditional cruise, the website boasts – and these are cruises that can only be booked on the company's website, rather than through the hands of a travel agent bearing glossy brochures – the ship stays in port in the evenings and sails late, allowing passengers to enjoy all the nightlife and facilities that the local destinations provide. Or indeed, to eat something other than the burgers and pizzas on offer on *easyCruiseOne*.

A warning note might be sounded to the wary on browsing the ship's facilities online, with its photo galleries of bars, gyms and restaurants. A small print disclaimer reads: 'All photographs shown are establishments located ashore, closely resembling those found on board easyCruiseOne.'

That was certainly true at the start of the ship's maiden voyage, when bad weather forced it to take refuge in the industrial port of Toulon, rather than the glamorous Riviera hotspot of St Tropez as advertised. It was a brief hiccup, soon to be forgiven – unlike the colour scheme. Orange is a colour long associated with all Stelios's offerings, but in its all-encompassing run of the ship, it was apparently grating on some passengers' senses.

As *The Guardian*'s correspondent wrote of his trip on *easyCruiseOne*'s maiden voyage:

> I've stepped into a hideous nightmare. No, it's not a dismembered body or a horse's head or anything. There are no sordid sex acts going on, no sex acts at all in fact. The cabin is empty. It's just that it's very very orange. Catastrophically orange.

The orange, reported a 'queasy' *Daily Mail* journalist, extended to the cabin's bathroom and even the ceiling.

Undeterred by its garish exterior – and indeed interiors – the ship sailed straight into Cannes harbour alongside the *QE2*, whose more upmarket patrons were, according to *The Times*, spilling their cocktails in disbelief:

> Stelios, easyCruise's ebullient founder waved at the *QEII* passengers, who had stopped what they were doing and were staring back in astonishment; it was close enough to see the looks on their faces. They did not wave back.

For all the carping of travel writers and the dismay of fellow cruisers, it looks like the concept is here to stay, for a while at least. The *easyCruiseTwo* was launched the following May, servicing the less exotic northern European ports of Antwerp, Amsterdam and Rotterdam. The new boat, a smaller vessel, had been already in operation under another company, but would be 'refurbished to easyCruise standards' before going into service with Stelios. There would also be, he promised, less orange. The inaugural sailing of *easyCruiseTwo* took place in August 2006 and was, by the account of an *Observer* writer on board, a somewhat bawdy affair.

Stelios, questioned whether the concept was a 'non-stop floating boozeathon', objected, pointing out that there were museums as well as clubs in Amsterdam. *The Observer* concluded though that most passengers were 'here more for the beer than Vermeer'.

Stelios has announced further expansion plans, commissioning two new cruise ships and retaining an option for two more, to be built in the owner's native Greece by Neorion Holdings. The 500-berth vessels are expected to be delivered in 2008. By then, easyCruise is planning to have expanded operations as far as the Greek islands, the southern Caribbean, the Bahamas and Dubai.

Meanwhile, a second series of *Cruise with Stelios* – a reality TV show for satellite channels, said to be focusing largely on customers using the jacuzzi – was in production. The man himself was preparing for a court showdown with a mobile phone company over a branding

. . . Or Cheap and Cheerful?

clash. The company? Orange. Stelios declared he would attend in an orange boiler suit.

13

Going Overboard

WHILE THE INDIVIDUALS at the centre of some of the notorious missing persons cases on cruise lines are suspected to have been the victims of foul play, and the disappearance of others remains a complete mystery, a whole other category of lost passengers remains: the jumpers.

Some of these tragedies may have been deliberate, planned in advance by the depressed and suicidal. But frequently, the leaps seem to have been sparked by a combination of impulse and alcohol – an argument, a domestic dispute, and possibly, the belief that jumping overboard would not necessarily be a dangerous thing to do. In fact, it usually proves fatal.

According to the crew of the *Carnival Legend*, the last conversation Ramesh Krishnamurthy, thirty-five, of Pennsylvania, had with his wife was an argument over the bar tab they were running up on board. Krishnamurthy would settle it in an unanswerable way, jumping over the rail of his balcony into the pitch black waters of the Atlantic, in front of his two children. A seventeen-hour search was launched by the Coast Guard. It was, according to one New York paper, an event that 'bogged down' thousands of US holiday-makers returning to port in Manhattan, and apparently soured the mood on board one of Carnival's so-called Fun Ships.

In similar circumstances, Australians have apparently taken a more phlegmatic approach to enjoying themselves while a passenger is missing. The *Pacific Sky*, P&O's ill-fated party ship, has seen men overboard more than once; passengers Dennis Hughson and Alan Welsh have been on board among parties of friends on two such occasions. In one of these instances, too, the leaper was a man pushed over the edge by an argument with his wife.

Hughson was enjoying the floorshow when the news broke. 'They can't stop the entertainment on the boat, because everything's got to go on,' he said. 'They were just in the middle of doing *The Rocky Horror Show* dance when – ping! – the PA came over the loudspeakers and the captain made an announcement.' The dancers on stage froze – 'they were like statues' – before continuing where they left off when the captain had finished. Soon afterwards the captain's voice broke in again – could the doctor report to the bridge? And a little while later, an appeal was issued for the rescue boat crew to prepare to go into action. The passengers in the theatre weren't aware of it, but the boat was turning round.

Any recreational jumpers should be warned of many possible hazards: firstly, the great distance to fall. While it may look like a simple dive into the sea, the plunge to the water's surface can equate to a leap from a fifteen-storey building. Hitting the sea alone could prove enough to kill. Secondly, in cold waters, the sudden icy chill can prove fatal by inducing vagal shock, or cold shock, which causes violent shivering and the contraction of muscles, making it impossible to swim. It also prompts a gasping reflex – one that can easily lead to inhaling water and drowning. In some cases, instant cardiac arrest may result. (Doctors believe that the average survival time of those flung from the deck of the *Titanic* was a mere few seconds.) Such physical reactions are likely to be exaggerated if the person has been drinking or eating excessively, as cruise passengers are apt to do. Even if jumpers survive the impact, they cannot expect the cruise ship to alter its course quickly: the time required to slow the ship down, turn around, and return to the scene may run into hours.

In the *Pacific Sky* incident related above, a further, chilling factor might have come into play. Leftovers and other food waste on cruise ships is often ground or pulped and then discharged at night, out of the back of the boat. It is a practice that can attract a few hungry sharks in the ship's wake. On this occasion, crew told passengers, there had been fins spotted in the water.

Incredibly, within a few hours, the leaper had been rescued – a passenger on deck spotting the man as the ship's searchlight scoured the waves. 'The crew said how lucky he was,' said Welsh, who added that it was rumoured that the man had 'been in the navy and learned floating techniques'.

A cheer went up as news of the rescue was announced. It is not known how pleased the man's wife was to see him again. However, Hughson relates that some passengers whose entertainment had been constantly punctuated by updates were unenthusiastic: 'People were so annoyed by the interruptions that they were just saying, "Leave him there!"'

Hughson and Welsh had witnessed another rescue in the warm waters of the South Pacific a year earlier, when a fellow passenger – believed to have been on medication – threw himself over the railings. Using sophisticated global navigation devices – and the low-tech practice of simply throwing a mass of plastic furniture overboard to mark the spot – the ship's crew were able to return to the site of his leap and locate him.

It is understandable that cruise companies are as reluctant to tell of survivors, as of fatalities. Any search is a costly business: delays and disrupted schedules can cost vast sums in fuel, port fees and compensation payments to passengers who miss flights. The *Legend*'s search caused such delays that even the following cruise from New York could not leave on schedule. Furthermore, survival stories create a false impression: bar a few miracle rescues, a jump is final.

The *Pacific Sky*'s third man overboard was not so fortunate. In January 2005, on the last night of a ten-day cruise ending in Brisbane, twenty-four-year-old Andrew Mark Gready, who had been drinking heavily, climbed over the railings on deck and jumped. People nearby had tried to dissuade him in vain. Crew lowered a rescue boat into what were described as treacherous seas, but failed to bring him back. The man's family, who hired a helicopter in a last attempt to find him after the ship gave up the search, said they believed that he did not realise how far the drop was; his decision to jump was 'a prank that went wrong'.

One passenger who made it overboard and survived was Tim Sears, a thirty-one-year-old man from Michigan, who found himself floating in the waters of the Gulf of Mexico after setting off on a cruise from Texas. Bizarrely, he had no recollection of how he had tumbled off the *Carnival Celebration*. The last thing he could recall was looking for his friend in the casino, after a day and night of heavy drinking.

Now he was in the sea – without his trousers or shoes, and unable to see properly without his glasses. His friend on board, assuming he was off somewhere enjoying himself, did not report him missing.

It was perhaps his ex-army paratrooper background that saved him. Sears swam in search of land or a boat to pick him out of the sea; but even when dawn came, revealing boats passing in the distance, none spotted him. Exhausted, fearing sharks and barracuda, at one point, he made his peace with God, decided he could swim no longer, and went under, but when he had let himself sink some metres and his lungs had started to fill with water, he decided he did not want to die after all. He chose to make one more push instead, fighting back to the surface. Several more hours elapsed. Eventually, he spotted another ship on the horizon. He swam a last desperate few hundred metres and screamed for help. The ship's crew heard his cries, and pulled Sears, badly burnt and dehydrated, from the water.

Sears, who believes he fell victim to drink spiking, is one of the few who has gone overboard and lived to tell the tale. His survival is particularly remarkable because no-one witnessed his fall. Without being sure that someone has definitely gone into the sea, cruise lines are reluctant to have a ship turn and mount an expensive search. Hoax calls have been known to happen, and the scope for passengers to go briefly missing – asleep, passed out drunk, happily engrossed in the facilities, or indeed, discreetly enjoying the attentions of another guest or crew member – are legion.

Tim Sears's remarkable escape from the seas is not an entirely victimless tale. As his repute spread, many have apparently attempted to trace the man from Lansing, Michigan – to the perpetual frustration of another Tim Sears, whose telephone number is actually listed in Lansing's *White Pages*. On being contacted, he said: 'What is it with you people? Do you think if I was some drunken idiot who fell off a cruise ship I'd have a listing? Just leave me alone!' On no account should this man be telephoned.

14

Not a Bang but a Whimper

A CAUTIONARY WORD for those daredevils now eager to book a cruise. Not every trip is enlivened by pirates, crime or disaster. All too often, a cruise really is just a boatload of passengers simply sailing into old age – and beyond.

One newspaper's travel editor, who wished to remain anonymous, advised as a rule of thumb that prospective passengers look at the models in the brochure and add twenty years. Faces alone may not be sufficient to form an accurate picture: on one trip, he believed he was on a boat largely populated by middle-aged women, until he reached the pool. Many who choose to cruise, it seemed, also choose facelifts.

If it is bliss to be alive and on a cruise ship, to be old is very heaven. Daina Brampton, a former *Fairstar* bar steward, has vivid memories of the afternoon teas on the longer voyages, the type that attracted a much older crowd than its more notorious jaunts. 'It was served in the Upper Zodiac lounge – a room with a circular hole in the middle where people could stand to watch the entertainment below.' Even though afternoon tea was just one of seven meals served during the day – from early morning pastries on the deck to breakfast, morning tea, lunch, dinner and finally the midnight buffet – the trays and trays of sandwiches exercised a magnetic appeal:

> These crowds of old people would start gathering before 4 pm, circling the table like sharks. You'd take the covers off and they would just come in at you, in a mass of walking sticks – it would be impossible to battle your way out. You couldn't get through the scrum.

Bev, another former *Fairstar* steward, believes there was a direct connection between the death rates on board and the overeating. 'They even used to snatch loads of biscuits when I walked through with plates. And they were just ordinary, plain biscuits.'

A similar rush would occur when the first tranche of nightly cabaret finished, Brampton said:

> At the end of the early evening entertainment shows you would just have to pin yourself to the walls, because there would be a stampede of old people trying to go to bed.

While some entertainment staff – cocktail pianists, bingo callers and the legendary gentleman hosts – are in their element among an ageing clientele, for others, such as the nightclub musicians, it can be trying. Murray Ferguson, fed up with schoolies and the party excesses of some trips, said he would initially appreciate the respite afforded by the longer Asian cruises with an older clientele, but it soon became 'mindnumbing':

> They would all go to bed at 9 pm and you'd be playing gigs to nobody. But they'd paid for entertainment and so you had to provide it, even if no one was there.

Yet the heady mix of music, sea air and sandwiches would move many to the most passionate of declarations. Brampton recalls that some of the older passengers, retired, neglected by relatives, but now finding attentive care and happiness on board, would announce: 'I'm coming here to die ... I can't think of a better way to go.'

This frequent refrain was no idle threat, as Brampton, who was initially quartered with other staff just around the corner from the *Fairstar*'s morgue, knew all too well:

> If someone died, we would have to walk past the bodies to get to our cabins – you knew because you'd hear the whirr of the refrigerator... On a longer cruise you'd expect it. Once we lost four or five going around Asia.

Older voyagers might like to look away now – but it seems that a common sport below deck is a crew sweepstake: just how many passengers will pass away on each cruise?

At larger ports of call, a few deceased passengers pose little problem. As most passengers shuffle off for sightseeing, corpses can be discreetly offloaded to be sent home. Otherwise, the stiffs stay on.

The *Fairstar* had room for two in its morgue, a big stainless steel refrigeration unit with a drawer for each body. Bigger ships, with a more geriatric clientele, have many more. On the great ocean liners operated by Cunard, boasting an atmosphere in which little has changed in the past fifty years, facilities are naturally a little more expansive. The *QE2* has space for eight prematurely departing passengers; the *QM2* can house twelve.

A Cunard spokesman 'did not know' if they have ever needed an overflow facility; but according to crew working for other companies on smaller vessels, a rush on the morgue has occasionally left staff embarrassed. One recalled a busy period: 'They had to fill a bathtub in a spare cabin with ice and put the body in there.'

Perhaps, though, these elderly passengers were the lucky ones – shuffleboarding off this mortal coil. Katie, another former *Fairstar* steward, recalls older guests leaving the ship weeping at *not* having ended their days in such enchanting surrounds.

For those who don't want to die, there is some good news. Despite the noroviruses and the memento mori of the morgue lurking just a few decks below the passenger cabins – and the fact that ships have no legal obligation to carry a doctor – facilities are often impressive, according to medical professionals.

Anita, a nurse who spent ten years at sea on various ships in the Caribbean and Mediterranean, says the medical facilities on many Princess ships were amazing. 'We could get results from blood tests in fifteen minutes – some things were better than in accident and emergency departments.' As a shipboard nurse, Anita often treated an ageing set of patients with complex medical histories, apt to take a tumble on a shore excursion. She says she was always more than adequately resourced; however, she counsels, 'If you're an elderly person on a cruise, it's really important to work out what facilities they've got, because they really vary.'

At least one cruise line is rumoured to have evicted a guest who booked back-to-back cruises for the twilight of her years. Her sunset age lasted over a decade, and her growing decrepitude put an increasing strain on their onboard medical facilities.

But then, as a study in the *Journal of the American Geriatrics Society* confirmed, the price of constantly going on cruises can compare favourably with that of living in many nursing homes. While cruise lines might baulk at the comparison, the experiences are similar enough for a chain of new retirement developments in Britain to market themselves as 'cruise ships on dry land'.

Nurse Anita said of all destinations, the Panama Canal cruises posed her biggest nightmare:

> It's one of those places, a wonder of the world, that a lot of people say they want to see before they die. So you get old people who literally are about to die . . . People would always be collapsing on the deck – it's very hot and tropical down there, but they'd be outside all day wanting to watch as we sailed through – you'd always have an emergency.

The health news, though, is not all bad for the elderly: according to Anita, motion sickness is apparently far more prevalent among younger, first-time cruisers. What older passengers may lose in general mobility, they apparently gain in the sea legs.

15

What Lies Beneath

THE INEQUALITY OF the world, say anti-poverty campaigners, is mirrored through the decks of a cruise ship.

For many westerners, a working life on the ocean wave can be grand. A whole offshoot of the industry has bloomed around arranging work for people on a cruise ship: agencies on the shore; extensive how-to books; even downloadable courses and contacts for sale over the internet. For many of those who do spend years at sea, travelling the world in some of the most luxurious surroundings possible, it can prove a fabulous experience.

Sandy, a former bar steward, said:

> The travelling appealed to me and I knew I could never afford to go on a cruise as a passenger, so I thought working on one would be fun. I had a blast and made many lifelong friends in the process.

The entertainers, bar staff, security officers and others can make a good wage – and with accommodation and food all provided on board the ship, most of it can be saved. While some may find themselves effectively employed at an hourly rate that many might sniff at on shore, it is rarely a long-term career for these young western staff, who are unlikely to have a family to support at home. Daina Brampton, who started work for P&O in the 1990s on $3 an hour, said: 'When you're young and have no responsibilities, it's just fun.'

Below deck, the deal is somewhat different. One website selling the secrets of landing a job on cruise ships also claims to give crucial advice on which posts westerners should never consider taking.

Some belowdecks jobs are the uncontested domain of unskilled staff from India, Bangladesh, Indonesia and other countries counted among the poorest in Asia and Africa. Many of these workers are rostered on around the clock for months without a break, in what the International Transport Workers' Federation has described as sweatshop conditions, often too intimidated to complain. Many are bonded to work, as the cruise firm retains a large portion of their wages until the contract is over. A further slice of their salaries goes to the agencies through which they are usually hired.

When ships sail in international waters under 'flags of convenience', there is little recourse for these members of the crew. A ship is said to sail under a flag of convenience when it is registered in a country that may have little or no connection with its owners, makers, crew, guests, operating cruise line, or itinerary. Registering a ship in a country such as Panama or Liberia allows businesses to avoid the stringent regulations and higher costs faced in Britain, the USA, Australia and other wealthy countries.

Industry leaders candidly admit that staffing considerations play a major part in the decision to fly such flags. Bob Dickinson, Carnival CEO, says that strict regulations and the unionised labour market found in countries such as Britain and the US prevent cruise lines achieving an 'optimal crew mix', and increase the companies' labour costs, so the cruise lines register their ships in the Bahamas, Panama or Liberia in order to be able to negotiate what he describes as 'fair and equitable compensation in the global market'.

Different nationalities usually take the jobs on different sections of the ships. Typically, officers come from a first-world seafaring nation such as

Italy or Portugal; the entertainment and front-of-house crew come from the same country as the majority of passengers on board, be it Britain, the US or Australia; and the rest of the crew are from the third world.

Each section of the crew must abide by different rules, governing where they can go on the ship and who they can talk to, creating a de facto class system on board. Many are banned from speaking to passengers. As an entertainer on Australian cruise ships admitted: 'It was hard for the crew to be a big happy family.' Another former crew member observed: 'The Italians are usually doing the bossing about, but the Indonesians do the hard yards.'

Officers and senior staff have their own private cabins, while the westerners who make up the front-of-house staff might share with one other; down below, it is typically more cramped. On the *Fairstar*, even the cocktail pianist had his own private quarters, while the Indonesian workers would share six bunks per windowless room.

While the quality of staff quarters varies from ship to ship, the 'galley rats' will find themselves billeted in the noisiest, smelliest parts of any vessel.

A British croupier, Richard Arghiris, who had initially shared a cabin and eaten in passenger areas when working for an Israeli cruise line, told of his disgust when the chef started making casino staff eat with the rest of the crew:

> We had to go down to the Russian sailors' quarters, these cockroach-infested, dingy places, where everyone was sitting smoking in the corridors. The cabins were cramped and dirty and noisy – and stank of engines, and diesel. The toilets were clogged almost constantly.

Even further down in the ship was a deck for the Filipino housekeeping staff.

In one case recorded by International Transport Workers' Federation investigators, a ship sailing in the Caribbean had just two showers and one working toilet for 100 male and female crew members.

Marine consultant Peter Burge said:

> Ratings [staff with no commissioned rank] are almost without exception from the likes of the Philippines and India, because they pay them a pittance. By first-world standards they are paid nothing. They are only required to be healthy – there is generally no qualification standard. They'll screen them to make sure they're clean and won't cause problems.
>
> But probably ninety per cent of the ships that are operated by leading shipping nations have been flagged out and can therefore pick up crews wherever they like. We've got ships running around with Senegalese, Bangladeshis . . . people [who] are truly desperate.

No matter how poor the conditions, complaints are not welcome. One Indian kitchen worker, doing eleven-hour shifts on board the Carnival ship *Festival*, said: 'If you speak from the heart, you are gone, fired. You just have to keep saying yes.'

Burge agreed that this was often the case:

> The ratings won't do anything; [because] they won't get another job. They're often employed by crew agencies in the countries they come from. If the cruise companies say they don't want any troublemakers, they won't get them.

This makes belowdecks crew vulnerable. The crew are far more liable than passengers to be the victims of crime, harassment and assault – especially female crew on a male-dominated ship.

An Australian woman who worked as a steward on cruises out of Sydney said: 'We were women that the Italian officers would just try to fuck. To them, we were scum.' As comparatively lowly crew members, stewards were not allowed to socialise in passenger areas. 'But when we went to try to relax in the crew bar, it would be male dominated, and there would be porno movies playing.'

Cruise ship security officer Randy Jaques, who claims sexual assaults are rife on ships, says that few crew would ever come to him to report offences, no matter how much he encouraged them to do so. Peter Burge agrees: 'There is a code of silence amongst the crew, if not amongst the officers. And that culture certainly translates internationally.'

Lawyer Charles Lipcon, whose firm represents many cruise ship workers on a contingent fee basis, is scathing in his assessment of cruise lines:

> I think they're very bad employers – you wouldn't work for them the way they demand eighteen hours a day, seven days a week, for fifty bucks a month plus tips. If you do anything at all the company doesn't like they fire you with ten minutes news. I don't know too many people who would want that.

Representation at sea is, he says, ineffective at best. 'They have unions; [crew] call them pretend unions.'

Anita, a nurse, who was employed through a British agency, on what she described as a good salary, with good conditions overall, said she looked into joining a union at one point but was unsettled to discover how little assistance she could call upon. 'You're kind of in limbo. What could I have done? You don't belong anywhere at sea.' That is why, she thinks, many have turned to litigation to get redress.

Such legal representation may be costly, if not impossible to obtain. While Earle Moulton, the barman who served alcohol to Lynsey O'Brien, the Irish teenager who went overboard on a *Costa Magica* cruise, may glean little sympathy, his firing and subsequent lack of work shows how powerless the crew can be. The fifty-six-year-old Jamaican claims to have served the young girl only after she showed him an ID card claiming she was aged twenty-three, but he was sacked by Costa Cruises five days after her disappearance and was still unemployed when he was tracked down by Britain's *Daily Mail* months later.

A father of four, he had worked for Italian-based Costa Cruises for fifteen years but was sacked without compensation. He said that his floor manager told him to stop working, and get off at the next port in Puerto Rico; he believed it was nothing serious, that he was just being suspended pending an investigation into Lynsey O'Brien's disappearance. But when Mr Moulton called his agent in Kingston for more work, he found that he had been marked 'NTR': not to be rehired. He had received no written notification of this. While Moulton's basic wage was only US$790 a month, commission and tips meant he could earn up to $2500. Now, he faced the loss of all earnings plus his pension, whether his firing was merited or not. Moulton said he tried to hire a lawyer in Miami, without success. His livelihood was gone.

While the conditions belowdecks staff face would deter most westerners, among workers in developing countries, jobs on cruise ships remain highly sought after, because the wages, though low, are better than those they can make at home. Between 2001 and 2003 a fraudster posing as a cruise ship agent managed to con 120,000 would-be applicants out of large sums of money across a number of nations in Africa and Asia.

Recently, cruise lines have started hiring staff from eastern Europe, from countries whose average wage still falls well below those in the west. Even on the *Hebridean Princess*, the luxury ship chartered by the Queen for an estimated £200,000 for her eightieth birthday celebrations, many of the crew are Latvians earning £40 a day. The personnel chief from the cruise line's hiring agency told *The Sunday Mirror* that it was all about the bottom line, adding: 'And you do find British people are more likely to tell you to stick your job up your backside. Latvians are more likely to crack on and keep their heads down.' He said most of the eastern Europeans he was hiring had the kind of qualifications that would land most Britons far better paid jobs.

Across all cruise lines, staff typically work at least a twelve-hour day, seven days a week. For many in service positions, their earnings are almost entirely made up of tips. A study by the Seafarers' International

Research Centre (SIRC) at Cardiff University showed that many were recruited on the basis of racial stereotypes, with Asians preferred for their friendliness. One recruiter told the report's author:

> Asians, especially the Filipinos, can smile very nicely. They seem to have been born with a wonderful service culture. They always greet the guests and always smile. And they do it so naturally.

The assumption that cruise staff will smile by nature carries over into the sales pitch; the latest Oceania Cruises brochure describes how the 'international staff' are not only trained to anticipate guests' every whim, but also that:

> It is simply their nature to exceed [...] expectations; pleasing you is what pleases them. Genuine sincerity and warmth show on their smiling faces and is sensed in every movement and every encounter...

Yet, as a waiter on a different cruise line pointed out, no matter how hard Asian staff members worked or smiled, their higher earning managers were usually European.

One Australian woman who had worked alongside Indonesians and Filipinos said:

> I don't know how they do it. They're so well educated – almost all the ones I worked with have been to university and got a degree – but they're just so desperate to get decent jobs.

After briefly leaving cruise ships, this woman was rehired in a managerial position – in charge of her former coworkers, many of whom had far more experience.

She said that since she had left, she had heard of an Indonesian woman being promoted to an assistant manager position. 'I was quite surprised. But maybe the cruise companies are moving forward into the real world with the rest of us.'

Ships can effectively become racially segregated. As one website giving advice about cruise ship jobs makes clear, the deckhand and able seamen positions are usually given to citizens of developing countries, who as a rule are not allowed to go into passenger areas or use any guest facilities, and can only ever drink in the crew bar. In contrast, it says, small US-registered ships and riverboats recruit young Americans for similar positions – and typically, these deckhands are allowed to socialise with the passengers.

In his book *Cruise Ship Blues*, Ross Klein recounts how he spoke to a Honduran busboy on a Regency cruise, and asked him how long it would take him to get a promotion; the busboy replied that he was too dark-skinned ever to be promoted as a waiter. Perhaps the part of the 2006 remake of the film *The Poseidon Adventure* that most strained viewers' credulity was the appearance of a black captain at the helm of the stricken cruise ship – although, as many critics pointed out, he was soon killed off.

For many workers, tips are their major source of income. On many cruise lines, passengers are requested to pay a specific amount per person per night, intended as a gratuity for two or three designated staff who will be serving them, such as their waiter and cabin stewards. This may even be paid upfront, although it is not usually included in the advertised fare.

Unfortunately for the people who need the money most, some passengers decide not to pay this – understandable perhaps in the context of cruise tickets becoming cheaper, attracting customers for whom the additional gratuity might represent a significant extra charge, particularly when it is a cost that they might reasonably expect the employer to cover.

An Indian worker who has worked on many ships said that although he enjoys working for Carnival more than other cruise lines, he and his colleagues in the restaurant service and housekeeping effectively have no wages – only US$46 a month. He works for tips; but since the company introduced a reverse gratuity system, charging for tips upfront and then allowing guests to claim back the money if they are not happy, many guests have chosen to do that:

> The guests take back the money just by saying that they did not enjoy the services though they have been getting the best services always. This causes our total pay to go down and we cannot send enough money home. It is like working for free.

One reason for this, he thought, was that guests are not sufficiently informed about the reason for the gratuity – they see it as an extra bonus for crew members, but for many of the staff, tips are virtually all the money that they will earn on the cruise.

Crew often have to pay a bond to their employer and also pay for flights and uniforms out of their own wages. On some ships, those who lose such items as their name badges have to pay US$80 to replace them.

Nevertheless, many of the jobs represent an opportunity for workers in poor countries to earn far more money than they might at home – albeit at a cost of rarely seeing the families they are frequently working to support. Both Carnival and Royal Caribbean point out that their tipping systems are hardly unique: it is not unusual for staff in land-based American resorts to earn the bulk of their income through tips. The cruise lines also say that their crew have such additional benefits as free accommodation, food and medical care.

P&O Cruises Australia says: 'Crew welfare is of paramount importance to us.' Staff remuneration details are, it says, 'confidential between our workforce and the company'.

Despite this, the practice of paying low wages to service staff has disturbed some who travel on cruise ships – both passengers and crew. One former P&O staffer, a westerner, said he would tip cabin stewards out of his own wages when working on board. A man from Liverpool in Sydney's western suburbs, disembarking with family and friends from a P&O *Pacific Sun* cruise that attracted media attention for a norovirus outbreak, said the real story was the scandalous wages paid to the staff. 'It's shocking what they're paid. And they were always up before us and after us working.' Despite having already tipped upfront, his family left their cabin steward more, he said. 'We're not rich people, but we wanted to make sure he got something.'

16

Love Boats

BOATS HAVE BEEN associated with love and sex since at least the days when Paris sailed off with Helen of Troy, and there is probably a good case to be made for stretching that history back to Noah. In modern times, from the cheesiest episodes of 1970s TV series *The Love Boat* to the celluloid romance of Kate Winslet and Leonardo DiCaprio, passions have run rife on the high seas. For some passengers, the rocking and heaving is not always seasickness.

Cruises are credited with sparking many a marriage: Australia boasts many couples who met upon the bawdy decks of the *Fairstar*. One Australian woman claimed to have met both her first and second husbands on the ocean (though presumably on different cruises).

Some cruise ship captains are now allowed to perform full marriage ceremonies at sea: namely, those on P&O ships registered in Bermuda, including ships of the Princess Line, the original TV love boats. Other cruisers normally have to wait for a priest when the ship hits port. Although captains are often called upon to conduct a renewal of vows for married couples, few ships or nations recognise marriages contracted out in the ocean.

Confusion about the rules has occasionally come to the aid of those who marry in haste. The actress Zsa Zsa Gabor was married to an eighth husband, Mexican screen star Felipe de Alba, by the captain of a cruise ship. However, the marriage was not legally binding and the following day Gabor had it annulled – recalling, no doubt, that she had yet to divorce husband number seven.

Cruise ships are magnets for newlyweds, but would-be cruising honeymooners might like to consider the cautionary tale of Stella Bates, a Kidderminster woman who married her long-time lover Michael in Barbados. At their exotic beach wedding, they invited a stranger, a fellow guest in the hotel, to be their witness. Soon, though, she would be playing a bigger role than that. The happy couple joined a cruise ship for their honeymoon – a week-long Caribbean cruise, on which witness Laura-Jo was also booked.

As the ship sailed on through the night, Stella was tucked in bed, but Michael found himself up and about with their new friend. At the end of the cruise, the women exchanged telephone numbers – which is how, when Michael disappeared, Stella was eventually able to confirm just where her new husband was; it was also how one of the witness's friends was able to text the now-jilted wife: 'It's only fair that you know. Laura has been sleeping with your husband. It all started when we were on the cruise ship.' Michael told *The Mirror* he was happy with Laura-Jo and felt he had found his 'true love'. For her part, Laura said of those balmy nights on the cruise: 'When we kissed on his honeymoon I fell head over heels.'

Onboard romances can be fraught with other unlikely risks. One new lovers' practice that has caused cruise ship crews great consternation in recent years can be blamed on Kate and Leonardo. Inspired by the 'King of the World' scene in *Titanic*, couples have been spotted climbing out onto the tip of ships' prows with their arms flung wide. The Passenger Vessel Association cautioned cruise operators in a 'Titanic Alert': 'Keep your crew members alerted to this potential problem and perhaps even close or rope off the extreme bow access area of your vessel.' Access is usually not possible on the largest liners, but smaller vessels have reported a spate of such incidents.

Other dangers are less romantic. An American nursing journal recently sounded a warning note to anyone considering an illicit liaison with a crew member: 'Many cruise line employees come from impoverished villages and could come aboard with undiagnosed or untreated conditions.' A cruise ship crew member's self-diagnosed 'fever blisters' were diagnosed by nurses as herpes.

Douglas Ward's Berlitz *Complete Guide to Cruising* also warns the single woman passenger to be wary of an easy fling with the officers: 'They get to see new faces every week (or every cruise) and thus the possible risk of sexually transmitted diseases should be borne in mind.'

Any crew members caught in flagrante could face dismissal. Often cruise lines, perhaps wary of lawsuits, prohibit sexual relations between staff and customers, or at least ban crew from entering passenger accommodation (although Carnival's CEO has noted publicly that a captain's reputed sexual prowess can be something of a moneyspinner, luring passengers on board).

Mere prohibitions or contractual requirements have not always come between seafaring hunters and their quarry. High-profile casualties of their own libido have included the Scottish captain of the *Hebridean Princess*, who was sacked from a previous post, reported the *Sunday Mirror*, after leaving the bridge of P&O's 46,000-tonne liner the *Sky Princess* to pleasure a female passenger, leaving junior staff at the helm to look after the rest of the 2000 people on board as the ship sailed along the Alaskan coast.

One woman who used to work for P&O has warning words for guests:

> You'd see female passengers flirting with the officers and think, don't go there. The Italians would have a wife at home, a girlfriend on the ship and be sleeping with the passengers. But you'd have girls going on a cruise with the intention of getting a stripe on their shoulder.

The uniform appears something of a trump card in love. One envious passenger, a veteran of many Australian cruises, confessed:

> You do find of an evening, late at night, all the women do tend to be attracted to the officers. My friends and I used to say, here they come, here come the whiteshirts. Three or four of them walk into a bar and all these girls come crowding around. We said we'd buy some shirts and try it next year. Then they disappear – I don't know where they disappear to. We all assume – but we'd only be guessing . . .

Another former P&O crew member, Sandy, confirmed:

> The female passengers were definitely on the prowl for a crew member to have a shipboard romance with . . . They showed no self respect – they were on the hunt!

One Australian sports star, a woman, remains notorious among former *Fairstar* crew. A female steward, who preferred to remain anonymous, described the celebrity as a 'dirty dog' after she and a colleague were subject to an unsolicited approach late one night. The two women were somewhat surprised to find the former Olympian's hands suddenly wrapping round their waists, and moving down into their groins. Both refused the invitation.

However, it is not just passengers who go after the crew. Perhaps inspired by the success of the officers, other crew members have been known to be emboldened into approaches that surpass passenger expectations. One passenger on an Australian cruise was astonished to find a note under the plate that her waiter had just set down, inviting her to meet him in her cabin in ten minutes. She didn't.

Stephen, a former crew member on the *Fair Princess*, could shed some light on the goings-on. Although he said he was 'never big on cracking on to the passengers', plenty of his colleagues were. It was the way they got through the monotony of life at sea. Some of the bands, in particular, were what he termed 'notorious rootrats': 'You'd see them when the passengers got on the ship, checking them out, planning ahead on the possibilities.'

Despite the shared cabins, crew usually found a way to enjoy some privacy with any lucky passengers:

> One of the real pains in the arse would be whenever the other guy I was sharing a cabin with would get it on with a passenger. We had a code whereby he'd hang a tie over the door. One night I actually did want to go back to my room, when we were at port in Noumea, and found I was going to have to roam the streets instead.

Cruisers should not, however, expect sexual services from the promisingly named 'gentlemen hosts' – men who are employed to attend to the needs of the many single women travellers of a certain age. These immaculate gentlemen, who usually pay a nominal fee to be on board, will take you for a fox trot, rumba, a cha-cha or even the occasional tango, but the twosomes are strictly limited to the dance floor. The Working Vacation Inc, an agency that supplies gentleman hosts to a range of cruise ships, specifies that they must be physically fit, kindly and moral. Even dancing with the same woman twice in an evening is frowned upon. Usually they are required to post bond with the ship: should these ageing Lotharios broaden the scope of their hosting duties with a lady, they are swiftly ejected from the boat at the next port.

Some of the older women apparently need to be kept in check, too. *The Wall Street Journal* has reported that some gentlemen have required all their diplomatic skills to repel the advances of overly aggressive women. One host, a sixty-five-year-old Scot, admitted: 'The women can be pushy.' Having frequently paid double the normal rate as single occupants in a cabin, they sometimes feel a sense of entitlement, he said: 'They say "I pay for this privilege to dance with you."'

Lauretta Blake, who runs Working Vacation Inc, said that even the fleet-footed hosts have been known to be ensnared. Ageing single female passengers who wish to latch on to these gentlemen of impeccable credentials may do so – but strictly after the end of the cruise.

Those who can't wait might try one of Saga's cruise ships. The holiday firm specialises in vacations for the over-fifties (a potentially youthful demographic on some boats). The TV presenter Esther Rantzen, having tried out one of their cruises, reported in the *Daily Mail* that the company's acronym, far from standing for 'Send A Granny Away', was in fact better known by her fellow passengers as 'Sex And Games At-sea'.

A constant theme in any discussion with both guests and crew who love the life at sea is that cruises are a way to forget the everyday and leave their mundane, landlocked lives behind. Sometimes, though, you can have too great a dose of unreality.

Guests on a 2005 Nile cruise were smitten with a dashing young military man, recounting tales of adventure in Kosovo and Afghanistan. A tour guide on a shore excursion even likened him to an Egyptian god. None was more smitten than his girlfriend, Shona, who knew that on this cruise, her beau, the war hero Captain Sir Alan Mcilwraith, planned to propose.

At least, that is, until a call came through from top brass: he was to be wrested away from his holiday on an urgent mission back to London to tackle terrorists. A dinghy and helicopter were being despatched to take him.

His would-be fiancée's tears were flowing – but Mcilwraith received a last minute reprieve. Fellow guests urged him to get on with it and propose. So that evening, the gallant soldier made his way to the lounge and, borrowing the compere's microphone, asked his Shona to marry him. To the cheers of the other passengers, she agreed.

Yet another romance had been sealed on the seas. Shona confided in other guests that she feared she could not live up to the dashing captain's life. Alas, neither could he. It turned out that the Sir Captain was nothing of the sort: his medals bought on eBay, his stories – even including a Wikipedia entry – fictitious, and his battlegrounds not Kosovo but a Glasgow call centre. His fiancée returned the ring, and the sorry story was reported in the British press.

Still, at least Shona's intended was rumbled before she tied the knot. Others have fallen for worse rogues. Perhaps the most notorious was Giovanni Vigliotto, whose career in winning the hearts of wealthy ladies is thought to have spanned several decades. Signor Vigliotto's fall came in the early 1980s. He had wooed and wed a real estate agent before disappearing. She tracked him down to a Florida flea market, where he was selling her possessions. During the resultant investigation and eventual trial, he would confess to having played a similar trick on 104 other women. His astonishing strike rate had been aided by the romance of the sea: no less than four women had fallen for his faux-Italian charms and tied the knot with Signor Vigliotto on one single cruise.

One great fear of first-time cruisers is the idea of being trapped on a boat with thousands of people with whom they have nothing in common. Many passengers try to alleviate the risk by putting out feelers on online message boards or even booking through a specialist agent attracting a certain type of clientele. This is all very well for those who are part of the target group; however, for other passengers who find themselves on a ship with a large party whose members share a similar interest, the situation can then become dire indeed.

In retrospect, it would have been good if a certain Diann from Florida had known that A&S Travel Center advertised cruises on the 4swinging.com website. The November 2005 cruise she took on the *Carnival Imagination* would have some particularly outgoing and friendly people on board. Namely, several hundred swingers.

For Diann, who shared her outrage via an online review at consumeraffairs.com two days after the cruise ended, it had clearly been a bit of a shock:

> OH MY GOD. I could not believe the outrageous open display of SEX that went on for 2 NIGHTS at the Disco ... My 16 yr old witnessed

lesbian and gay behavior as well as group participation and YES offers of marijuana. What the hell is going on? ... the SWINGERS were even easily identifiable by their ORANGE wrist bands.

A&S Travel were advertising another Playful Swingers cruise for late 2006. The ship wasn't explicitly identified – but, it seems safe to say, passengers would probably know once they are aboard. As Carnival Cruises boasts on its website: 'Our passengers have more fun!'

It wouldn't happen on the upmarket boats. But then, why swing when you are rich enough to bring along a choice of lovers? Among the passengers on the ultra-luxurious Seabourn boats was one British man who became well known to regular fellow guests. He would cruise virtually all year round, accompanied by two women: one his wife, the other his mistress. The immaculately turned-out ladies were booked into two separate cabins, but otherwise the threesome went everywhere together, before, as one fellow passenger put it, 'he would decide which one he would bestow his favours upon that evening'. The wealthy man died recently, but his mistress was reportedly still enjoying a Seabourn cruise habit.

When it comes to hosting the most Dionysian of rituals, the Greeks remain firmly centre stage – albeit with the help of partying Europeans. Lurid headlines were garnered by one boat, the *Ayia Napa Queen*, that sailed out of the Greek Cypriot port Ayia Napa: it was investigated by police in 2004 after TV footage of onboard sex games in which, according to *The Observer*, 'whipped cream, watermelons and cucumbers played a central role'. However, reports of 'sex cruises' in the Mediterranean were slightly overegged: the culprit turned out to be a single, daytripping pleasure boat.

While the name Ayia Napa would ring warning bells for many – as a resort with a certain reputation for uninhibited nightlife – few would expect any such troubles from a 'proper' Mediterranean cruise ship. Yet one such was the venue for one of the most astonishing complaints that has been levelled by a passenger against a cruise line.

Shelley Sparkman, thirty, of Malibu, California, splashed out on a three-day trip on Royal Olympic Cruises for herself, sailing from the capital Athens to a variety of Greek islands. At lunch on the very first day, it became obvious to Ms Sparkman that a good number of her fellow passengers were extremely familiar with one another. Before dessert had been polished off, several women had made themselves comfortable to the point of removing virtually all their clothes, bar G-strings, rubbing suntan lotion onto one another. And these particular passengers did not seem at all put out by the camcorder that another – male – passenger was pointing at them. This might be Europe, but for Ms Sparkman and others, it was a bit much. They decided to eat inside.

Back on the main deck to sunbathe later, she was surprised to see the camera still busily filming passengers – including herself. Something fishy was going on, and she decided to investigate. As she wandered the boat, she became aware of two men hanging up towels on the top deck, creating an improvised screen. A second cameraman was in the vicinity, apparently filming couples as they descended out of general view behind the towels. From below, Ms Sparkman's incredulous ears heard what she could only describe as 'a series of unsettling groans and grunts coming from the area'.

She had heard enough. But her ensuing complaints yielded the remarkable explanation from the ship's crew that, indeed, a group of passengers from Holland and Belgium were aboard, shooting a porn film, starring two 'celebrities of the genre'. And the understandably angry and disgusted Ms Sparkman was potentially an unwitting, unwilling extra.

After returning home, she complained to the Royal Olympic cruise line requesting a full refund. Hearing nothing, she took her case to *Condé Nast Traveler*. Their Ombudsman column advised:

It's true that European ships tend to be more relaxed on the subject of toplessness than U.S. lines, but what Sparkman encountered falls outside the boundaries of what is acceptable.

Even by the standards of the notoriously uninhibited Dutch, these had been strange fellow travellers. Royal Olympic said the episode was 'an anomaly', and eventually offered Ms Sparkman a voucher for a future cruise.

17

Mutiny!

ONE OF THE many curious foibles of cruise passengers is that, while they spend up to tens of thousands of dollars to pass weeks on a slow-moving ship whose whole appeal is the possibility of ultimate relaxation on board, they don't seem to like it when they can't get off.

No matter if that ship is regarded as the biggest and best in the world, a megaliner with a choice of fifteen restaurants and bars, endowed with five swimming pools, a casino, a state-of-the-art gym, a ballroom, a theatre with West End–style shows, live music, a basketball court and even a planetarium, for those who can't be bothered to nip up on to deck to see the real thing. No matter that, according to Cunard, 'athletes will find one of the best-equipped playing fields anywhere'. Or that 'sybarites', no less, could 'enjoy the rejuvenating treatments of the world-renowned Canyon Ranch SpaClub'. It is, according to their trademarked description, a 'veritable City at Sea'. This ship even has virtual reality golf. What more, in the name of Poseidon, could any passenger want?

What they want, apparently, is to have all the joy of docking for a few hours at a Caribbean island, complete with purpose-built jetties, tax-free shopping and desperate locals trying to flog them overpriced tat. It is, after all, in the brochure. And when that pleasure was denied to passengers on the *Queen Mary 2*, the ship's owners, Cunard, soon felt their wrath.

From the beginning of its young life, the *QM2* appeared slightly jinxed. Billed in advance as the biggest and best ocean liner ever seen, its construction in France's Saint-Nazaire shipyard, Nantes, was a subject of much local pride. Around 3000 craftsmen worked for a total of 8 million hours on the ship; 20,000 people contributed in some way to the final result. Its construction was marred by tragedy in the autumn before the *QM2* sailed. Sixteen people, including workers and their families on a visit to see the new ship, died when a gangplank collapsed.

The *QM2* was launched nonetheless to great fanfare in 2004, officially christened by Queen Elizabeth II – Mary's granddaughter – in a ceremony in Southampton, before setting sail on its maiden voyage. This first journey suffered due to technical problems, the ship returning late after bow doors covering propellers failed to shut. Some passengers sought compensation for missed flights – a minor portent of the mutiny to come.

In January 2006, the *QM2* set off from New York en route to Rio de Janeiro and sailed down the North American coast as far as Fort Lauderdale without incident; however, after stopping to pick up some more passengers at the Florida port, the ship, considerably broader than most, managed – despite the assistance of a local pilot – to bump its gigantic flanks on the side of the shipping lane. An enormous shuddering sound was heard.

Dr Stuart Romm, a former CEO from Sydney who joined the *QM2* in Fort Lauderdale, recalled the moments when the cruise started to go wrong:

> A lot of the people on the condominiums on the side were waving. We thought they were saying goodbye, but it turned out they were saying get away from the channel.

The ship returned to port in Fort Lauderdale to check on the damage, and passengers were offered a program of shore excursions. A British passenger, Peter Normanton, was one of those who spent two hours walking around a mall. He later told *Holidays Undercover*: 'We didn't realise then that this would be the highlight of the cruise.' Divers established that one of the *QM2*'s four propeller pods had been hit and would be out of action until full and proper repairs could be done, but the ship could sail on the remaining three propellers.

The *Queen Mary 2* resumed its voyage two days later, but it was soon clear to the commodore that the damaged boat would never reach a speed sufficient to get the boat to Rio on time. The passengers were told that there would be one or two slight alterations to the schedule. The island of St Kitts in the Caribbean? They wouldn't be going there. Barbados, the British holiday-makers' favourite? No, not that one either. Nor indeed, Salvador, the city on the beautiful white-beached coastline of Bahia in northern Brazil. In fact, they wouldn't be getting off at all until Rio. It was full steam ahead – or more accurately, three-quarter steam ahead.

One might imagine that customers whose idea of travelling was to idle in secure comfort might be relatively docile. Not these. Instead, the news sparked fury. Mutiny was afoot. Like the sans-culottes of revolutionary Paris, the passengers gathered in their thousands, barracking the commodore, who held meetings with them in the planetarium and theatres – and tried to placate them with a miserable offer of a fifty per cent refund.

Dr Romm said: 'I think the problem from a Cunard point of view was that they didn't tell us what was going on.' The majority of passengers were either working-class British in their sixties or elderly Americans and Canadians:

> The North Americans kicked up a bit of a fuss but the British got more incensed by the day. They regarded it as a high speed ferry ride from New York to Rio de Janeiro.

Cunard continued with a full program of entertainment – musical shows, and cultural lectures on places that the passengers would no longer have the opportunity to visit – but the mood was turning decidedly nasty.

The commodore – Ronald Warwick, a senior captain in the fleet who was approaching retirement and no doubt had expected to see out his final few working months in peace – could only stand and take the wrath of the *QM2*'s guests. 'A 20,000 mile journey for nothing!' shouted one to loud applause. There were further cheers for another sarcastic sally: 'Surely as master of the ship you must be able to make some decisions!'

Many passengers concluded that it was a waste of time to attend the formal meetings called by the commodore: he was taking no questions and the microphone would be removed as soon as he finished speaking.

Dr Romm said:

> There is a certain British discretion – they're not known for being open and frank – but when they got nasty it was terrifying. It really was poisonous, there only was one subject of conversation, whenever you sat down with anyone new. Everyone's little story came out – how they needed to get off because relatives had died . . . or they'd start saying 'I'm not going to get off in Rio, I'm going to chain myself to the bathroom.'

The BBC reported that 'militants' were attempting to disrupt the cruise. According to Dr Romm, 'It snowballed completely out of control . . . The passengers took over. The discussions going on were all about the mutiny.' Events planned by the cruise ship's staff were swept aside or ignored as the irate mutineers plotted:

> In the ballroom they tried to hold a Latin American dance class but passengers turned them away . . . And as we crossed the equator, there was a ceremony with about 300 people on deck to mark the occasion.

In the ballroom, simultaneously, 1800 were having a meeting to work up a petition.

A plan was formed: those who were supposed to disembark at Rio, making way for other passengers who would be sailing back up the South American coast via Montevideo, would simply refuse to leave. The great tradition of protest, the sit-in, was about to be replayed in the unlikeliest surroundings.

Not even the presence of RADA-trained theatre workshoppers and a daily harpist could alleviate the pain. 'People have got stress, anxiety and depression on board,' a British passenger, Penny Freemantle, told the BBC:

> We've travelled 16,000 miles [25,700 kilometres] since leaving home and seen nothing at all apart from ocean. People would have caught a plane straight to Rio if they'd known the cruise wouldn't be stopping.

As an added gesture, Cunard had offered guests free access to the internet and premium TV channels – 'even the dirty videos', according to one woman. Some passengers made use of the internet facilities to send emails to the media.

'And then,' said Dr Romm, 'I'm not paranoid, but – the wi-fi was gone. Then the TV reported a Cunard statement that there were only thirty-odd people dissatisfied.'

It was a red rag to the sailing John Bulls. A few wealthy passengers had satellite phones, allowing them to keep the media informed. The mutineers went to CNN and told them there was a petition that thousands had signed.

The cable news services, Sky and CNN, disappeared from television sets – but documentaries were still playing, said Dr Romm. 'The crew were saying it was down to bad reception but everyone suspected it was deliberate – that communications were being pulled. It was like a police state.'

Cunard was holding firm, and going on its own publicity offensive in what had become a media war. 'We obviously have missed these ports of call, but our passengers have had twelve days on the most luxurious liner in the world,' protested Cunard's president, Carol Marlow, on television, adding, lamely, 'We felt there was value in that.'

There were allegations of seasickness caused by the dash for Rio, rumours that stabilisers had not been deployed – claims categorically denied by Cunard. Their medical facility had only had to inject ten people – very few, they said.

Meanwhile, the ambulance chasers had stepped in. In Cardiff, Wales, a law firm was arranging a class action for some 200 people on board – and more were putting their names to it every day, the lawyers said.

Rio was drawing near. More passengers were threatening to lock themselves in their cabins, with nothing but the minibar for company. Now there were two or three meetings a day, word of mouth taking mutineers in their hundreds to the ballroom.

'Many people on the ship are happy to force Carnival and Cunard to recognise that they can not push us around,' passenger Andy Horler told the BBC. 'I'm waiting for one of the ninety-year-olds to be escorted off in handcuffs!' The media held its breath.

Tensions were high. 'One lunch, we sat down with a retired couple and a lady in her late fifties on her own – she was just a bit of a chatterbox but going on and on about the situation,' Dr Romm recounted:

> Then, in the middle of this extremely posh restaurant, with white-jacketed waiters and silver service, another guy just exploded: he threw his plate down and shouted, 'Shut up, I can't stand it, I've had enough – is this all we can talk about?' Everywhere fell silent. That was the level of tension, and it just rubbed off on everybody.

Something had to give, and – alas – it was Cunard, before the world could enjoy the spectacle of Brazilian police storming the ship and enforcing summary justice on the elderly upstarts.

On the eve of the *Queen Mary 2*'s arrival, Cunard's president flew to Rio, and announced that the company would be making munificent amends. 'This wasn't a true Cunard voyage,' Carol Marlow declared, 'and we wanted to put that right.' A full refund was offered, including the airfares of many passengers who had flown to join the ship. Mutiny was averted.

Some claimed their emotional scars would take longer to heal. 'We were prisoners on a luxury ship,' one passenger said. Others were more philosophical. Neville Smith, a retired engineer, said: 'They came up with the full refund and we don't think we can get any more than that.'

The promised revolution never came. Echoes would linger: the *QM2* did perhaps serve as an inspiration for a short but sweet outbreak of passenger power a few months later, when the spirit of the mutiny was, albeit briefly, revived on a Celebrity ship, the *Summit*. Passengers who were hoping to see Seattle and Sitka, Alaska, were angered to discover that their ship would be heading straight through from California to Ketchikan. Many believed that mechanical problems should have been revealed earlier; but the cruise line said that the difficulties were only confirmed once the ship had left port. With passengers complaining of being held captive, talk of a sit-in in the ship's casino reached the shore. However, Celebrity seemed to have headed off militant action with a $200 refund.

As for the *QM2*, life returned much to normal after the threat of revolution had passed. Dr Romm sailed on the next two legs of its voyage, round to Los Angeles, enjoying the rest of his trip; it was, he said, a 'beautiful boat'.

A planned party to celebrate the passing of the *QM2* by the *QM1* on the American west coast was quietly shelved; but life was much more peaceful after the departure of most of the British contingent. However, even this comparatively uneventful journey north was not unblighted for some unfortunate passengers. Before reaching LA, the ship contacted the US Centers for Disease Control vessel sanitation program with sad news: over 100 people on board had gone down with severe diarrhoea, caused by enterotoxigenic *Escherichia coli* or ETEC – a type of E. coli.

Later in 2006, Cunard would cancel two more trips to allow for full repairs to the ship. Other schedules had to be altered, well in advance, and the great mutiny on the *Mary* was not – yet – repeated. But the memory must have been fresh in the mind of Cunard's president when she publicly unveiled the plans for the next ship in the fleet, the *Queen Victoria*, on order for delivery in late 2007. Cunard didn't do cruises, Marlow insisted – they did voyages. In ocean liners. Built to get from A to B.

18

Short and Sweet

IN THE BATTLE of jinxed British boats, the *Aurora* might well stake a claim. It first shot to fame after spending a disastrous Mediterranean cruise barred from ports with hundreds of vomiting, diarrhoea-stricken passengers on board (see chapter 2), but like the *QM2* it had already got off to an unpromising start. On its maiden voyage, the liner only made it from Southampton to the Bay of Biscay, where it broke down and turned to limp back home. The compensation bill for passengers topped £6 million on that occasion.

Perhaps the German-built ship was ill-fated: it suffered what seafarers regard as the most unlucky of omens at its launch, when the champagne bottle swung by Princess Anne in the blessing failed to break on the ship's side and simply fell into the sea. Whether cursed or otherwise, its maiden mishap would pale beside another mechanical debacle it suffered through in early 2005.

On 9 January, 1752 passengers boarded the *Aurora* for the ship's greatest adventure yet — a grand world cruise. They would take in twenty-three countries — crossing the Atlantic to Brazil, rounding South America, then sailing the Pacific to South-East Asia, returning home via San Francisco and the Panama Canal. En route, they would call at the world's exotic ports — Funchal, Acapulco and Honolulu and thirty-seven others.

All in all it would be an extraordinary, 103-day journey, far from the dark winter of England, returning only in the sunshine and light evenings of spring. Worth paying up to $100,000 a head for.

Passengers boarded with evening wear, cocktail dresses and dancing outfits for hot sultry nights in Rio, but soon found they would have to wear their winter coats a little longer. There was something up with an electric motor – and despite the frantic efforts of engineers, there was little chance of setting off across the ocean that day as planned.

There would, however, be some test sailings. And so the *Aurora*'s grand cruise started: a circumnavigation of the Isle of Wight, as mechanics grappled with the problems. P&O anxiously looked on, but managing director David Dingle announced that the cruise would still go ahead. They might just have to tinker with the schedule a little bit.

By day five of viewing the Solent (the narrow stretch of water between mainland England and the Isle of Wight), oil refineries and the twinkling lights of nondescript Hampshire towns, some passengers had had enough, and were sufficiently ill-at-ease to abandon ship for Barnsley, but the overwhelming majority stayed on.

In the interim, passengers were being treated royally, kept aboard with that most alluring of invitations: a free bar. The *Aurora*'s bartenders, suddenly unexpectedly busy, dispensed 12,853 bottles of beer, 12,626 of champagne or wine, and 1246 of spirits. As for the cocktails, they lost count after the first 10,000 served.

P&O arranged daytrips to destinations previously unlisted among the cruise line's global highlights: the New Forest area and shopping in Southampton. A retired banker in one of the two-storey penthouses – complete with its own grand piano, butler and spiral staircase – told *The Times* that passengers were 'pretty phlegmatic' and 'still staring at Blighty'.

Details of the new route emerged: there would be a mere ninety-three days at sea, and the ship would sail in five days' time. They would have to skip a few ports and come back via the Suez Canal – but the voyage was on. It wasn't good enough for many, and around 350 took off, taxied home with a full refund and a voucher for next time.

Hoping against hope, the vast majority stayed. P&O gambled on calling in what they termed a 'comedy cavalry' – a select band of entertainers who had last been seen on primetime TV many years before: magician Paul Daniels and ageing comedians Jimmy Tarbuck and Tom O'Connor. It was, some ventured, the cruellest cut of all. But back on land, O'Connor told the *Daily Mail*:

> The mood is very up. I have done five shows and they are getting the best of everything. It's nearly like the Blitz; the elements are against us, but let's stick with it.

The day of sailing approached. Spirits remained high, although sorties into the waves to test the engines were inconclusive. And then the ship set off: passengers, wrapped up against the chill of the Channel, optimistically waving goodbye to England for the umpteenth time. Next stop Madeira.

It was not to be. Having travelled just 110 miles of their planned 39,250-mile journey, the crew finally gave up. The ship was chugging along, getting up to 20 knots – but it was not a speed that would see it around the globe on schedule. P&O announced the cancellation of the *Aurora*'s first attempted global cruise, citing insurmountable technical problems.

The remaining passengers disembarked, displaying a generosity to their hosts that Cunard would later find sorely lacking on the *QM2*; but then, the *QM2* customers would have to fight for their full refund, let alone a free bar.

There was, as one passenger, Margaret Smith, fifty-nine, from Manchester, said, 'something of the Dunkirk spirit' on the ship. She added: 'It is very disappointing but we all stuck together and we were treated very well.' As another put it: 'We were going nowhere, but in style.'

It was estimated that the whole affair would cost P&O more than

US$50 million. The cruise line promised to honour all contracts for the ship's staff, many of whom came from India, and compensate them for lost tips.

In the scheme of things, finishing the year in similar circumstances was perhaps of little consequence for the *Aurora*; and certainly no surprise. The ambitions of all those setting off just before Christmas 2005 were somewhat more limited in scope: not to see the magic of the Orient, nor even make it to the Mediterranean; simply to visit Belgium, for a spot of gift shopping. Passengers awoke expecting to see Zeebrugge, but were greeted by a landscape that seemed to exert a magnetic pull on the ship: the English south coast.

Inclement weather, this time, was the reason. Happily for P&O, that meant no compensation claims, as they had simply needed to divert the ship for safety purposes.

The Times reported that a spokeswoman for Carnival, the owners of P&O Cruises, said: 'We hope everyone enjoyed their weekend on *Aurora*. We have had many positive reports from passengers that they had an excellent time on board.' Better, perhaps, than could be found in Belgium.

19

Storms in the Ports

FOR ALL THE things that can, and do, go wrong on board, cruise ships offer passengers a place where all the trappings of home – be that an American diner or a genteel restaurant – miraculously exist in the far-flung reaches of the planet. You may well be standing on the deck overseeing the Panama Canal below – a clean swathe cut through a country known for malarial jungle, crime, and the occasional military uprising – but inside in the lounge there will still, somehow, be scones and jams for tea.

Every now and then it can become all too apparent that this teatime sense of security is at odds with reality; that ports of call are not necessarily part of some stable, peaceful democracy, but potentially far more volatile places.

In the year 2000, partying Australians cruising around the South Pacific were skirting political unrest in islands all around them. Revolution had already broken out on the Solomon Islands, and tensions had grown so high in Fiji that news had even filtered down to cruise ship entertainment staff.

Ahead of the stopover in Fiji, all the crew of the *Fair Princess* were warned that there was word of a protest, recalled a young Australian, Stephen, a staff member on the ship. Crew were to tell passengers to steer clear of the courthouse. 'When we got into town we knew that something was amiss, because people were putting up bars on the windows,' he said. It was, in fact, not just a minor protest but a fully fledged coup in progress: it was the day of George Speight's uprising in Fiji. 'We suddenly had this situation where we had to round up all the passengers.'

For the crew, though, the coup could have devastating consequences, Stephen explained. 'The other problem was that Fiji was where we stopped to get our weed – so me and another guy volunteered to go and find some passengers.'

The riots that would accompany the coup by the Fijian businessman Speight were under way, and buildings were already burning; the coup would see hostages taken, but this was an emergency. 'We jumped in this cab in the middle of the riots, and got him to drive us to the residential area of Suva where our dealer lived.'

Having carried out the necessary transactions, they returned to the taxi. 'He drove us up to the top of the hill above the town, where we could look down and see all these buildings on fire and the looting happening below.' When the two crew members returned from their own personal mission, the passengers – over 900 of them – had been accounted for. Afternoon tours were cancelled, but the managing director of P&O Cruises Australia said that, far from being disgruntled, the passengers were in good spirits. 'They were sort of fascinated that they had been involved in something like that and had seen it firsthand.' Enough was enough, though, and the ship sailed out for less tempestuous shores.

Even in times of peace, passengers can find their way to danger once they are down the gangplank. A spate of incidents in 2006 had insurers and consumer groups lining up to warn passengers: just don't do the daytrip. At the very least, they cautioned, passengers should be aware that the temptingly cheap unofficial excursions – those not sanctioned by the cruise lines – were not as likely to be safe and well regulated as similar tourist trips in their home country.

In April 2006, P&O Australia's *Pacific Sky* was once again the scene of a tragic early death, in its final months before the stigmatised ship was offloaded to a Spanish cruise line. The passengers had disembarked for the day on the northern tip of the island of Penang. Some went jetskiing with a local operator. Three young women from Melbourne and a crew member from Mexico were racing two jetskis, riding pillion, when they collided. One, Kathryn Sheppard-Irwin, twenty, died from her injuries.

The third of three separate deaths in quick succession from cruise ship snorkelling excursions occurred at the beginning of 2006. Two of the three separate incidents occurred in the same area off Belize, the other near St Martin. One man's body was never found.

Two months later, in Chile, another daytrip ended in disaster when twelve American cruise passengers from the *Celebrity Millennium* died when returning from a tour of a national park. The bus they were in plunged 80 metres over a cliff on a notoriously dangerous stretch of road leading back to the port of Arica. All but four on board were killed by the crash.

Celebrity issued a statement that made clear that this was not an official tour. While many passengers choose to find their own transportation for daytrips – often finding local operators or taxi drivers who will put on a similar excursion at far lower rates than the packages sold on board – cruise lines point out that they have normally vetted their chosen partners and the decision to go elsewhere is made at the passengers' greater risk.

It is not just passengers who can find themselves in trouble when the ship reaches foreign ports. Captains and officials often need to be prepared for the attentions of local officials who may not always be entirely scrupulous in their demands.

When one of the small luxury Hebridean ships added certain Indian ports to its itinerary, the chief purser was obliged to stock up with several thousand cartons of cigarettes, as well as bottles of whisky, to be presented as gifts before port authorities would allow the boats to dock.

These 'gifts' paled beside the sums that some of the better known, larger liners have had to cough up. Passengers on one *QE2* voyage down to South America were informed at one point that there would be a slight delay, because the authorities at the Central American port at which they had docked were claiming that the water supply on board was not of sufficient cleanliness. It was, the captain said, patently ridiculous, because the ship's water had been restocked in New York – by reputation, the cleanest water supply in the world, he reckoned. A 'fine' of $30,000 was to be imposed. The captain said they had no choice but to pay an official the money. Later, he related, the same official came up to him and said that it would be a lovely gesture if the captain were to invite him, his wife and family to come and dine aboard the *QE2* that evening while it was in port. The captain told him he would indeed be welcome – but it would cost him $30,000.

20

That's Entertainment

THE FORMER ITALIAN prime minister, tycoon, and media mogul, Silvio Berlusconi, has long been a controversial figure. He has been variously accused of corruption, turning his country into an elective dictatorship, and creating a culture of cronyism; of controlling the airwaves and dumbing down the media; of being cynical, uncaring, chauvinistic, shady and undemocratic. He has been investigated over allegations of tax fraud and for his business dealings, and spared other investigations only due to the immunity granted to politicians, especially prime ministers. He offended many of Italy's European Union partners with a brand of diplomacy that saw him liken German politicians to Nazi guards and make obscene gestures for the cameras behind the Spanish foreign minister's back.

But no single blot on his past seems quite so pertinent to those who report on him as one particular fact, destined to stain his CV forever. In a phrase that should surely be etched on his gravestone, Signor Berlusconi was – as the world's newspapers never tire of reminding their readers – a 'former cruise ship crooner'.

Just what is it about being a cruise ship entertainer that carries such stigma? Commentators on Berlusconi seem to believe his former profession is inextricably linked with a certain oleaginous, superficial charm, a lack of trustworthiness. This could be due to the fact that cruise ship entertainers, star turns or otherwise, remain primarily employees looking after guests, obliged to retain a happy smile and kind word for all punters even in the mornings, when the entertainer based on dry land might be indulging a hangover and a foul temper. Perhaps anyone on the high seas wearing a fixed grin for all comers can only appear suspicious.

Berlusconi's early career is mentioned with such a frequency as to almost imply that the later years of mendacity and egomania sprang from strolling the decks. Certainly, some of the associations he formed would be for life. Fedele Confalonieri, the chairman of one of Italy's biggest TV companies, Mediaset – owned by Berlusconi – shared his murky historical shame: accompanying on the cruise ship's piano while the young Silvio strummed guitar and crooned, numbers by French songsters Charles Trenet and Charles Aznavour being among his favourites.

Berlusconi himself played up this episode in his life, having included the detail in a 128-page picture album entitled *Una Storia Italiana*, distributed to every Italian household in his 2001 election campaign.

To be a politician and to have worked on a cruise ship appears unfortunate. Britain, too, has its own political cruising connection in the shape of the deputy prime minister, John Prescott – though no entertainer he, but a former steward. He would not be allowed to forget his early life either, taunted in the House of Commons by rich Conservatives such as Nicholas Soames – 'Mine's a gin and tonic, Giovanni, and would you ask my friend what he's having?' Right-wing commentators have referred to Prescott as the 'former Cunard waiter'. Oddly enough, Mr Prescott narrowly avoided political downfall in 2006 when an affair with his secretary, Tracey Temple – herself the daughter of a cruise ship entertainments officer – became public.

It is not only politicians who are somehow tarred by association with the cruise ship entertainment industry. Some actors have apparently tried to airbrush a cruising past from their personal history.

According to an interview in the *Mail*, Nigel Harman, a former star of the BBC's biggest soap, *East Enders*, who first worked after graduating as a dancer on a cruise ship, apparently found the episode so embarrassing that he would not own up to it for many years.

Those who have stepped from the sea to the stage are few – though much vaunted by entertainment recruitment agencies. The best most can come up with are Claire Sweeney – a British soap actress and TV presenter – and singer Jane McDonald, who rose to prominence in a TV documentary, *The Cruise*; that is, because of, rather than in spite of, her background. Despite albums, tours and acting gigs, 'cruise ship singer' is a tag that she has not quite shaken off.

Entertaining cruise passengers can also be the fate of a certain type of fallen light entertainer. Despite the industry's insistence that cruising has recently been rejuvenated, the ghosts of the past linger. From the peculiar sub-genre of family-led bands that charted in the 1970s and 80s, Denise of the Nolan Sisters has returned to the waves, while Jimmy, child star of the Osmonds, now appears on, and organises the entertainment for, cruise ships, sharing his vision with the unwary public.

In critical terms, 'cruise ship entertainer' remains a term of abuse. In the space of a few months in *The Times*, for example, one review damned a pop group for sounding 'like a drunken cruise ship band'; another called Cybill Shepherd's singing so bad that 'she wouldn't even get a booking on a cruise ship'; a third called an artist's songs 'as flaccid as a cruise-ship covers band'; while a fourth dismissed a West End show as having production levels 'worryingly reminiscent of a Seventies cruise ship'. (Ironically, many cruise lines claim that they perform 'West End quality shows'; as one long-term guest lecturer on cruises put it, 'It really depends on which part of the West End you're talking about.')

Weathermen and game show hosts have traditionally been brought on board as celebrity guests to lure passengers of a certain age. Nicholas Parsons (a British doyen of the daytime TV show, not to be confused with the Australian writer-director of the same name) is one such regular, a man who was once duped into appealing to the British public on behalf of an elephant whose trunk was allegedly stuck in its own anus.

On some European cruises, there are worrying signs of modernity. P&O tailors its offerings for the different clientele it expects on different ships (the *Aurora*, incidentally, is described as contemporary), and promises 'credible' entertainment. The *Oceana* now runs a show called *Seven* that the cruise firm has described as 'a bit of a more risqué show' than those on offer elsewhere; and the ship's band, a spokesman said, will play covers of songs by Arctic Monkeys, giving P&O passengers an unexpected slice of indie rock-cum-post-punk revival thrash.

Yet for all the talk of engaging the hippest talent, in times of crisis – such as the *Aurora*'s breakdown (see chapter 18) – the 'comedy cavalry' hired by P&O was straight from the old drawer. And when one of Britain's oldest entertainers, the actor Sir Norman Wisdom, recently announced his retirement from the stage, the blow was cushioned by the announcement that he would still be seen elsewhere: he would, in fact, be performing for cruise ship audiences on his ninetieth birthday.

The irredeemable scent of seaside-resort glitz remains: feather boas on dancers are as common a sight as an elderly passenger with a stomach bug. For every cruise line that pumps money into a state-of-the-art theatre, another is looking at getting in a cheaper comedian. Fares on many ships are, the cruise lines constantly point out, as affordable as other types of holiday and value for money – but lower prices mean passengers can't really expect a deluge of both great food *and* top quality entertainment; if it's lobster in the buffet, it will be spandex at the show.

A large swathe of the cheaper cruise lines take it upon themselves to whip their guests into a party spirit, enforced by the cruise director. Responsible for all the entertainment on board, putting together the programs and managing the staff, the cruise director will often take to the microphone to lead the entertainment, maybe even a singsong. The kind of recreational opportunities thrown up on the larger resort ships might not be everyone's taste, involving such highlights as bikini stuffing, sex quizzes and hairy chest competitions: as Douglas Ward, a pre-eminent global cruising critic, puts it, they tend to 'cram lots of people into small cabins and provide non-stop activities that insult the intelligence and assault the wallet'.

By and large cruise lines insist that stereotypes of cheesy antics and party games on board are long outdated; although certain activities appear live and well. Fear not: there will be bingo.

One relic that persists today, even on some of the poshest liners, is the tradition of toasting the baked alaska. On the penultimate night of a cruise, the ship's staff darken the dining room before parading in with the dessert, adorned with lighted sparklers. According to one regular passenger, this even occurs on Cunard's *Queen Mary 2* in the main 'Britannia' dining room. 'Everyone cheers, and they sing Auld Lang Syne,' he grimaced. 'I try to avoid it. It doesn't happen in the Grill Rooms.'

The Grill Rooms are Cunard's last vestige of a class system on board: passengers in the more expensive suites or staterooms are automatically served in the better restaurants. But upstairs or downstairs, no Cunard guest is ever confronted with a waiter's antics as undignified as those drilled into the serving staff of Carnival Cruise Line, who are trained to perform song and dance routines. Mealtimes are regularly punctuated by a stream of waiters bursting in singing numbers such as 'Hot! Hot! Hot!', to the perceived delight of the American guests. (Cabin stewards escape this indignity, merely having to turn tricks such as making animals from folded towels.)

Other British cruise ships still indulge in 'Sail Away' parties at which songs like 'Land of Hope and Glory' and 'Rule Britannia' are sung over glasses of Pimms. 'They definitely maintain the traditions,' a P&O spokeswoman said. 'Although we're having to cater for a new market, we'll always be an inherently British cruising company.'

The baffling practice of shuffleboard continues, she confirmed: 'You'd struggle to find a cruise ship in the world that doesn't have shuffleboard on it.' This, for the uninitiated, is a game played on deck with a puck and mallet and a scoring area marked out in squares.

Not so quaint are the drinking games: a staple of some American cruises, and as natural as a sea breeze in Australia. Passengers cannot expect to find such goings-on aboard any luxury liners — and should be particularly wary of mooting them at any apparently impromptu parties on board. Alcoholics Anonymous meetings at sea are announced in the ship's daily program in code: 'Friends of Bill Jones' (or someone with a similarly innocuous name) will be invited to meet in the lounge.

Perhaps more and more Australian passengers will be diverted Bill Jones's way, as P&O's vaunted crackdown on drinking kicks in. But many cruise lines will be loath to curb alcoholic revelry: it is a large source of revenue for staff and ship alike. One regular practice on some lines that has surprised the unwary is to offer passengers a welcome drink on boarding, a cheap cocktail on a tray proffered by waiters. Welcome! Now sign the bill. Gotcha.

It is not all drinking: there is gambling too. Virtually all ships have a casino and slot machines, popular with Americans and pokie-fixated Australians in particular; Britons so far are said to be relatively uninterested. In Australia, where gambling has become a lucrative industry and a growing social problem in recent years, casino owners have expressed concern that cruise ships — exempt from gambling taxes offshore — may take their trade.

For those who may not get enough gambling on board, P&O Princess Cruises last year agreed to support a $1.5 billion project to build a huge resort casino in Singapore, signing a memorandum of understanding with gambling giants Tabcorp to push cruise customers their way. In the meantime, P&O have done their bit for the gamblers: when a recent cruise from Sydney was postponed, waiting passengers were issued with vouchers to spend in the nearby Star City casino.

Beyond the bars, show lounges and casinos, most ships do have libraries. *Death on the Nile*, Agatha Christie's tale of cruise ship killing, is said to be a popular choice in some liners' libraries and bookshops; and the *Pacific Sun*'s Churchill library features knights in suits of armour.

An Australian couple who enjoyed a cruise on the *Carnival Inspiration* said they were very impressed by the Shakespeare Library, with its oak panelling and olde English design: 'But we never saw any books there, only paintings being sold.' Selling paintings is one of the more bewildering offshoots of cruise ship culture: a bizarre stab at quasi-refinement, the strange phenomenon of art auctions.

The world's most famous – and probably most valuable – painting, Leonardo da Vinci's *Mona Lisa*, once made a transatlantic crossing on the SS *France*. That fact should not be enough to make passengers believe that a cruise ship such as the *Pacific Sun* is just the place to find a great work of art, but it seems some do. The art auction, reviled by many, is a growing feature of cruising life, popular with passengers looking to bring back a souvenir of more apparent durability than a postcard, hangover or irritated bowel. Regular cruisers, some of whom complain of being hustled aggressively to attend by crew, report seeing many of the same masterpieces from ship to ship. Bidders should be aware that the price paid at auction will normally have a framing and shipping fee slapped on top.

And while some more upmarket ships bring on scientists, historians and broadcasters as lecturers, resort ships have their own speciality: shopping talks before impending ports of call, with plugs for preferred partners on the shore.

21

Captive State

THERE IS A thin line between feeling cosseted in an exclusive, secure ship – or feeling trapped out at sea. When things have gone wrong, passengers have often complained of being held captive on a prison ship: whether on the mutinous *Queen Mary 2* direct sailing from the US to Rio, or sick ships such as the *Aurora* or the *Black Prince*.

Passengers who have been perturbed by the drunken excesses of others, or even by the conversation of fellow diners with whom restaurant seatings will typically keep them for the duration of the cruise, have similarly talked of being trapped on board, suddenly being conscious of the limitations of the space on board and the deep blue sea surrounding the ship. Cabins are generally smaller than they sometimes appear in holiday brochure or website photographs, and walls are thin enough to hear the antics in the corridors or neighbouring rooms. There is normally no getting off (on many cruise lines, passengers who decide to leave a cruise early can be liable for a fine on top of any extra expense).

As the cruise industry association, the ICCL, states proudly: 'A cruise ship is inherently secure because it is a controlled environment with limited access.' It is little wonder then that cruise liners have often been utilised or requisitioned for somewhat different uses over the years: from warships to prison ships.

In the wake of the Russian revolution, Lenin, the first Bolshevik leader, would be one of the first to harness their possibilities as a way of casting enemies into exile. In the autumn of 1922, seventy Russian thinkers were rounded up, along with their families. The *Preussen*, a cruise ship whose previous role had been to take tourists around the Baltic Sea, was one of two boats used by the Russian secret police to deport the intelligentsia to Germany. It was a life sentence; any returnees, by special order of the Politburo, would be shot.

The cruise ship offered a great opportunity to trammel crowds of people and regiment their holidays, if not their lives. One boom in modern cruising occurred in Hitler's Germany, where the Nazis ordered two new cruise liners to be built to escort the Fatherland's workers on vacation. In 1938, these ships took around 180,000 Germans to destinations such as Madeira and the Norwegian fiords as part of the Nazi *Kraft durch Freude* – 'strength through joy' – program.

One of them, the *Wilhelm Gustloff* was torpedoed in the Baltic towards the end of the second world war, and over 7000 of the people on board died. It was not an isolated event: in the context of wartime casualties, the sunken cruise liners brought down by enemy torpedoes barely registered as maritime disasters, although many had far more passengers aboard (including civilians) than the *Titanic*.

The sinking of the *Gustloff*, in terms of the numbers who perished, was the world's worst ever shipping tragedy. Its association with the Nazis might explain why it is so little known; it was named after the leader of the Swiss Nazi party, who was assassinated in 1936. It could have been worse: it was originally to be called the plain old *Adolf Hitler*, which might have made it ripe for torpedoing even earlier.

The Allies also made use of liners during the war: they were perfect for military discipline or as prisoner-of-war ships. The SS *America*, built as an ocean liner before the USA entered the war, was soon pressed into military service. Later it returned for passenger cruises, but on several occasions in its later life owners sought to convert the liner into a prison ship. Once, a buyer planned to take it to Phuket, Thailand, on the basis that it could be either a hotel or a prison.

In Britain, the *Queen Elizabeth* was due to be launched as a cruise liner in 1938, but preparations for war changed all that. It wasn't completed until 1940, by which time it had been designated a troop ship. After the war it was turned into the passenger liner which it had originally been intended to be, and remained so until the late 1960s. In 1971 it became, of all things, a floating university campus moored off the island of Tsing Yi near Kowloon, Hong Kong, before an arsonist set the old liner on fire. It burned for a week before sinking; eventually part of the hulk was dredged up and used as landfill for one of the runways of the new Hong Kong airport.

Recent events have again shown how cruise liners are regarded as part of a nation's emergency infrastructure, with the controversial chartering of Royal Caribbean ships in the aftermath of Hurricane Katrina in 2005, and the evacuation of foreign nationals from Lebanon on board cruise ships in 2006.

One astonishing story from 1970s Britain came to light only in 2006. Among British society's deeply conservative establishment was a group of military officers who were appalled by what they saw as a dangerously left-wing Labour government, elected under Harold Wilson for a second time. Although the prime minister had been known to refer to possible coup plots against him, such talk seemed more the product of paranoid rumour than reasonable fear in democratic Britain.

Yet, it turned out, such plots existed. A retired major would eventually explain to BBC documentary makers just when his own tipping point came: on his return from a cruise. Major Alexander Greenwood came home from a cruise down the Rhine to be appalled by high interest rates and strikes. He sounded out contacts in the military and captains of industry who might be prepared to step in.

And where would the democratically elected government go under these plans? Army and secret service people had already located the ideal place, and just needed to get permission. So a senior executive of Cunard was approached: could they borrow the *QE2*? The ship was set to be a 'floating prison' for Harold Wilson and his cabinet.

In April 2006, a headline told how John Howard's government would be dealing with asylum seekers heading for the mainland in a similar fashion. The 'tough new Pacific Solution' would see refugees stopped and sent on a P&O cruise. This story was from the satirical website, The Chaser.

By August, the idea appeared less outlandish. A plan was indeed announced to intercept illegal fishermen and asylum seekers in Australian waters and hold them for up to a month on a prison ship. Australian Customs said they were searching for a vessel to be converted. Labor's customs spokesman, Joe Ludwig, one of the opposition politicians who denounced the plans as unworkable, said: 'The only thing that might actually fit that is a P&O cruise liner.'

22

Disaster! From Rogue Waves to Infernos

SAILORS WHO CLAIMED to have seen them were long derided by scientists on shore. It wasn't possible, they said. It could only have been the rum. And yet the legends persisted: beasts more than 100 feet tall, capable of snapping a boat in two with their power, coming from nowhere. But such enormous rogue waves did not fit with the maths.

Until lately, that is. In the movies, New Yorkers are used to seeing their home smashed around by fictional monsters, from Godzilla to King Kong, but a boatload returning to Manhattan from Florida on a cruise in 2005 were left shaken after coming face to face with another supposedly legendary force: a monster rogue wave.

The *Norwegian Dawn* had been sailing through a storm off the coast of Georgia a few hours earlier, but one of little consequence; free drinks were served to raise the passengers' spirits.

And then, at daybreak on Saturday morning, 16 April, with the waters apparently calming, out of nowhere came a wave over 70 feet or more than 20 metres high. It crashed through windows on the ninth and tenth floors of the ship, sent furniture flying, smashed a jacuzzi-style whirlpool, and wrenched out railings with its force. Water flooded through sixty-two cabins. In twenty years of sailing, said the captain, he had never known anything like it.

Terrified passengers reported that the luxury liner bobbed around 'like a cork in a bathtub'. A gift shop, a theatre, and much of the glassware in the bar took particularly damaging hits – but, remarkably, only four passengers were injured. One single, huge wave had swept through the boat. Battered but still functioning, the *Norwegian Dawn* sailed on. It took shelter in the port of Charleston, where many of the guests decided to disembark, some vowing never to return to the sea.

It was not the first time, in fact, that a cruise liner had been hit by such a wave – but it had only been recently that any captain could say his ship had been buffeted by a rogue wave without his story being filed with the fish that got away. Scientists believed a rogue wave was something that would come along once only every 10,000 years.

Increased reports from ships and offshore oil rigs prompted research by the European Space Agency, using radar satellites that could map wave forms even through storms and clouds. It revealed that not only did these waves exist – but they also occurred in far higher numbers than anyone had expected. Ten waves measuring 25 metres or more – far higher than the one that left the *Norwegian Dawn* limping and its passengers in panic – were spotted in just three weeks.

The disappearance of more than 200 enormous ships (supertankers and container ships over 200 metres long) in just two decades suddenly had a plausible explanation: not just the catch-all phrase 'bad weather', but the rogue wave. Now it is believed that these freaks of nature may loom as large as 60 metres.

Even a wave half that size could be terrifying – such as the one encountered in 1995, by the *Queen Elizabeth 2*, when a hurricane whipped up the North Atlantic. Ronald Warwick, the captain that day, talked of seeing a great wall of water coming towards the ship. 'It looked as if we were going into the White Cliffs of Dover,' he said. Although it was probably less than a minute, he said the wave seemed to take an age to arrive; but when it did, it broke with tremendous force over the bow, sending an incredible shudder through the ship.

Two other, smaller cruise ships had felt the force of rogue waves in the South Atlantic within a week of each other in early 2001. Both the *Bremen* and the *Caledonian Star* had their bridge windows smashed in by the force of water alone. The *Bremen* lost all power and electronic instruments: for two hours it drifted out at sea, its crew fearing the worst.

According to German researchers who studied the incident, they were lucky: many ships have been sunk by lesser waves. 'I never met, and hope I never will meet, such a monster,' Dr Wolfgang Rosenthal told *The New York Times*. Yet out there now, at any given moment, he estimated, ten of these shipwreckers would be crashing their way along. It's the kind of statistic that lends a new urgency to Dr Rosenthal's work. In 2004, the U.S. Naval Research Laboratory measured a 100-foot (30-metre) wave in US waters, surging through the Gulf of Mexico in the wake of Hurricane Ivan.

The scientists say that they now know rogue waves exist; but they still can't be sure what causes them, and are at a loss how to predict them. Marine physicists at the University of Miami, the cruising capital of the world, are applying themselves to the question now.

So far, no cruise ship – bar the fictional SS *Poseidon* – has been brought completely down by a rogue wave, but fatalities have occurred. In 1966, an Italian cruise ship, the *Michelangelo*, lost one crewman and two passengers en route to New York. A giant wave ripped into it; its magnitude evidenced by the fact that it smashed heavy glass almost 25 metres above the normal level of the sea.

Of course, rogue waves aren't always to blame; on occasion, ships have been known to achieve terrifying lurches without any help from the elements.

This happened as recently as July 2006: the *Crown Princess* was the newest ship in the Princess Cruises fleet, with only four voyages under its belt. The sparkling superliner was making its way back to New York from the Caribbean, and had not long left its last port of call, Port Canaveral, carrying around 3000 passengers north up the tranquil coast of Florida.

There was nothing to worry unsuspecting passengers, some sunbathing around the pool, others in the ship's Movies Under the Stars cinema. Perhaps, though, there was an omen in the blockbuster the cinema was preparing to show, the story of the definitive sinking ship: *Titanic*.

Without warning the ship took a massive tilt to one side. On deck, dozens of swimmers were washed out of the pool. Passengers clung to railings to stop themselves falling overboard. Water poured down stairwells and lift shafts; furniture was flung across cabins. Equipment in the ship's gym was uprooted, and casino slot machines knocked over. One passenger described seeing the grand piano come rolling by.

Another passenger, Gillian Bogush of London, was resting in her cabin when the lamps started sliding towards her. Then even the armchairs started flying across the room. One caught her sixty-seven-year-old husband in the chest. 'It was absolutely terrifying,' she told reporters later. 'Many people thought the ship was going to sink.'

Outside, there was panic. Everything was sliding across the deck, passengers said. Windows were smashed, and bloodied and injured guests feared the worst. The British captain made an announcement assuring them that the ship would not sink, but some who heard it thought his voice was so edgy that they still feared the ship might go down, and seized life jackets. 'You could hear the terror and fear in his voice,' one American passenger said.

After an agonising thirty seconds, the ship slowly returned to an upright position. Two hundred and forty people were injured, two of them critically. Under escort from US Coast Guard vessels, the *Crown Princess* limped back into Port Canaveral, where the wounded were treated. Some were airlifted to hospital, more were stretchered off.

The traditional remedy – a free bar – was laid on for the shaken, but Princess Cruises announced that the voyage would end there and all passengers would be refunded in full. A technical steering malfunction was blamed for the ship's sudden list, with a full investigation promised.

It was a freak incident, said cruise experts. However, just a few months earlier, the *Crown Princess*'s sister ship, the *Grand Princess*, had made a similar lurch when taking a sudden turn back to Galveston, Texas, for emergency treatment for a passenger who had suffered a heart attack. On that occasion, twenty-seven passengers were injured; a Princess Cruises inquiry said that the ship had turned too fast. The sudden listing of the ships may have terrified those on board, but the ships, analysts concluded, were never in danger of sinking.

Nonetheless, passenger liners have been brought down by a combination of human error and natural hazards; the ever-present dangers of the sea. Most famous of all was of course the supposedly unsinkable *Titanic*, but other cruise liners have gone down in similar circumstances in the more recent past.

Many of the cruise ships out on the seas today – including P&O's very own *Pacific Sun* – had entered service by 1986, when the *Mikhail Lermontov* was sailing out of Sydney, and yet, in geopolitical terms, it was very much a different era.

If anyone had used the words 'Russians' and 'cruise' in the same sentence in the 1980s, many westerners would have assumed, incorrectly, that they could only have been referring to nuclear missiles. Bizarrely, at the height of the Cold War, with international tensions rising and the arms race spiralling out of control, Russian cruise ships were plying the seas around Australia. Despite the deep suspicions and hostility dividing the Communist east and the capitalist west, the Soviet flagship *Mikhail Lermontov* – one of five liners named after famous literary Russians – had even been allowed to cruise to New York, before being banished from American waters by Ronald Reagan after the Soviet invasion of Afghanistan.

Tagging along with the Russian crew was a shadowy consignment: KGB agents. As the boat sailed out into the blue waters of the west, the agents were a constant presence – checking that no member of the crew was set to defect or engaging in 'excessive fraternisation with foreigners' – a practice that many cruise lines have apparently been unable to deter their officers from indulging in to this day.

As the years went by, and Gorbachev's policies of reform had effect, surveillance became less rigid, but the crew's cabins, it was believed, were still bugged. The *Mikhail Lermontov* underwent a massive refurbishment in 1982 to bring her up to international standards – private ensuite facilities for passengers, and an overall ambience that was a little less starkly Soviet.

In February 1986, she was in Australia, and set out on one of a series of cruises from Sydney to New Zealand. Passenger Nicole Blaser (now Ristev) was just ten years old, a Sydney schoolgirl on her first cruise, accompanied by her mother. At that time, she said: 'We didn't really know about Russians over here. But they were nice people.' As the youngest passenger on the ship, she was well looked after by the Russian crew:

> The ship was really nice and the food was really good. A lot of crew had children the same age as me. The waiter in the restaurant would give me double dessert, and when the adults were having fancy meals they'd give me a plate of chips. As a kid you'd think, 'Oh, wow!'

Ten pleasant and uneventful days elapsed, passengers taking in ports on the North Island before the ship headed for New Zealand's capital, Wellington. Then, sailing out of Picton through the Marlborough Sounds, the local harbour pilot decided to take the ship on what would prove a perilous course – slipping between a lighthouse and land, all too close to the rocks.

The bars on Russian boats were more famed for their vodka than any other alcoholic drinks, but it was a wine-tasting session that was keeping the generally elderly passengers on board entertained in the early evening of 16 February when a loud thud vibrated through the ship, followed by a crashing and shaking of plates and glasses.

Down below, the ship had hit solid rock. A 12-metre gash had been ripped into the *Lermontov*, letting water into the bulkheads and stopping the engines.

On the surface, the crew tried to preserve a veneer of calm. Dinner, it was announced, would be slightly delayed, but there was no reason for alarm. The wine tasting would continue – at least, until the glasses started sliding off the tables.

Nicole recalled:

> An announcement said they had run aground, a tiny hole in the ship, no need to panic. No one quite believed it – and then we saw crew members running around with life jackets on. So that was a sign for everyone to go and get on their life jackets. There was a bit of a language barrier problem, so asking the crew didn't generally help.

The crew assembled everyone in the main lounge, and the captain attempted to beach the ship. Darkness loomed, and still the passengers remained on board. Other ships, including a large oil tanker, saw the cruise liner in evident difficulty and offered assistance, only to be rebuffed. The tanker stood by, regardless, and others arrived, too, convinced their help would soon be needed.

Nearly three hours after the crash, as the ship began to tilt ever more heavily, the evacuation of passengers started.

'It was so calm; no one panicked. It was partly the age range. Maybe they'd had a few vodkas,' said Nicole.

The *Lermontov* had left port well under capacity – a fact that may have saved many lives. Evacuating a ship of elderly people was no swift feat:

> A lot of the older people were saying 'We're not walking any more! We've had enough!' People behind were yelling, 'Just keep going!' I remember thinking *if those people in front of me move, I'll get off.* We were calm, but I knew the ship could sink . . .

Even after the procession of pensioners had made it on deck, getting them into the lifeboats proved tricky. By now, the ship was tilting so much that the crew had to get the passengers down to the lifeboats on rope ladders or even ask them to make a leap. Heavy rain was falling. A good number of the elderly were injured in the transfer to the jam-packed lifeboats. Night had fallen and the *Lermontov*'s lights had gone, the ship illuminated only by the spotlights from rescue boats.

Nicole was one of the first passengers to be evacuated, picked out by the ship's crew. 'A crew member saw me in the crowd, a Russian, and said "You. Come here now." He put me on the second lifeboat.'

The lifeboat took its first load of passengers to safety on the tanker and Nicole watched as the evacuation continued.

It was barely fifteen minutes after the last passenger had finally made it onto the crammed lifeboats that the unthinkable happened – a modern liner went down in the middle of a cruise. 'It didn't look real . . . It was like watching a scene from a movie.'

There was a deafening noise. Six-foot-high bubbles erupted from the sea. And slowly, the *Mikhail Lermontov* sank to the bottom of Port Gore.

Debris from the ship was washed up all around; hundreds of deck-chairs floated in the sea, to be picked up as souvenirs for the sundecks of nearby houses.

Amazingly only one person died – a Russian engineer, believed to have gone down with the ship. More people would die diving in the wreck in the years to come, as the *Lermontov* became a prime site for scuba divers to explore.

Most passengers seemed to suffer few ill effects, although lawsuits relating to the case would drag on for many years afterwards, with some claiming damages for their ruined holiday – although, lawyers said, some claimants ruined their chances by admitting that the episode had furnished them with enough stories with which to regale dining companions for life. Some claims for lost luggage raised a few eyebrows – an astonishing number of the guests seemed to have packed family heirlooms for their two-week cruise.

A New Zealand government inquiry into the *Lermontov*'s last moments pinned the blame for the disaster on the local pilot, Don Jamison, who had taken the ship through a channel normally only used by much smaller craft. Jamison's only explanation for his fateful decision was that a punishing workload had left him suffering from mental and physical exhaustion. He claimed to have been working an average of eighty hours a week over the previous four months.

☆☆☆

Rocks, hurricanes and mighty waves account for three of the four natural elements that ships contend with. The final element, fire, has also claimed its victims. Engine room blasts have been a notable cause of fire, often fatally for ships' crews. Four died on a Norwegian Cruise Line ship, the SS *Norway*, in 2003, when a boiler explosion set the engine room on fire while the boat was docked in Miami.

The potential for disaster on ships out at sea with passengers aboard was highlighted again in June 2006, when a similar engine room fire left a cruise ship burning in the English Channel. Firefighting teams were called from the British mainland to tackle the blaze on Louis Cruise Lines' *Calypso*. The terrified, mainly Dutch passengers reported how they had been woken in the middle of the night, their cabins plunged into darkness as smoke drifted through the ship. Trijintje Bos was one of those who was told to gather on the deck. She explained to *Holidays Undercover*: 'We thought soon we would have to jump.' Helicopters winched firefighters and paramedics aboard as volunteer lifeboat crews and merchant ships stood by ready to evacuate passengers. This time, the fire was extinguished by crew after it gutted the engine room. It emerged that the ship, which was towed into port in Southampton, had been inspected twice in recent weeks and numerous faults had been found on both occasions. The owners, Louis Cruise Lines, said all the faults had been corrected and all deficiencies rectified before the fire.

A fatal inferno had occurred on another ship only a few months earlier. One man died of a heart attack and eleven passengers were injured, some as a result of smoke inhalation, when fire ripped through cabins on Carnival's *Star Princess* off Jamaica during a Caribbean cruise. It was thought to have been started by a smouldering cigarette. More than 100 cabins over three decks were left blackened by the blaze.

Fire regulations on board have been tightened up in recent years: the UK Maritime and Coastguard Agency required the *QM2* to install new sprinklers and replace panels in all of its 1300 bathrooms within just six months of its launch date.

Fires breaking out in passenger cabins have been comparatively rare compared to accidents in ships' laundries and engine rooms, which accounted for a series of blazes in the 1990s, requiring the evacuation of several ships and causing the deaths of several crew members from smoke inhalation.

The biggest, most dramatic conflagration that has taken place on a cruise ship in modern times was the one that sealed the fate of the Italian liner, the *Achille Lauro*, whose notoriety had been forever guaranteed by its hijacking in the 1980s.

The *Achille Lauro*'s final hours had already been foreshadowed in the late 1970s, when its sister ship, the *Angelina Lauro*, caught fire while moored in St Thomas in the British Virgin Islands, eventually ending that ship's cruising life.

Early in the morning of 30 November 1994, en route to South Africa, the *Achille Lauro* was sailing off the coast of Somalia in the Indian Ocean, far from safe harbour, when fire took hold in the engine room. By daybreak, the captain had given the order to abandon ship.

The 1090 passengers and crew were all evacuated into lifeboats. The evacuation was a dangerous exercise: two people died and eight were injured. However, a tanker, the *Hawaiian King*, answered the captain's mayday call, along with a US Navy cruiser and several other ships, taking the vast majority to safety.

The *Achille Lauro*, though, was burning out of control. It began to tilt at a 40 degree angle, huge flames and black smoke engulfing its decks. The fire burnt for nearly three days before the inevitable happened: the ship so long associated with drama and death slipped from view, sinking forever beneath the waves.

23
Diving In

LIFE AT SEA is not democratic. Just like plankton, drifting at the mercy of the current, passengers and crew are ultimately at the whim of an omnipotent, and sometimes unseen, entity: the ship's captain. It can normally be assumed that he – and it is nearly always a he – is a benevolent guiding force. Of course, every now and then you find out differently and then all hell can break loose.

☆☆☆

It had not been an auspicious start to the eight-day cruise on the *Reef Explorer*. The so-called luxury dive boat left Cairns seven hours late on its way out to the Great Barrier Reef. The passengers weren't too pleased, but then there were marvels ahead: many had come all the way from the United States and Europe, paying $3000 a head, to explore the world's most renowned coral reef.

Then there were one or two minor technical hitches. The dinghy leaked. The hoist on board broke. The winch? Its seals exploded. Well, it wasn't going to spoil the passengers' enjoyment too much – though they couldn't help noticing when the batteries failed, taking down much of the lighting on board, and even the navigation system. There were always the stars, on a clear night anyway.

Losing the gas stove was a bit of a blow. For a week, the passengers would be strictly on cold meals, never ideal after a long day of physical activity in the water. Not great when you've got flu. One of the crew was the first to succumb and the virus quickly spread throughout the passengers, laying them low one by one for twenty-four hours or so each. The expected four dives a day didn't really materialise. In the circumstances, it was only a matter of time before someone on board cracked up.

Unfortunately, that person was the captain. And how.

Having successfully and safely surfaced after a dive in the Coral Sea, 275 kilometres off the coast, the passengers climbed back on deck to discover a scene more chilling than circling great white sharks: the captain raving at crew members because they had not complied with his demands to sail away and leave the dive party to their fate on the reef.

'He had clearly lost it,' one passenger later told *The Courier-Mail*. The captain ordered one of his crew to saw through the anchor chain. Then, bizarrely, he tried to enlist the help of the passengers against the crew, ordering them to tie them up. They were trying to mutiny, he claimed. To make sure things went his way, the captain brandished a flare gun, uncapped it, and pressed it against the head of an American passenger.

The gun would never be fired. The drifting boat crashed into a coral reef. It was just distraction enough. Passengers and crew jumped on him, wrestling him to the ground. He never had the chance to lash his mutinous crew.

As though on a latter-day *Bounty*, the crew had done the unthinkable and overthrown their captain. He was dragged inside, confined to a cabin, and for good measure, tied to a bunk.

Who would steer this faulty ship, now stripped of its main boatsman, back to port? A dive instructor navigated as best he could to Thursday Island, a twenty-four-hour voyage. Passengers came to the assistance of a battle-weary crew: they had no choice.

Island police were called. The cracked captain was taken, sedated, to hospital and later checked himself into a psychiatric facility on the mainland.

It was the captain's first outing in the job. The tourists later filed civil suits against the dive company. The company offered to take the passengers on another trip for free. None of them fancied it. The captain was charged with three counts of assault, but the case was dismissed when the judge heard that he had been of unsound mind. The captain finally decided to sue the dive company instead.

Such an incident was the last thing Australia's dive industry needed at the time. Earlier that year, something had happened to two passengers on a dive boat that would send shivers through any diver for years to come, adding a whole new nightmare to everyday worries about equipment failure or succumbing to nitrogen narcosis or the bends. Two divers surfaced from exploring the Barrier Reef to find that, surreally, their boat was no longer there.

It was an event that inspired the chilling film *Open Water*, yet the film-makers would only base the story loosely on the Australian case – the true-life event containing elements too far-fetched for a script.

The diving trip was part of a holiday that the young Americans, a married couple from Baton Rouge in Louisiana, took to mark the end of a stint doing charitable work abroad. Tom and Eileen Lonergan had been volunteers in the Peace Corps in Tuvalu, and were on their way back to the States. In Port Douglas, the couple joined the MV *Outer Edge* for a daytrip to Crispin Reef, part of the Great Barrier Reef. All the passengers would make three dives that day, before the boat would head back at 3 pm. A British diver was the last to see the Lonergans, under the water: together, the three of them had admired a giant clam in the reef.

The crew would never be quite clear about just how they failed to count all back on board. What is sure is that the *Outer Edge* headed back to the mainland without the Lonergans on board.

Fishermen reported seeing many fins in the area that day. A large number of tiger sharks were circling. The Lonergans were stranded.

Back in Port Douglas, the crew of the *Outer Edge* were oblivious to their depleted passenger numbers. No-one ascribed much significance to the odd extra shoe on deck. It was only two days later when a bag was found on board containing not just the couple's belongings but their passports that the alert was sounded.

A huge air and sea search was set in motion, but no traces of the Lonergans' bodies would ever be found. Some of their diving gear was later discovered washed up on the mainland, several miles from the site of their disappearance. And several months later, a fisherman found a diver's slate, a piece of equipment used for writing messages in the water. In what would be identified as the handwriting of Tom Lonergan was the message:

> Monday Jan 26; 1998 08am. To anyone who can help us: We have been abandoned on A Reef by MV Outer Edge 25 Jan 98 3pm. Please help us come to rescue us before we die. Help!!!

They had made it through the first night, but help had not come in time. A coronial inquest found that the couple must almost certainly have died of dehydration or drowning, or been taken by the many sharks.

The coroner recommended that the captain of the dive boat, Jack Nairn, be tried for manslaughter, but the jury cleared him, the prosecution failing to prove that he was criminally negligent.

Confusion reigned over how the miscount had occurred. At the inquest and trial, conflicting accounts surfaced, and a dive instructor told of the difficulty crew had in accounting for tourists who were constantly moving around, chatting.

Extracts from the Lonergans' diaries, found in their room at a hostel in Cairns, were leaked to the press. Tom, suffering from depression, had once written, 'I feel as though my life is complete and I'm ready to die,' and barely two weeks before the fateful trip, Eileen had noted: 'Tom's not suicidal, but he's got a death wish that could lead him to what he desires. And I could get caught in that.'

Because the bodies were never found, some from the Queensland dive industry claimed that the Lonergans were not in fact dead. A host of myths and rumours spread: Elvis-like sightings of the balding engineer and his younger, blonde wife; theories that the Lonergans had faked their own disappearance to start a new life. Some even claimed that the couple had been assassinated by the CIA. It was suggested that their Peace Corps postings were cover for a spy operation in the South Pacific, and that a CIA hit squad in a submarine was sent to deal with the couple before they could share any classified secrets.

The explanation that the coroner's court would finally uphold was the simplest: that no-one could survive floating in shark-infested seas for long.

It would be comforting for most divers to dismiss this as a one-off. Most well-run dive boats have systems for checking all passengers on or off the vessel, and simple, seemingly foolproof precautions such as headcounts, buddying and tags to be hung on boards on the dive deck. Unfortunately, there are several other instances of divers never making it back to their boat — and their absence not being noted.

In Florida in 2000, a similar sized boat, the *Aqua Nut 11*, left two passengers out on a reef outside Key Largo. Michael and Lynda Evans surfaced after their first dive to find that the boat had already departed to a second site, out of sight.

Neither the presence of the Evans's belongings nor the full compressed air cylinders that were set ready for their next dive alerted anyone on the boat. Out at sea, the Evans managed to swim for a small tower and climb onto a small platform where they huddled for the night. At daybreak, a yacht spotted them and called the coastguard. The Evans were saved; the dive company was prosecuted.

The British magazine *Diver* relates how similar events once occurred during the kind of excursion in which any dive company would be expected to pull out all the stops — a press trip, arranged to show off the holiday to journalists to garner favourable coverage. Instead, the liveaboard vessel *Tiger Lily* managed to leave two dive journalists stranded in the Red Sea. Only by suppertime did the other divers realise that they were missing. Fortunately, the pair had managed to haul themselves aboard a rocky outcrop. When the boat eventually returned, it was in darkness. Luckily one of the journalists had a camera, whose flash signalled their whereabouts to the boat. As *Diver*'s writer concluded, such incidents show that no diver – no matter how well they think they know the crew or their fellow passengers – can assume they'll be missed.

In Cuba, two experienced divers, Robert and Olga Kazarian, were abandoned at sea, even though they'd been on a small boat carrying fewer than a dozen passengers. It was their hundredth dive. They were waiting just a few metres beneath the surface, on a regulation 'safety stop', allowing their bodies to adjust to water pressure and avoid the bends, when they saw the engines start. No-one realised they were missing. The couple were left treading water miles from land.

They were rescued, *Diver* reported, after three hours, by alerting unlikely saviours – the occupants of a pedal boat. But since then, the Kazarians would always tell their story on every new dive boat and say, 'Don't forget us!' to their shipmates. It was at most only half a joke.

24

The New Dawn

I F THE SEAS have been occasionally turbulent of late, this can still be regarded as something of a golden age for the cruise lines. While some Australian travel agents were reported to be stripping cruise holidays from their shop windows during the worst of the adverse publicity resulting from the Brimble case in 2006, the industry has remained buoyant in stormy waters. A bigger threat might be the effect of rising oil prices: this was the reason Carnival cited earlier in the year, when issuing a profits warning, which was followed by a drop in their share price.

Any such blip should be put in context, though: passenger numbers keep growing year on year and profits have been rolling in for the giant corporations. With new, ever-larger ships on their way, the lines are seeking and finding new markets to fill the berths of their expanding fleets.

Some expansion is geographical: in July 2006, Costa Cruises – a division of Carnival – became the first major international cruise line to start operating out of China. The *Costa Allegra* started cruises from Shanghai exclusively for Chinese guests, and there are two more ships to follow. The *Allegra* is expected to take 55,000 passengers in its first year. As ever, Italian officers are in charge of a third-world crew: this time, Chinese workers sent for training at a hospitality institute in Manila.

Other new markets are niche: cruisers are becoming an increasingly diverse breed. More and more special interest cruises are being dreamed up, some by firms targeting repeat business from their existing customers (for example, P&O in the UK schedule special, separate cruises for people interested in gardening, bridge, dancing and wine tasting on board the *Artemis*), but also by groups who are chartering ships for themselves.

The first all-gay transatlantic cruise will take place in May 2007 – carrying 2600 gay men and women on board the *Queen Mary 2* for a six-day crossing from New York to Southampton. In Australia, a gay travel firm is planning to completely hire out P&O's *Pacific Sun* for the first time next year. (At least in Sydney, such charters are unlikely to meet the hostility that passengers on the 'first ever gay and lesbian family cruise' encountered in Nassau, the Bahamas, in 2004, when more than 100 protesters led by Christian pastors stopped them disembarking from the *Norwegian Dawn*.)

Naturist cruises are also taking to the waves. In Australia, cruises setting out from Brisbane and up the coast of Queensland have become established. In the US, one Texan travel company specialises in nude cruises, chartering ships as big as the 2200-berth Costa Cruises liners. Passengers are required to wear clothes in port, and the cruise video, a staple souvenir on American ships, is for once not available.

Religious cults, too, have often chartered ships, while the Scientologists even have one of their own, *Freewinds*, that is used as a retreat and training centre.

Other organisations are booking out parts of ships for their own clientele. One firm, GeekCruises, holds computer training courses on cruises with such enticing titles as 'Linux Lunacy' and 'Photoshop Fling', fitting seminars around mealtimes and shore visits and laying on extended classes to fill days spent at sea.

Royal Caribbean has even joined forces with Sydney's Macquarie University and other educational institutions around the world to establish a floating academy at sea, the so-called *Scholar Ship*, which will set sail from Piraeus, Greece, in 2007 and travel to five continents over a period of four months. Up to 700 students – paying around US$20,000 each – are expected to be on board alongside the ship's academic staff. Students will earn credits for courses completed on board that go towards undergraduate and postgraduate degrees. They are promised 'experiential learning', including the chance to interact with people in their various ports of call through voluntary work. On the first global trip, the passengers – or as the promoters call them, the 'mobile transnational learning community' – are scheduled to stop off in Morocco, Argentina and South Africa, reaching Perth in Western Australia halfway through, before returning via Asia to Greece.

Perhaps the ultimate cruise is that which never ends. *The World*, which started its perpetual global circumnavigations in 2002, contains the apartments of the ultra-rich who sniffily decry the captain's cocktail party world of everyday cruising, but choose instead to live at sea, one season meandering down the coastline of South America, another exploring the South Pacific and Asia.

Holiday-makers can still join the ship for shorter periods – at a price ranging from US$1200 to $4200 a night. But the real point of the project, as described by the billionaire founder Knut U. Kloster Jr, is to live on board, allowing residents to travel the world without leaving their own home.

Most of the 110 apartments – valued at between US$2.5 and $8.5 million – have now been sold by ResidenSea, the Bahamas-based consortium behind *The World*, with middle-aged Americans making up around half of the owners. Golf is, unsurprisingly, a big preoccupation: cruising schedules are timed to coincide with Open championships, and the ship has a full-time onboard coach and a golf centre with a virtual reality simulation as well as a real grass putting green, and two detachable greens for extra challenges when in port. (*The World* also provides special biodegradable golf balls.)

The ship is not to everyone's taste: it is marked by a 'pervasive emptiness', said one journalist who made it on board a couple of years after the initial launch; a place where one walks 'through the ship's deserted lobby to the sound of an automatic grand piano playing Elton John medleys'.

The neverending residential cruise is not the limit, no matter how extreme it might seem. There are plans afoot for a whole new breed of cruise liner – one which will sail in the skies. The Aeroscraft, a new type of airship, will have the kind of scale and amenities seen in cruise ships and be able to fly thousands of miles without refuelling at a speed and height that would let passengers enjoy the view of landmarks below. Worldwide Aeros Corporation, the American company behind the project, expects a prototype to be ready sometime in 2007 and says that several cruise ship companies are watching with interest.

Back at sea level, new routes will continue to open up. Antarctica has been converted in an astonishingly short time from a barely accessible remote wilderness to a destination cruise tourists can travel to on whim – and the North Pole could be next. As the polar caps melt, thinning the ice in the Arctic Ocean, Russian icebreaker ships are already lined up to take holiday-makers to the extreme north for about US$30,000. In Russia, this kind of money might put off all but the mafia, but it is less than the fares already paid for the best rooms on long luxury cruises by wealthy people in other countries. Global warming saw the first icebreakers reach the North Pole little over a decade ago, but Canadian government officials say that if the ice continues to melt at the current rate, cruise liners will be able to sail straight over the pole within thirty years.

The last part of the planet – bar the dry bits – will be conquered by that unlikely pioneer, the cruise ship passenger. As the ICCL puts it, cruise ships will 'visit – literally – all corners' of the big, round world.

So how did cruises get to be so big? Cheaper air travel may have originally killed off the need for passenger liners, but it has also allowed many more people to fly to cruise ports, get on board and discover the delights of life at sea.

As Carnival's CEO Bob Dickinson has said, the core attractions have remained more or less constant since the first cruises sailed in the nineteenth century — a constant social buzz, wining and dining, and no need to keep repacking to move on to a new destination.

Nevertheless, while the oceans may still look the same, little on board today would be familiar to a nineteenth-century passenger. Cruise holidays have been democratised, even if some vestigial ideas of aspiration and exclusivity remain: cruise lines and travel agents walk a fine line between making any customer feel she or he can come on board and selling a cruise as a dream holiday. Dickinson relates how advertisements showing a handsome couple in an idyllic scene divided his industry; many felt it would be off-putting to a new clientele who couldn't picture themselves in that way. The strange combination of aspiration and ambivalence is epitomised by a British woman who recently went on a reality TV show to have radical plastic surgery, saying she wanted to be remade so she could 'fit in on a cruise ship'.

There are horses for courses, and the culture — and price — of some cruise ships means they remain the domain of the super-rich. Certain brochures and websites shamelessly hark back to days of Empire and supposedly gentler times: regally named ships, classical music, gentlemen hosts, crystal glassware; an era when one could imagine a Poirot being called upon to investigate foul play at sea.

Despite the west's ageing populations, the industry isn't simply waiting for passengers to reach their dotage before getting on board. It is looking towards the next generation now.

Companies such as Royal Caribbean have gone to great lengths to reposition their ships as places for the young and active. Since 2005, Royal Caribbean's advertising campaigns have shown fit young things engaged in sporty pursuits on their cruises, to the soundtrack of Iggy Pop's 'Lust for Life' (voted the worst match of any song and advertised product by readers of *Slate* magazine). Even if guests occasionally get active, though, cruising is by nature a choice for the passive; surrendering to an itinerary, being shepherded from place to place for the briefest of stops, barely scraping inland.

Why then, cruising's enormous and booming popularity now? Partly, a more affluent population, with an older profile overall; partly, perhaps, trends towards longer work hours, making a cosseted holiday more desirable. Short cruises offer a chance to visit a number of destinations, however briefly, and particularly suit an American population that typically enjoys only two or three weeks of annual leave.

In the USA, the size of the industry has reached the point at which consumers don't so much choose whether to cruise, but which cruise to take. In Europe, companies like Ocean Village are aggressively marketing their products as 'cruises for people who don't do cruises'. The concept of being aboard a ship is being relegated from centre stage: cruises are instead presented as new worlds, where various lifestyles and desires can be catered for.

More and more, the big cruise ships are being sold as floating resorts, and it's a good analogy: places where holiday-makers can eat and enjoy the entertainment and facilities in the same place that they sleep, insulated from the world – arguably, from the world they are ostensibly paying to see. However, as in the gated communities in the crime-ridden cities that ships leave behind, bad experiences are proportionally more terrifying when they happen on the inside.

As their populations grow to rival those of towns, the ships are more than ever just a slice of life; evolving as surely as TV costume dramas have given way to the *Big Brother* house. And just as reality TV's constant monitoring of people in a confined space reveals the kind of human behaviour that even Australian Prime Minister John Howard has specifically denounced, the goings-on aboard certain cruise ships have not stood up to much scrutiny.

The cruise's illusion of complete safety is what makes the intrusion of a dangerous reality so hard to bear. More than any other holiday, a cruise promises the ultimate in air-conditioned security; everyone and everything coming in and out is screened and scrutinised, monitored on CCTV; ships sell familiar brands in their onboard shopping malls, and even the vendors at ports are pre-approved. Passengers can stay in contact with their families on shore at all times, while sequestered in an environment that promises to be safer than their home cities and offers a sanitised version of foreign countries and their cultures.

It is precisely because cruise ships promise a secure, carefree world that any incidents of crime, death, tragic loss, disease, exploitation and abuse on board can seem so shocking.

Millions of passengers do and will enjoy trouble-free cruises each year. Cruise lines maintain that they offer one of the safest kinds of holiday, and not even the relatives of victims dispute that cruising is a relatively safe experience. Even so, every passenger is only the height of a handrail away from going overboard.

Acknowledgements

I would like to thank all those people, especially at *The Sydney Morning Herald*, who got me started on the story and helped me on my way with ideas, advice, encouragement, research and contacts for this book. They include Amanda Wilson, Tim Dick, Lisa Pryor, Jenny Cooke, Brigitte Mahler-Mills, Nora Martin, Helen Bayliss, Marianna Papadakis, Sean Nicholls, Ian Verrender, Richard Coleman, Mick Millett, Keith Austin and Geesche Jacobsen at the *Herald*, and elsewhere, Hannah Griffiths, Louise Hall, Colleen Hughson, Helen Hutcheon and Joan Lownds.

I would also like to thank *The Guardian* for sending me to Sydney, and all the people who made my time there such a happy one.

Much of this book could not have been written without information given to me by a number of people who talked to me at length about their experience working on cruise ships. I appreciate all their input, and while some are recognised by name in the book, I am equally grateful to others who preferred to remain anonymous. I would like to thank all those who spoke to me – and particularly, the International Cruise Victims. Their campaign is ongoing and can be found at www.internationalcruisevictims.org; their partner sites, www.cruisebruise.com and www.cruisejunkie.com, document ever-growing caseloads of incidents at sea.

This book would not have happened without Meredith Curnow at Random House, who first saw the stories' potential, nor turned out so well without Elizabeth Cowell's fabulous editing.

Thanks too to Amy McLean and to David and Avril Topham. Thanks, most of all, to Katharine Viner.

Thank you to all those who gave their permission to quote materials originally published elsewhere, including Reuben Goossens, www.consumeraffairs.com, *The Sydney Morning Herald*, News Limited and the UK *Daily Telegraph*.

While every effort has been made to contact all copyright holders, the publishers will be glad to make good in future editions any errors or omissions brought to their attention.

Notes

Introduction

Page xi: They were to sail for months over the breezy Atlantic ... Twain, Mark, *The Innocents Abroad*, 1869, p 6, http://mark-twain.classic-literature.co.uk/the-innocents-abroad/ebook-page-06.asp

Pages xi–xii: If the nightclub is jumping ... Cornford, Philip and Jacobsen, Geesche, 'Culture of cruise neglect exposed', *The Sydney Morning Herald*, 24 June 2006

Page xiv: It sounds too good to be true! Is it? ... Cruise Lines International Association, online FAQs, www.cruising.org/planyourcruise/faqs/qna.cfm?ID=37

1: The Missing

Page 1: In 1975, during the last days of the Vietnam War ... Author's interview with Son Michael Pham

Pages 1–2: One day in 1999, Gregory Miller ... Kerr, Joseph, 'Man missing at sea', *The Newcastle Herald*, 15 April 1999; 'Teased gay "jumped overboard to his death"', *The Sydney Morning Herald*, 21 September 1999

Page 3: Disappearances reported by the International Council of Cruise Lines included ... International Council of Cruise Lines (ICCL), press release: 'Cruise industry releases crime statistics', 4 March 2006; Gibson, William, 'Cruise casualties go overboard', *The Courier-Mail*, 9 March 2006

Page 4: Two American citizens with no personal or financial problems ... Pham, Son Michael, testifying before the Congressional

Subcommittee on National Security, Emerging Threats and International Relations, transcript of hearing: 'International maritime security II: law enforcement, passenger security and incident investigation on cruise ships', Washington, DC, 7 March 2006

Page 4: Ocean travel puts passengers and crew in a distant, isolated environment ... Shays, Christopher, address to Congressional Subcommittees on National Security, Emerging Threats and International Relations, and Criminal Justice, Drug Policy and Human Resources, transcript of joint hearing: 'International maritime security', Washington, DC, 13 December 2005

Page 5: Mr Pham was one of those who appeared ... Other witnesses told of cases ... Congressional Subcommittee on National Security, Emerging Threats and International Relations, transcript of hearing: 'International maritime security II: law enforcement, passenger security and incident investigation on cruise ships', Washington, DC, 7 March 2006

Pages 5–7: The committee also heard about the case of Lynsey O'Brien ... O'Brien, Paul and Byrd, Kurt, interviewed on ABC News *Primetime*, 'A 15-year-old girl served alcohol on cruise ship falls overboard', 13 April 2006, www.abcnews.go.com/Primetime/story?id=1837441&page=1; *Holidays Undercover*, ITV1 (UK), broadcast 25 July 2006; Vousden, Petrina, 'Father of teen who died on cruise ship still fighting for justice', *Daily Mail*, 20 March 2006; Fergus, Lindsay, 'I want justice for my precious Lynsey', *The Mirror* (Ireland), 15 March 2006

Page 7: A family friend, Brian Mulvaney, told the congressional hearings ... Mulvaney, Brien, testifying before Congressional Subcommittee on National Security, Emerging Threats and International Relations, transcript of hearing: 'International maritime security II: law enforcement, passenger security and incident investigation on cruise ships', Washington, DC, 7 March 2006

Page 7: In an internal report ... 'Cruise ship company: Don't blame us for tragic teen's death', *Irish Independent*, 21 April 2006

Pages 8–10: On 5 July 2005, a week into their honeymoon ... Murphy, Dennis, 'Few clues in honeymoon cruise disappearance', *NBC News*, 13 December 2005, report based on *Dateline NBC*, broadcast 16 September 2005; 'George Allen Smith', Wikipedia, http://en.wikipedia.org/wiki/George_Allen_Smith (viewed May 2006); Day, Elizabeth, 'Murder on the high seas?', *The Sunday Telegraph* (UK), 22 January 2006

Page 8: I remember being at the casino ... Hagel Smith, Jennifer, speaking on *The Oprah Winfrey Show*, quoted in 'Two sides of the honeymoon cruise disappearance', *ABC News*, 26 January 2006

Page 10: In the words of the dead man's sister ... Smith, Bree, 'George A. Smith IV', International Cruise Victims website, www.internationalcruisevictims.org/OurStories/tabid/53/ItemID/6/View/Details/Default.aspx

Page 11: We're going to continue until our dying day ... Smith, Bree, 'Justice for George', International Cruise Victims website, http://community.internationalcruisevictims.org/blogs/jfg/about.aspx (viewed 19 August 2006)

Page 11: George's life will not be taken in vain ... Smith family, 'Justice for George', International Cruise Victims website, http://community.internationalcruisevictims.org/blogs/jfg/about.aspx (viewed 19 August 2006)

Page 11: Royal Caribbean eventually issued a statement ... Royal Caribbean, press release: 'Top 10 myths regarding Royal Caribbean's handling of the disappearance of George Smith', 27 January 2006

Page 12: As many great peace and spiritual teachers have said ... Hagel Smith, Jennifer, statement: 'Our continuing journey of seeking answers and peace, in memory of George Allen Smith IV', US Newswire, 4 July 2006

Page 14: Mr Carver pointed out that the case was still open ... Author's interview with Kendall Carver

Page 14: We don't want to go dealing with our tragic loss in public ... Author's interview with Son Michael Pham

Pages 15–16: I've been thirty years suing cruise lines ... Author's interview with Charles R. Lipcon

Page 16: We live in the United States and we thought we had rights ... Author's interview with Son Michael Pham

Page 17: Thomas Dickerson, a US judge and expert on travel law, has put it bluntly ... Luzadder, Dan, 'Passenger disappearance leads to scrutiny in cruise industry', *Travel Weekly*, 21 February 2006

2: Now Wash Your Hands ...

Page 19: 'We suspected there was going to be a problem,' a passenger related ... Martin, Nicole, 'Land at last for passengers on the bug cruise', *The Daily Telegraph* (UK), 4 November 2003

Page 19: They looked like the blokes from *ET* ... Jeffery, Simon and agencies, 'Spain shuts border to virus ship', *Guardian Unlimited*, 3 November 2003

Page 19: Andrew Williams from South Wales took six days to succumb ... Martin, Nicole, 'Land at last for passengers on the bug cruise', *The Daily Telegraph* (UK), 4 November 2003

Page 21: It sparked a furious response ... Jeffery, Simon and agencies, 'Spain shuts border to virus ship', *Guardian Unlimited*, 3 November 2003

Page 22: An elderly passenger described the scene to the UK *Daily Telegraph* ... 'Holidaymakers' dream shattered by cruise virus', *The Daily Telegraph* (UK), 7 September 2003

Page 23: Another 200 were struck down with the bug on the *Aurora*'s sister ship ... '200 passengers hit by cruise ship bug', *Daily Mail* (UK), 27 May 2005

Page 23: But just how clean are the ships? One Nile cruise ship, the *Karim Palace* ... *Holidays Undercover*, ITV1 (UK), broadcast 25 July 2006

Pages 23–24: It doesn't necessarily follow that the grander the ship, the cleaner ... Centers for Disease Control, QE2 inspection report, 23 January 2006, http://www.cdc.gov/vsp/InspectionQueryTool/Forms/InspectionSummaryView.aspx?int InspectionID=5816101 (viewed July 2006)

Page 24: More unpleasant were some of the unhygienic parts of ships ... *Which?* survey, quoted in 'Flies and out-of-date food sink cruise ship hygiene standards', *Daily Mail*, 1 September 2005

Page 24: ... a report in an American scientific journal showed a definite correlation ... Center for Advancement of Health, press release: 'Inspections sharply reduce diarrhea outbreaks on cruise ships', 12 December 2002

Page 25: Another, David Cordon, from Wakefield, Yorkshire, related ... 'Wedding "spoilt" by cruise virus', BBC News Online, 2 June 2006, http://news.bbc.co.uk/nolpda/ifs_news/hi/newsid_5041000/5041890.stm

Pages 25–26: *Holidays Undercover* **reporters spoke to Paul and Fran Hughes** ... *Holidays Undercover*, ITV1 (UK), broadcast 25 July 2006

Page 26: The mother of Joshua Woodcock, twelve, appeared on the same program ... *Holidays Undercover*, ITV1 (UK), broadcast 25 July 2006

Page 27: David Forney, chief of the Vessel Sanitation Program ... Clark, Cheryl, 'Cruise ship told to follow own rules after outbreak', *The San Diego Union-Tribune*, 29 March 2006, quoted by Cruise Ship Report website, March 2006, www.cruise-ship-report.com/News/032906.htm

Page 27: It's little wonder that the ship's captain had apparently already turned to drink ... 'Cruise-ship captain pleads guilty to drinking', *The Seattle Times*, 1 August 2006

Pages 27–28: *The Times* **reported that in late May, a twelve-night Baltic cruise** ... 'Cruise passengers may sue over curse of the Black Prince', *The Times*, 6 July 2006

Page 28: According to the CDC's statistics ... Centers for Disease Control and Prevention Vessel Sanitation Program, 'Updates of gastrointestinal illness among passengers and crew for international cruise lines', www.cdc.gov/nceh/vsp/surv/GIlist.htm

Page 28 ... several hundred passengers and crew fell sick with the Norwalk virus ... Cruise Junkie website, www.cruisejunkie.com/outbreaks2006.html

Page 28: The CDC's David Forney told a medical inquest ... Forney, David, quoted by Centers for Disease Control, transcript of telebriefing: 'Outbreak of gastrointestinal illness aboard cruise ships', 27 November 2002, www.cdc.gov/od/oc/media/transcripts/t021127.htm

Pages 28–29: The Public Health Agency of Canada issued a report ... Public Health Agency of Canada, 'Statement on cruise ship travel', *Canada Communicable Disease Report*, 15 October 2005

Page 29: In 2005 a report was issued by the CDC to raise medical awareness ... 'Cruise-ship-associated legionnaires disease, November 2003 – May 2004', *Morbidity and Mortality Weekly Report*, 18 November 2005

Pages 29–30: With such an array of infectious diseases ... New South Wales Department of Health, 'Disease control on international cruise ships', 21 April 2006

3: Oil on Troubled Waters

Page 32: In a single week, a typical cruise ship will rack up a good 210,000 gallons ... Figures from the Bluewater Network, quoted in Hickman, Leo, 'Is it OK ... to go on a cruise?', *The Guardian*, 7 March 2006

Page 33: In the 1990s, Royal Caribbean launched ... Klein, Ross A., *Cruise Ship Blues: the underside of the cruise industry*, New Society Publishers, Gabriola Island, BC, 2002

Page 33: US Attorney General Janet Reno was moved to say ... United States Department of Justice, press release, 21 July 1999, www.usdoj.gov/opa/pr/1999/July/316enr.htm

Page 33: 'This case,' promised Reno, 'will sound like a foghorn' ... United States Department of Justice, press conference, 21 July 1999, www.usdoj.gov/archive/ag/speeches/1999/royalcaribbean.htm

Page 34: Tom Sansonetti, Assistant Attorney General for the Department of Justice said ... European Policy Centre, 'The role of enforcement in environmental protection', 1 July 2004, www.theepc.be/en/er.asp?TYP=ER&LV=293&see=y&t=2&PG=ER/EN/detail&l=&AI=430

Page 35: There was, then, no law flouted ... Arakawa, Lynda, 'Cruise company violated accord', *Honolulu Advertiser*, 12 March 2005

Page 35: The *Queen Elizabeth 2* itself came under investigation in 2006 ... 'Cruise ship pollution investigated', *Edmonton Sun*, 2 May 2006

Page 35: A somewhat less refined ship was prosecuted under the MARPOL Convention ... Australian Maritime Safety Authority, 'Fairstar owners prosecuted for garbage discharge', www.amsa.gov.au/Marine_Environment_Protection/Protection_of_Pollution_from_Ships/Prosecutions_for_Ship_Sourced_Pollution/Garbage_pollution_prosecutions/Fairstar_Prosecuted.asp

Page 36: According to estimates from the Port of San Francisco ... Reuters, 'San Francisco aims to reduce cruise ship emissions', 11 July 2006

Page 37: More than any others they were touting their green credentials ... Author's interview with Jackie Savitz

Page 37: In Carnival's most recent publicly available environmental report ... Carnival Corporation & plc, 'Environmental Management Report: fiscal year 2005', p 15

Page 38: *The Daily Telegraph* **reported that the captain described the accident** ... 'QE2 "spears" 40ft whale in the dark', *The Daily Telegraph* (UK), 19 September 1996

Page 38: Carnival recently endorsed a new project in San Francisco ... Reuters, 'San Francisco aims to reduce cruise ship emissions', 11 July 2006

Page 38: Bob Dickinson, Carnival CEO, recalls a time ... Dickinson, Bob and Vladimir, Andy, *Selling the Seas: an inside look at the cruise industry*, John Wiley & Sons, New York, 1997

Page 38: All the garbage was stacked on the crew deck ... Author's interview with former cruise ship crew member

Pages 38–39: The cruise industry is definitely more aware of environmental concerns ... Author's interview with Teri Shore

Page 39: It's singling out an industry that has already taken the steps to minimise ... *Background Briefing*, ABC Radio, 8 May 2005

Page 39: But campaigners say the laws are still necessary ... Author's interviews with Teri Shore and Jackie Savitz

Page 39: According to Royal Caribbean's senior vice-president of marine operations ... 'A cruise line starts to clean up after itself', *The New York Times*, 28 January 2004

Page 40: The standard marine sanitation devices mainly used elsewhere ... Author's interview with Jackie Savitz

Page 40: ... some observers believe that the cruise industry will one day ... Ward, Douglas, *Complete Guide to Cruising & Cruise Ships 2006*, Berlitz, London, 2006, p 25

4: The Unwelcome Guests

Pages 41–42: A local tour director told the *LA Times* **of his shock** ... Dickerson, Marla, 'Curse of the daytrippers', *Los Angeles Times*, reprinted in *The Sydney Morning Herald*, 1 April 2006

Page 42: Holland America was fined $300,000 by the Virgin Islands ... 'Action Atlas Coral reef', MotherJones website, www.motherjones.com/news/special_reports/coral_reef/cayman.html (viewed July 2006)

Page 42 ... one visitor recounted seeing other people clambering over colonies ... Rowe, Mark, 'Tourism "threatens" Antarctic', *The Daily Telegraph* (UK), 11 February 2006

Pages 42–43: Such fears took on a whole new dimension ... Squires, Nick, 'Liner takes tourist hordes to Antarctica', *The Daily Telegraph* (UK), 5 September 2006

Page 43: In Australia, the little-touched Kimberley region has been identified ... *Background Briefing*, ABC Radio, 8 May 2005

Page 43: Graham Watkins, the director of the Charles Darwin Foundation ... Nicholls, Henry, 'Caught in the eco-tourist trap', *The Guardian Weekly*, 28 April 2006

Page 44: In 1933, P&O distributed a letter to its passengers visiting Papua ... P&O Australia, 'Take me away: 70 years of cruising from Australia', P&O Cruises Australia website, www.pocruises.com.au/html/history.cfm

Pages 44–45: Journalist Ian Verrender used to live on the Pacific island of American Samoa ... Author's interview with Ian Verrender

Page 45: In 2003, campaigners persuaded the cruise industry to drop plans ... Oceana, 'Contamination by cruise ships', www.oceana.org/fileadmin/oceana/uploads/europe/reports/cruise_ships_eng.pdf

Page 45: Hotels have to go through years of permitting, mitigate their effects ... Save Kahului Harbor website, www.savekahuluiharbor.com/cruise.php (viewed April 2006)

Page 45: Ross Klein notes in *Cruise Ship Blues* that in recent years ... Klein, Ross A., *Cruise Ship Blues: the underside of the cruise industry*, New Society Publishers, 2002, p 45

Page 46: Spend time in a cruise ship port and you'll see more of the world than you will ever see travelling ... Portside Living website, www.portsideliving.com.au/content/cms/Cruise+Wharf/53/ (viewed May 2006)

Page 46: A sustained campaign of protest helped prevent another planned cruise terminal ... Save our Spit website, www.saveourspit.com/index.html; ABC News Online, 19 August 2006

Pages 46–47: Tourism Queensland research found that cruise passengers ... Tourism Queensland, 'Cruise ship passenger research', August 2004, www.qttc.com.au/shadomx/apps/fms/fmsdownload.cfm?file_uuid=6E0FF79D-DAA4-5C5A-88BE-815AC5DD9EF3&siteName=tqcorp_06

Page 47: The cruise lines are 'selling' Alaska ... Cohen, Gershon and Geldhof, Joe, Responsible Cruising in Alaska, 'Statement in support', Division of Elections, Alaska, www.elections.state.ak.us/forms/03ctax_pro.pdf

Page 48: The measures had been vigorously opposed by the cruise industry ... Dobbyn, Paula, 'Cruise ship industry funds Alaska tax fight', *Anchorage Daily News*, 13 June 2006

Page 48: One man who eked out a living diving for and hawking starfish ... Torres, John A., web special report: 'Canaveral's crews: the people and profits behind the port's cruise ship party', *Florida Today*, 18 July 2006, www.floridatoday.com/apps/pbcs.dll/article?AID=/99999999/NEWS01/512110310/0/news07 (viewed July 2006)

Page 48: Nevertheless, cruise ships provide only an insecure source of livelihood ... Belize Channel 5 news report, broadcast 10 July 2006, http://new.channel5belize.com/archive_detail_story.php?story_id=16584 (viewed July 2006)

Page 48: Nobody in the Caribbean owns a cruise ship ... Pattullo, Polly, quoted in newsletter: 'The cost of tourism in the Caribbean', Latin American Bureau, spring 2004

Pages 48–49: This, Ross Klein recounts in *Cruise Ship Blues*, was the fate of Grenada ... Klein, Ross A., *Cruise Ship Blues: the underside of the cruise industry*, New Society Publishers, 2002, pp 113–114

Page 49: There is no competition ... Klein, Ross A., *Cruise Ship Blues: the underside of the cruise industry*, New Society Publishers, 2002, p 41

Page 49: As Robert S. McIntyre of Citizens for Tax Justice told *The Washington Post* ... Weisman, Jonathan, '$236 million cruise ship deal criticized', *The Washington Post*, 28 September 2005

Page 50: *The Washington Post* reported that Carnival's CEO wrote to the United States Treasury ... Weisman, Jonathan, '$236 million cruise ship deal criticized', *The Washington Post*, 28 September 2005

Page 51: The ship was sent first to Bangladesh's shipbreakers ... O'Connor, Ashling, 'Anger greets toxic liner ruling', *The Times*, 31 July 2006

Page 51: One man who was still trying to make a living at Alang ... Nair, Rupam Jain, Reuters, 'A dying industry in India's graveyard of ships', 5 July 2006

Page 51: But Greenpeace activists in India and beyond are demanding ... Joseph, Anto, 'For India, breaking up is hard to do', *The Observer*, 22 January 2006

5: Down Under and Dirty

Pages 53–56: A P&O spokeswoman claimed that they don't do booze cruises ... Topham, Gwyn, 'The plan: party for three days, don't get drugged and raped', *The Sydney Morning Herald*, 1 April 2006

Page 56: At other times, the law has tried to head off trouble ... Maley, Jacqueline, 'Holiday drug crackdown', *The Sydney Morning Herald*, 30 November 2004

Pages 56–57: The *Herald* had also reported on another particularly notorious trip ... Brown, Malcolm, 'Disruptions mar cruise', *The Sydney Morning Herald*, 18 December 2003

Page 57: Former crew member Daina Brampton worked on many schoolies trips ... Author's interview with Daina Brampton

Pages 57–58: According to passengers on board the particularly anarchic 2003 cruise ... Vaughan, Craig, 'How our trip turned ugly – schoolies tell of horror booze cruise', *The Daily Telegraph* (Sydney), 20 December 2003 (extract reproduced with permission of News Limited)

Pages 58–59: Still, as one security guard told *The Sydney Morning Herald* ... Cornford, Philip and Jacobsen, Geesche, 'Culture of cruise neglect exposed', *The Sydney Morning Herald*, 24 June 2006

Page 59: But then, not all security guards themselves appear ... Weaver, Clair, 'Cruise of sex, booze, brawls', *The Sunday Telegraph* (Sydney), 2 July 2006

Page 59: Jeff Dobjeckie, a former security manager on the *Pacific Sky*, told a reporter ... 'Cruise ship was like wild west', *The Daily Telegraph* (Sydney), 4 July 2006

Page 60: Even the government felt obliged to get involved ... 'Cruise ships told to retrain bar staff', *The Sydney Morning Herald*, 6 July 2006

6: *Fairstar* the Fuckship

Pages 61–62: Maritime historian Reuben Goossens, who sailed from Melbourne ... Goossens, Reuben, 'TSS Fairstar', ssMaritime.com website, www.ssmaritime.com/fair1.htm (viewed May 2006)

Page 62: Sandy, an ex-stewardess who went on to work for Norwegian Cruises ... Author's interview with Sandy, former steward on the *Fairstar*

Pages 62–63: Murray Ferguson was a musician on the *Fairstar* ... Author's interview with Murray Ferguson

Page 63: A *Sydney Morning Herald* journalist took a cruise ... Fife-Yeomans, Janet, 'One ship, lot of passes in the night', *The Sydney Morning Herald*, 16 August 1991

Page 63: Ian Verrender, a former resident of Pago Pago in American Samoa ... Author's interview with Ian Verrender

Page 64: An ex-crew member relates: 'You'd never get much time in Oz' ... Author's interview with former cruise ship crew member

Page 64: Most of the time, says Murray Ferguson ... Author's interview with Murray Ferguson

Page 65: On return, one former US soldier from San Francisco ... Hewett, Tony; Bishop, Karin; and Date, Margot; 'It was a bloody disaster', *The Sydney Morning Herald*, 25 June 1991

Pages 65–66: Of all the ships assessed ... Ward, Douglas, *Complete Guide to Cruising & Cruise Ships 2006*, Berlitz, London, 2006

Page 66: The *Fairstar*'s last cruise was, fittingly, described as a 'raucous affair' ... Angelo, Jesse and Smith, Mike, 'Nothing retiring about fun ship's farewell to Sydney', *The Daily Telegraph*, 1 February 1997

7: Dianne Brimble

Pages 68–69: ... the events of one night in September 2002 ... *Australian Story*, ABC, broadcast 8 May 2006

8: The Enemy Within

Pages 75–76: Charles R. Lipcon, a lawyer specialising in cruise ship suits ... Author's interview with Charles R. Lipcon

Page 75: Cruise lines operate within a very strict legal framework ... ICCL, statement: 'Cruise industry policies: personal safety & security', www.iccl.org/policies/personal.cfm

Page 76: As another maritime law specialist, Brett Rivkind, explained ... Rivkind, Brett, addressing the Congressional Subcommittees on National Security, Emerging Threats and

International Relations, and Criminal Justice, Drug Policy and Human Resources, transcript of joint hearing: 'International maritime security', Washington, DC, 13 December 2005

Page 76: The cruise industry places the highest priority ... ICCL, briefing memo: 'The safest way to travel, cruise ship security', www.iccl.org/pressroom/securityfinal.pdf

Pages 76–77: One mother, however, refused to sign such a document ... Carlton, Alexandra, 'Cruise ships: the perfect place to commit a crime?', *Madison*, June 2006; testimony on International Cruise Victims website, www.internationalcruisevictims.org

Page 77: Janet Kelly, a forty-nine-year-old estate agent ... Congressional Subcommittee on National Security, Emerging Threats and International Relations, transcript of hearing: 'International maritime security II: law enforcement, passenger security and incident investigation on cruise ships', Washington, DC, 7 March 2006; Rawe, Julie, 'Crime rocks the boats', *Time*, 13 March 2006

Pages 77–78: Rehiring is not uncommon, according to industry insiders ... Author's interview with Randy Jaques

Page 78: Sydney maritime consultant Peter Burge agrees ... Author's interview with Peter Burge

Page 78: The ICCL says that it has a 'zero tolerance' policy towards crime ... ICCL, statement: 'Cruise industry policies: personal safety & security', www.iccl.org/policies/personal.cfm

Page 78: A British security officer, Geoff Furlong, who spent ten years working on cruises ... *Holidays Undercover*, ITV1 (UK), broadcast 25 July 2006

Pages 78–79: To call the FBI direct, said Jaques, was 'above my pay grade' ... Author's interview with Randy Jaques

Page 79: Charles Lipcon agreed: 'There's a lot of use of date rape drugs now ...' Author's interview with Charles R. Lipcon

Page 80: Speaking with *The Daily Telegraph*, Jeff Dobjeckie ... 'Cruise ship was like wild west', *The Daily Telegraph* (Sydney), 4 July 2006

Page 80: Security officers generally have crime scene investigation experience ... Author's interview with Randy Jaques

Page 80: After one incident of violent assault on a ship ... Cornford, Philip and Jacobsen, Geesche, 'Culture of cruise neglect exposed', *The Sydney Morning Herald*, 24 June 2006

Page: 81 What happens afterwards? If a crime happens ... Author's interview with Son Michael Pham

Page 81: On *Holidays Undercover*, Geoff Furlong put it bluntly ... *Holidays Undercover*, ITV1 (UK), broadcast 25 July 2006

Page 81: Even breaking up fights is sometimes further than staff go ... Author's interview with David (not his real name), a cruise ship security officer

Pages 81–82: Another marine expert, consultant Peter Burge, gives a flat answer ... Author's interview with Peter Burge

Page 82: David, the young Canadian security officer quoted above, agrees ... Author's interview with David

Pages 83–84: The ICV has drawn up a wide-ranging blueprint ... International Cruise Victims, press release: 'Increasing security and passenger safety', June 2006

Pages 84–85: In Australia, P&O responded promptly to the plan ... Gavin Smith (Managing Director, P&O Australia), 'Statement from P&O Cruises Australia re International Cruise Victims' 10-point plan', 21 June 2006

Page 85: Even Arthur Frommer, the man behind the global tourism guidebooks ... Frommer, Arthur, 'On a trip, it's all about risk assessment', *Los Angeles Times*, 16 April 2006

9: The Smugglers

Page 86: The US Department of Justice says cruise ships frequently carry drug couriers ... National Drug Intelligence Center, 'Florida Drug Threat Assessment', July 2003, www.usdoj.gov/ndic/pubs5/5169/cocaine.htm

Page 87: Charges extended to smuggling offences on at least twenty other cruises ... United States Department of Justice, 10 June 2005, www.usdoj.gov/usao/fls/050610-01.html (viewed July 2006)

Page 87: Another trafficking organisation using cruise lines was exposed in September 2000 ... United States Drug Enforcement Agency, press release: 'Operation Creole', June 2001

Pages 87–88 : Three passengers on board the Cunard liner *Caronia* were found to have ... '$2.6 million bust on cocaine cruise', *Herald Sun* (Melbourne), 13 March 2003

Pages 88–89: Detectives had been alerted to the possibility ... '11 cruise ship passengers busted for drugs', Cruise Bruise website, www.cruisebruise.com/January_06_2005_Drug_Bust_Carnival_Celebration.html (viewed July 2006)

Page 89: People smugglers have also been known to use cruise ships ... Brinkley, Joel, 'For aliens, a Bahamas cruise is an easy way into the US', *The New York Times*, 29 November 1994

Page 89: The Caribbean has also been fertile territory for animal smuggling ... United States Department of Justice, news release, 15 November 1999

Page 89: A World Wildlife Fund investigation into how foreign species ... Reynolds, James, 'Scottish ports targeted by wildlife traffickers', *The Scotsman*, 9 December 2002

10: Under Attack

Page 90: In April 2006, crews on ships around the world ... 'QE2 ups security after "threat"', BBC News Online, 12 April 2006

Page 91: Perhaps the least successful of cruise ship bomb hoaxes was perpetrated ... Bernardo, Rosemarie, and Associated Press, 'Feds say lovesick woman threatened cruise ship', *Honolulu Star-Bulletin*, 29 April 2003

Pages 92–95: Despite such hoaxes and false alarms ... 'A hijack on the high seas', BBC h2g2 website, 7 May 2002, www.bbc.co.uk/dna/h2g2/A730900 (viewed July 2006)

Page 93: Abbas, who was finally captured by American forces in Iraq in 2003 ... 'US slammed over hijacker's death', BBC News website, 10 March 2004, http://news.bbc.co.uk/1/hi/world/middle_east/3498668.stm

Page 94: In August 2005, an alleged al-Qaeda militant ... Bagenal, Flora, 'Bigley "buried in Falluja ditch"', *The Sunday Times*, 23 April 2006

Page 94: Fears have grown to the extent that even the Queen ... 'Royal cruise terror alert', *The Sun* (Scotland), 19 April 2006

Page 95: Still, a report from a US Department of State conference ... Institute of Defence and Strategic Studies and Office of the Coordinator for Counterterrorism, 'Terrorism in Southeast Asia: the threat and response', US Department of State, Washington, DC, 12 April 2006, www.ntu.edu.sg/IDSS/publications/conference_reports/NEW%20TerrorismSEAConference05.pdf

Page 96: In an email to his family, later published in *The Newcastle Herald* ... Pain, John and Associated Press, 'Cruise missiles', *The Newcastle Herald*, 12 November 2005

Page 96: Your immediate reaction is that it could not possibly be true ... Author's interview with a *Seabourn Spirit* passenger

Page 97: The woman was in tremendous shock. She kept saying she had glass in her hair ... Author's interview with a *Seabourn Spirit* passenger

Page 98: Mike Rogers of Vancouver, told CNN ... 'U.S. Navy boards ship after pirate attack', CNN.com, 8 November 2005, www.cnn.com/2005/WORLD/africa/11/05/somalia.pirates/index.html

Page 98: Australians Gayle and Bob Meagher, from Sydney, told Channel 7 television ... Timms, Aaron and Proudman, Dan, 'For your cruise entertainment, pirates on the starboard bow', *The Sydney Morning Herald*, 8 November 2005

Page 98: Another Australian passenger, Paul McGhee, who saw four of the pirates ... Timms, Aaron and Proudman, Dan, 'For your cruise entertainment, pirates on the starboard bow', *The Sydney Morning Herald*, 8 November 2005

Page 99: 'They would love to take a cruise ship,' a Carnival officer said ... Author's interview with David (not his real name), a cruise ship security officer

Page 99: ... the area remains far from under control ... Associated Press, 'Japanese vessel foils pirates, UN ships less lucky', 5 July 2006

Page 99: Soon after the incident with the *Seabourn Spirit* ... Howden, Daniel, 'Somali "mother ship" directs attacks by pirates', *The Independent*, 12 November 2005

Page 100: Mark Dickinson of NUMAST, the British maritime workers' union ... Dunbar, Polly, 'The real pirates of the Caribbean', *Daily Express* (UK), 5 July 2006

Page 100: One British MP, Louise Ellman, said in April 2006 ... 'Pirates to raid Brits', *Sunday People*, 9 April 2006; House of Commons Transport Committee, 'Eighth Report', 28 June 2006, www.publications.parliament.uk/pa/cm200506/cmselect/cmtran/1026/102602.htm

Pages 100–101: According to Llew Russell, a security specialist ... Author's interview with Llew Russell, CEO of Shipping Australia

Page 101: The security guys started carrying revolvers ... Author's interview with Richard Arghiris, former cruise ship casino croupier

Page 102: Peter Chalk, a security analyst for the RAND Corporation ... Chalk, Peter, 'Africa suffers wave of maritime violence', Rand Corporation website, www.rand.org/commentary/040101JIR.html

Page 102: The UK's *Daily Express* reports that maritime unions believe ... Dunbar, Polly, 'The real pirates of the Caribbean', *Daily Express*, 5 July 2006

Page 103: Thanks to Gary's leadership, our country is much better prepared ... Royal Caribbean, statement: 'Royal Caribbean Cruises Ltd. names top federal security expert to head worldwide security', 5 June 2006

11: Bigger and Better?

Page 105: It is, enthused a reporter who had a preview ... Hardman, Robert, 'Monster of the seas', *Daily Mail*, 29 April 2006

Pages 106–107: In July 2006, the Costa *Concordia* was launched ... Reuters, 'New cruise ship has biggest spa at sea', 6 April 2006

Page 108: A retired marine manager for shipping underwriters Lloyds Register ... Stieghorst, Tom, 'Massive new cruise ship holds 5,000 people – and bigger potential for safety problems', *The Seattle Times*, 8 May 2006, http://seattletimes.nwsource.com/html/traveloutdoors/2002980817_webcruiseship08.html

Page 108: Maurizio Cergol, chief designer for Italian shipbuilders Fincantieri ... 'Just when you thought ships couldn't get bigger', *Los Angeles Times*, 30 April 2006

Page 109: Carnival president Bob Dickinson told a Seatrade conference ... 'All aboard the megacruisers: but where will they put 6,000 deckchairs?' *The Mail on Sunday* (UK), 19 March 2006

Page 109: ... in *The Times***, Adam Goldstein, CEO, stated ...** Jameson, Angela, 'Royal Caribbean steers course for more giant ships', *The Times*, 29 April 2006

Page 109: Norwegian's CEO Colin Veitch likewise noted ... Martinez, Amy, 'NCL strikes its biggest ship deal', MiamiHerald.com, www.miami.com/mld/miamiherald/business/15464901.htm?source=rss&channel=miamiherald_business (posted 8 September 2006)

12: ... or Cheap and Cheerful?

Page 111: As *The Guardian's* **correspondent wrote ...** Wollaston, Sam, 'And it was all orange', *The Guardian*, 14 May 2005

Page 111: The orange, reported a 'queasy' *Daily Mail* **journalist ...** Moore, Victoria, 'Bargain ... or sleasycruise?', *Daily Mail*, 17 May 2005

Page 112: Stelios, easyCruise's ebullient founder waved at the QEII passengers ... Chessyre, Tom, 'Is the future of cruising orange?', *The Times*, 7 May 2005

Page 112: The inaugural sailing of *easyCruiseTwo* **took place in August 2006 ...** Robbins, Tom, 'Cruising for some serious boozing', *The Observer*, 20 August 2006

Page 112: Stelios has announced further expansion plans ... 'Easy does it', *The Sunday Times*, 14 May 2006

Pages 112–113 Meanwhile, a second series of *Cruise with Stelios* **...** Silver, James, 'Branding a decade of easy', *The Independent*, 19 June 2006

13: Going Overboard

Pages 115–116: ... Dennis Hughson and Alan Welsh have been onboard ... Author's interviews with Dennis Hughson and Alan Welsh

Pages 116–117: The *Pacific Sky's* **third man overboard was not so fortunate ...** Lawrence, Jessica, 'I'll keep looking – father's vow on son lost overboard', *The Sunday Herald Sun* (Melbourne), 16 January 2005

Page 117: One passenger who made it overboard and survived was Tim Sears ... 'Cruise survivor: "I made peace with God"', *ABC News*, 26 January 2006

14: Not a Bang but a Whimper

Pages 119–121: Daina Brampton, a former *Fairstar* bar steward, has vivid memories ... Author's interview with Daina Brampton

Page 120: Bev, another former *Fairstar* steward, believes there was a direct connection ... Author's interview with Bev, a former *Fairstar* steward

Page 120: Murray Ferguson, fed up with schoolies ... Author's interview with Murray Ferguson

Page 121: A Cunard spokesman 'did not know' ... Author's interview with Cunard spokesman

Page 121: Katie, another former *Fairstar* steward, recalls ... Author's interview with Katie, a former *Fairstar* steward

Pages 122–123: Anita, a nurse who spent ten years at sea ... Author's interview with Anita, a former cruise ship nurse

Page 122: ... as a study in the Journal of the American Geriatrics Society confirmed ... Lindquist, Lee, *Journal of the American Geriatrics Society*, November 2004, quoted in 'Till death us do part', *The Economist*, 28 October 2004

15: What Lies Beneath

Page 124: The inequality of the world, say anti-poverty campaigners ... Wazir, Burhan, and Mathiason, Nick, 'Cruise liner crews slave below decks', *The Observer*, 8 September 2002

Page 124: Sandy, a former bar steward, said ... Author's interview with Sandy, a former bar steward

Page 125: Daina Brampton, who started work for P&O in the 1990s ... Author's interview with Daina Brampton

Page 125: Bob Dickinson, Carnival CEO, says that strict regulations ... Dickinson, Bob and Vladimir, Andy, *Selling the Seas: an inside look at the cruise industry*, John Wiley & Sons, New York, 1997

Page 126: A British croupier, Richard Arghiris, who had initially shared a cabin ... Author's interview with Richard Arghiris

Page 126: In one case recorded by International Transport Workers' Federation ... Wazir, Burhan, and Mathiason, Nick, 'Cruise liner crews slave below decks', *The Observer*, 8 September 2002

Notes

Page 127: Marine consultant Peter Burge said ... Author's interview with Peter Burge

Page 127: One Indian kitchen worker, doing eleven-hour shifts ... Wazir, Burhan, and Mathiason, Nick, 'Cruise liner crews slave below decks', *The Observer*, 8 September 2002

Page 127: An Australian woman who worked as a steward ... Author's interview with former cruise ship steward

Page 128: Cruise ship security officer Randy Jaques, who claims ... Author's interview with Randy Jaques

Page 128: Peter Burge agrees ... Author's interview with Peter Burge

Page 128: Lawyer Charles Lipcon, whose firm represents ... Author's interview with Charles R. Lipcon

Page 128: Anita, a nurse who was employed through a British Agency ... Author's interview with Anita, a former cruise ship nurse

Pages 128–129: The fifty-six-year-old Jamaican claims to have served ... Culliford, Graeme, 'Lynsey jumped', *Daily Mail*, 18 April 2006

Page 129: Between 2001 and 2003 a fraudster posing as a cruise ship agent ... Byrne, Eileen, 'Moroccan jobless left adrift', *BBC News*, 12 June 2002; 'Fraudster must be caught', *International Transport Magazine*, January 2003

Page 129 Even on the *Hebridean Princess* ... Smith, Thomas, 'Lat of luxury', *The Sunday Mirror* (UK), 9 July 2006

Pages 129–130: A study by the Seafarers' International Research Centre ... Whitfield, Martin, 'Smile please', *Transport International*, March 2004

Page 130: It is simply their nature to exceed ... Oceania Cruises, brochure: 'Impeccable service comes naturally', 2006, p 4

Pages 130–131: One Australian woman who had worked alongside Indonesians ... Author's interview with former cruise ship worker

Page 131: In his book *Cruise Ship Blues*, Ross Klein recounts ... Klein, Ross A., *Cruise Ship Blues: the underside of the cruise industry*, 2002, New Society Publishers, p 125

Pages 131–132: An Indian worker who has worked on many ships ... Author's interview with Carnival cruise ship crew member

Page 132: Crew often have to pay a bond to their employer... Torres, John A., web special report: 'Canaveral's crews: The people and profits behind the port's cruise ship party', *Florida Today*, 18 July 2006, www.floridatoday.com/apps/pbcs.dll/article?AID=/99999999/NEWS01/512110312/0/news07 (viewed July 2006)

Pages 132–133: A man from Liverpool in Sydney's western suburbs ... Author's interview with P&O passengers

16: Love Boats

Pages 134–135: The actress Zsa Zsa Gabor was married ... 'Short shelf life of celebrity marriage', BBC News website, 16 September 2005, http://news.bbc.co.uk/2/hi/entertainment/4252290.stm

Page 135: ... consider the cautionary tale of Stella Bates ... Roper, Matt, 'My husband ran off on honeymoon', *Daily Mirror* (UK), 13 May 2006

Page 136: An American nursing journal recently sounded a warning note ... Ericksen, Anne Baye, 'Career Cruisin' ', *Minority Nurse*, 14 February 2001, www.minoritynurse.com/features/nurse_emp/02-14-01a.html

Page 136: Douglas Ward's Berlitz *Complete Guide to Cruising* also warns ... Ward, Douglas, *Complete Guide to Cruising & Cruise Ships 2006*, Berlitz, London, 2006, p 72

Page 136: Carnival's CEO has noted publicly ... Dickinson, Bob and Vladimir, Andy, *Selling the Seas: an inside look at the cruise industry*, John Wiley & Sons, New York, 1997, p 75

Page 136: High-profile casualties of their own libido have included ... Martin, Stephen, 'Queen's cruise ship captain was sacked for being a jolly rogerer', *The Sunday Mirror*, 12 February 2006

Page 136: One woman who used to work for P&O has warning words ... Author's interview with Katie, a former *Fairstar* steward

Pages 136–137: One envious passenger ... Author's interview with Dennis Hughson

Page 137: Another former P&O crew member, Sandy, confirmed ... Author's interview with Sandy, former cruise ship steward

Pages 137–138: Stephen, a former crew member on the *Fair Princess*, could shed some light ... Author's interview with Stephen (not his real name), a former crew member on the *Fair Princess*

Page 138: *The Wall Street Journal* **has reported that some gentlemen** ... Stringer, Kortney, 'Cruise Lines Offer A Unique Opportunity', *College Journal* (from the Wall Street Journal Online website), www.collegejournal.com/salarydata/hotelrestaurant/20030328-stringer.html (viewed May 2006)

Page 139: The TV presenter Esther Rantzen, having tried out one of their cruises ... Rantzen, Esther, 'Water way to get away', *Daily Mail*, 9 July 2005

Page 139: Guests on a 2005 Nile cruise were smitten ... Weathers, Helen, 'An officer and a conman', *Daily Mail*, 15 April 2006

Page 140: Perhaps the most notorious was Giovanni Vigliotto ... 'Man with 105 Wives is sentenced to 34 years', *The New York Times*, 29 March 1983; Anecdotage website, www.anecdotage.com/about.php (viewed May 2006)

Pages 140–141: In retrospect, it would have been good if a certain Diann from Florida ... www.consumeraffairs.com/travel/carnival_cruise_lines.htm (viewed May 2006); www.4swinging.com/DESTINATIONS/playful.htm (viewed May 2006)

Page 141: Among the passengers on the ultra-luxurious Seabourn boats ... Author's interview with Lawrence (not his real name), a British cruise industry insider and regular passenger on cruise ships

Page 141: When it comes to hosting the most Dionysian of rituals ... Smith, Helena, 'Greek police investigate "sex party" cruise', *The Observer*, 27 June 2004

Pages 142–143: Shelley Sparkman, thirty, of Malibu... 'Ombudsman: sex sails', *Condé Nast Traveler*, September 2004, www.concierge.com/cntraveler/articles/detail?articleId=5909

17: Mutiny!

Pages 145–150: Dr Stuart Romm, a former CEO ... Author's interview with Dr Stuart Romm

Page 146: A British passenger, Peter Normanton, was one ... *Holidays Undercover*, ITV1 (UK), broadcast 25 July 2006

Page 148: People have got stress, anxiety and depression ... 'QM2 passengers begin legal action', BBC News website, 26 January 2006, http://news.bbc.co.uk/1/hi/world/americas/4645316.stm

Page 149: **Many people on the ship are happy to force** ...
' "Mutiny" cruise to dock in Brazil', BBC News website,
26 January 2006, http://news.bbc.co.uk/1/hi/world/
americas/4651322.stm

Page 150: **We were prisoners on a luxury ship** ... Downe, Andrew
and Iggulden, Amy, 'Cunard foils QM2 mutiny with full refund offer',
The Daily Telegraph (UK), 28 January 2006

Page 151: **But the memory must have been fresh** ... Hamilton, Alan,
'New queen designed to rule the seas', *The Times*, 17 February 2006

18: Short and Sweet

Page 153: **A retired banker in one of the two-storey penthouses**
... Naughton, Philippe, 'Still staring at Blighty', Times Online, 12 January
2005

Page 154: **But back on land, O'Connor told the** *Daily Mail* ...
Mouland, Bill, 'Busy going nowhere', *Daily Mail*, 13 January 2005

Page 154: **... Margaret Smith, fifty-nine, from Manchester, said**
... Smith, Laura, 'Ultimate booze cruise went nowhere in style', *The
Guardian*, 22 January 2005

Page 155: *The Times* **reported that a spokeswoman for Carnival**
... Pavia, Will, 'Jinxed cruise ship hits trouble again', *The Times*,
30 December 2005

19: Storms in the Ports

Pages 156–157: **Ahead of the stopover in Fiji** ... Author's interview
with Stephen (not his real name), former crew member on the *Fair
Princess*

Page 158: **The third of three separate deaths in quick succession**
... 'Events at sea', Cruise Junkie website, www.cruisejunkie.com/events.
html

Page 158: **When one of the small luxury Hebridean ships added
certain Indian ports** ... Author's interview with Lawrence (not his real
name), a British cruise industry insider and regular passenger on cruise
ships

Page 159: **Passengers on one** *QE2* **voyage down to South
America** ... Author's interview with Lawrence

20: That's Entertainment

Page 161: He would not be allowed to forget his early life either ... Johnson, Boris, 'Admit it, Blair', *The Daily Telegraph* (UK), 27 July 2006

Page 162: In the space of a few months in *The Times* ... Beautiful South review, 16 October; Cybill Shepherd review, 30 September; 'On his Todd: Rundgren live lacks the polish of his latest CD', 17 July; 'Songs my mother taught me', 8 July; *The Times*, 2004

Page 164: ... as Douglas Ward, a pre-eminent global cruising critic, puts it ... Ward, Douglas, *Complete Guide to Cruising & Cruise Ships 2006*, Berlitz, London, 2006, p 105

Page 164: According to one regular passenger ... Author's interview with Lawrence (not his real name), a British cruise industry insider and regular passenger on cruise ships

Pages 164–165: They definitely maintain the traditions ... Author's interview with P&O UK spokeswoman

Page 165: In Australia, where gambling has become a lucrative industry ... Allen, Lisa, 'Gambling laws all at sea', *The Australian Financial Review*, 21 April 2006

Page 165: ... P&O Princess Cruises last year agreed to support ... Kruger, Colin, 'Tabcorp, P&O book casino trip', *The Sydney Morning Herald*, 22 June 2005

Page 165: ... waiting passengers were issued with vouchers ... Gibbs, Stephen, 'Passengers sent to casino', *The Sydney Morning Herald*, 3 July 2006

Page 166: An Australian couple who enjoyed a cruise ... Author's interview with Dianne Pryor

21: Captive State

Page 168: In the autumn of 1922 ... Burleigh, Michael, review of *The Philosophy Steamer* by Lesley Chamberlain, *The Sunday Telegraph* (UK), 12 March 2006

Page 169: One astonishing story from 1970s Britain came to light ... Levy, Geoffrey, 'A very British coup', *Daily Mail*, 13 March 2006

Page 170: In April 2006, a headline told ... 'Tough new Pacific solution: refugees to be sent on P&O cruise', The Chaser website, 19 April 2006, www.chaser.com.au/index.php?option=com_content&task=view&id=3121&Itemid=26

Page 170: A plan was indeed announced ... 'Govt under fire over prison "mother ship" plan', ABC News Online, 3 August 2006, www.abc.net.au/news/newsitems/200608/s1704803.htm

22: Disaster! From Rogue Waves to Infernos

Pages 171–172: The *Norwegian Dawn* had been sailing through a storm off the coast of Georgia ... Broad, William J., 'Rogue giants at sea', *The New York Times*, 11 July 2006

Page 172: Increased reports from ships and offshore oil rigs prompted research ... 'Ship-sinking monster waves revealed by ESA satellites', European Space Agency website, 21 July 2004, www.esa.int/esaCP/SEMOKQL26WD_index_0.html

Page 173: According to German researchers who studied the incident ... Broad, William J., 'Rogue giants at sea', *The New York Times*, 11 July 2006

Page 173: In 2004, the U.S. Naval Research Laboratory measured ... Sherriff, Lucy, 'Hurricane Ivan prompts rogue wave rethink', *The Register*, 5 August 2005

Pages 174–175: There was nothing to worry unsuspecting passengers ... Reuters, 'Florida, passengers injured', 18 July 2006, quoted in *Daily Mirror* (UK), 20 July 2006, and *Daily Mail* (UK), 20 July 2006

Pages 175–179: Despite the deep suspicions and hostility ... 'The Mikhail Lermontov', *The New Zealand Maritime Record*, New Zealand National Maritime Museum, www.nzmaritime.co.nz/lermontov.htm (viewed May 2006); 'Mikhail Lermontov (ship)', Wikipedia, http://en.wikipedia.org/wiki/Mikhail_Lermontov_(ship) (viewed May 2006)

Pages 176–178: Passenger Nicole Blaser (now Ristev) was just ten years old ... Author's interview with Nicole Ristev

Page 178 ... lawsuits relating to the case would drag on for many years afterwards ... Cahalan, Adrienne, *Around the Buoys with Champion Yachtswoman and Navigator Adrienne Cahalan*, Random House Australia, Sydney, 2006, p 109

Page 179: Trijintje Bos was one of those ... *Holidays Undercover*, ITV1 (UK), broadcast 25 July 2006

Page 180: Fire regulations on board have been tightened up ... 'Giant liner refitted after fire safety alert', *The Times*, 25 June 2004

23: Diving In

Pages 182–184: It had not been an auspicious start ... O'Malley B., 'Crew lock up skipper on cruise from hell', *The Courier-Mail*, 30 October 1998; Meade, Kevin, 'Skipper "unfit" for trial after mutiny', *The Australian*, 17 December 1998; Meade, Kevin, 'Hell cruise skipper freed', *The Australian*, 6 May 1999

Pages 184–186: Earlier that year, something had happened ... Fickling, David, 'The cruel sea', *The Guardian*, 23 July 2004

Pages 185–186: Extracts from the Lonergans' diaries, found in their room ... Foggo, Daniel, 'A mystery resurfaces', *The Age*, 7 August 2004

Pages 186–187: In Florida in 2000, a similar sized boat ... Warren, Steve, 'Missing', *Diver Magazine*, September 2004

24: The New Dawn

Pages 189–190: Royal Caribbean has even joined forces ... 'FAQs', The Scholar Ship website, www.thescholarship.com/home/facts_at_glance/

Pages 190–191: ... it is marked by a 'pervasive emptiness', said one journalist ... Burkeman, Oliver, 'The World at war', *The Guardian*, 13 July 2004

Page 191: The Aeroscraft, a new type of airship ... Bowes, Gemma, 'Cruise ship of the skies', *The Observer*, 5 March 2006

Page 191: As the polar caps melt ... Vidal, John, 'Arctic meltdown open to abuse', *The Guardian*, 1 February 2006

Page 192: As Carnival's CEO Bob Dickinson has said ... Dickinson, Bob and Vladimir, Andy, *Selling the Seas: an inside look at the cruise industry*, John Wiley & Sons, New York, 1997

Page 192: ... voted the worst match of any song and advertised product ... Stevenson, Seth, 'What's the worst ad song ever?', *Slate*, 6 June 2005, www.slate.com/id/2120229/

Index

abandonment at sea 184–7
Abbas, Abu 93
academic cruises 189
accidents 173–5
Achille Lauro 92–3, 180–1
Adonia see Sea Princess
Ahern, Dermot 7
al-Qaeda 90, 94, 99
al-Sakka, Louai 94
Alaska 12, 34, 38, 42, 47, 48
alcohol 1–2, 5, 7, 8–9, 17, 27,
  52–60, 62, 70, 71, 77, 79,
  117, 153, 165, 167, 176
Alexandria 90, 92, 95
SS *America* 168
Angelina Lauro 180
Antarctica 42
Aqua Nut II 186
Arghiris, Richard 126
Arnold, Katie 66–7
Artemis 189
Askin, Josh 8
assault 52, 58, 80
Aurora 18–21, 24, 26, 152–5,
  163, 167
Australia 29, 52–60, 61–7,
  85, 189
Ayia Napa Queen 141

Background Briefing 39
Bahamas 17, 48, 74
Bald, Gary 101
Bates, Stella 135
Beattie, Peter 46
Belize 41, 48
Berlusconi, Silvio 160–1
bird flu 30
Black Prince 27–8, 167
Blue Lady 50
Bluewater Network 38

Bogush, Gillian 174
Bos, Trijinte 179
Brampton, Daina 57, 66,
  119–21, 125
Bremen 173
bribes 158–9
Brilliance of the Seas 8, 9
Brimble, Dianne *vii*, 68–72, 80,
  82, 88, 188
Brimble, Mark 72, 83
Brisbane 46, 69, 86, 106, 116
Burge, Peter 78, 81, 82, 127,
  128
Byrd, Kurt and Sharon 6

Caledonian Star 173
Calypso 179
Caribbean 46, 87, 105, 122,
  173
Carnival Celebration 117
Carnival Cruise Lines 33–4,
  37, 48, 49, 65, 76, 101,
  132, 141, 149, 155, 164,
  188
Carnival Destiny 1, 3
Carnival Festival 127
Carnival Imagination 140
Carnival Inspiration 166
Carnival Legend 114, 116
Carnival Pride 2–3
Caronia 24, 87
Carver, Kendall 13–14, 17
Carver, Merrian 12–14
Celebration 24, 88
Celebrity Cruises 13, 26, 29, 87
Celebrity Millennium 158
Centers for Disease Control
  (CDC) Vessel Sanitisation
  Program 23, 27, 150
Cergol, Maurizio 108

Chalk, Peter 102
Coburn, Tom 50
USS *Cole* 90, 95
computer training cruises 189
Concordia 106
Condé Nast Traveler 142
Confalonieri, Fedele 161
contamination 21, 22
Cordon, David 25
Costa Allegra 188
Costa Cruises 7, 106–7, 128–9,
  188, 189
Costa Magica 5, 128
Courier-Mail, The 183
crashes 176–9
crimes 73–85
Crown Princess 173–4
cruise ship industry, future of
  188–94
Cruise with Stelios 112
Crye, Michael 15, 39
Crystal Cruises 34
cultural insensitivities 44–5
Cunard 24, 90, 101, 104, 107,
  121, 144–51, 154, 164,
  170
Cunningham, Dwayne 89

Daily Express 100, 101
Daily Mail 24, 111, 128, 139,
  154
Daily Telegraph, The (Sydney),
  57, 59, 66, 80
Daily Telegraph, The (UK),
  19, 22
Daniels, Paul 154
de Alba, Felipe 135
death 3, 7, 20, 92–3, 121,
  145, 158, 178, 179,
  180

Brimble, Dianne 68–72
Death on the High Seas Act (DOHSA) 16–17
development of cruise terminals 46
Diamond Princess 104
diarrhoea 151
Dickerson, Thomas 17
Dickinson, Bob 109, 125, 192
  Selling the Seas 38
Dickinson, Mark 100
Dingle, David 153
DiPiero, Daniel 17
disappearances 1–17
  Carver, Merrian 12–14
  DiPiero, Daniel 17
  Hue Pham and Hue Tran 1, 3–4
  Kanesaki, Micki 17
  Mazey, Mark Anthony 1–2
  Mizener, Annette 2–3
  O'Brien, Lynsey 5–7
  Smith, George Allen IV 8–11
disasters 171–81
Discovery 43
disease *see* illness
Disney Cruise Line 87
Disney Magic
Diver 186, 187
Dobjeckie, Jeff 59, 80
drink-spiking *see* alcohol
drugs 5, 56, 69–70, 79, 86–9

easyCruiseOne 110–12
easyCruiseTwo 112
Elation 48
elderly travellers 119–23
Ellman, Louise 100
Enchantment of the Seas 87
entertainment 2, 124, 154, 160–6
environmental awareness 38–9
  see also pollution
Environmental Protection Agency 33, 39
epidemics *see* illness
Essef Corp 29
evacuations 177
Evans, Michael and Lynda 186

facilities 104–9, 122, 144, 190
Fain, Richard 103, 106
Fair Princess 30, 65–6, 137, 156
Fairstar 35, 60, 61–7, 119, 121, 134
Fairstar Shipping Corporation 35

falls/jumps overboard 5–7, 114–18
FBI 3, 10, 12, 15, 73, 75, 77, 78, 101, 102, 103
Ferguson, Kelley Marie 91
Ferguson, Murray 62, 64, 120
Fiji 156–7
Fincantieri 108
fires 7, 108, 179–81
Florida Today 48
food poisoning 22
Forney, David 27, 28
SS *France* 50–1, 166
Fred. Olsen Cruise Lines 27–8
Freedom of the Seas 37, 104, 105, 109
Freemantle, Penny 148
Freewinds 189
Frommer, Arthur 85
Furlong, Geoff 78, 81

Gabor, Zsa Zsa 134
gambling 2, 165
gay cruises 189
GeekCruises 189
Genesis 106
Gibraltar 21, 100
Golden Princess 42
Goldstein, Adam 12, 109
Goossens, Reuben 61
Grand Princess 175
Gready, Andrew Mark 117
Greenpeace 51
Greenwood, Major Alexander 169
Guardian, The 25, 43, 111

Haji-Ioannou, Stelios 110, 112
Harman, Nigel 162
Hatzistergos, John 30
Hawaiian King 180
Hawn, Goldie 26
Hebridean Princess 94, 129, 136
Herzigova, Eva 106
hijacking *see* terrorism
Ho Chi Minh City 65
hoaxes 57, 91, 139
Holidays Undercover 23, 25, 78, 81, 146, 179
Holland America Line 37, 42
Horizon 29, 87
Horler, Andy 149
Howard, John 170, 193
Hughes, Paul and Fran 25–6
Hughson, Dennis 115, 116
Hurricane Katrina 48, 49, 169
Hyman, Clete 9

illness 18–31, 122–3, 152, 167, 183
influenza 29, 30
International Convention for the Safety of Life at Sea *see* SOLAS Convention
International Council of Cruise Lines (ICCL) 3, 15, 39, 75, 76, 78, 167, 191
International Cruise Victims (ICV) 11, 14, 72, 80–1, 83–4
International Maritime Bureau 99
International Transport Workers' Federation 125, 126
Interpol 74
Island Escape 17

Jamison, Don 177
Jaques, Randy 77–9, 80, 81, 82, 128
Journal of the American Geriatrics Society 122

Kanesaki, Micki 17
Karim Palace 23
Kazarian, Olga and Robert 187
Klein, Ross A.
  Cruise Ship Blues 45, 48–9, 131
Klinghoffer, Leon 92–3
Knerler, Wally and Heidi 2
Krishnamurthy, Ramesh 114

Lawracy, Robert 89
Lee, Dr Henry 10
Legend of the Seas 91
legionnaire's disease 29
Liberty of the Seas 105
life on board 53–5, 58–9
Lipcon, Charles R. 15, 75, 79, 128
litigation 7–8, 11–12, 16–17, 22, 29, 33–4, 75–7, 128, 149, 184
Lonergan, Eileen and Tom 184–6
Los Angeles Times 41, 49, 85
Louis Cruise Lines 91, 179
Ludwig, Joe 170

McBride, Grant 60
McDonald, Jane 162
McGhee, Paul 98
Mcilwraith, Captain Sir Alan 139
McIntyre, Robert S. 49

Mail on Sunday 108
Majesty 87
mal de debarquement (MDD) 29
Malaysia 99
Malta 100
Mariner of the Seas 17
Maritime Investigations International 80
Marlow, Carol 149–50
MARPOL Convention 32, 34, 35
marriages *see* weddings
Mazey, Mark Anthony 1–2
Meagher, Bob and Gayle 98
Mediaset 161
Mediterranean 18, 19, 25, 26, 122, 141
meningococcal disease 30
Mercury 13, 26–7
Mexico 1, 5, 27, 91
Michelangelo 173
Mikhail Lermontov 175–9
military use of cruise ships 168–70
Milledge, Jacqueline 72
Millennium 87
Miller, Gregory 1–2
Mirror, The 135
missing persons *see* disappearances
Mizener, Annette 2–3
morgues 121
Moulton, Earle 128–9
Mukundan, Captain Pottengal 99
Mulvaney, Brian 7
mutinies 144–51, 167, 183–4

Nairn, Jack 185
Neorion Holdings 112
New Caledonia 56, 63
New York Times, The 173
Newcastle Herald, The 96
niche interest cruises 189
Nordic Empress 87
Normanton, Peter 146
norovirus outbreaks 18–22, 30, 31, 121
NorthWest CruiseShip Association 48
Norwalk virus 18–21, 28
SS *Norway* 50, 179
Norwegian Cruise Line 34, 35, 49, 62, 87, 109
Norwegian Dawn 171–2, 189
Norwegian Star 1
Noumea 62, 63, 70
nudity 59, 70, 142–3, 189
NUMAST 100

O'Brien, Kelly 5
O'Brien, Lynsey 5–7, 16, 128–9
O'Brien, Paul 5–7
Observer, The 51, 112, 141
Oceana 23, 24, 163
Oceana Cruises 36, 130
O'Connor, Tom 154
MV *Outer Edge* 184–5
Oxfordshire 61

P & O 18, 24, 26, 30, 35, 44, 58, 60, 65, 66, 71–2, 84, 88, 125, 132, 136, 154, 155, 157, 163, 164, 189
Pacific Dawn 66, 106
Pacific Islands *xiv*, 63
Pacific Sky vii, 30, 56–9, 66, 68–72, 80, 115, 116, 158
Pacific Sun 30, 52, 62, 66, 133, 166, 175, 189
  Runaway to Sea cruise 53–5
Palestinian Liberation Front 92–3
Panama 45, 49, 87
Parry, Rear Admiral Chris 100
Parsons, Nicholas 162
Passenger Vessel Association 135
Pattullo, Polly
  Last Resorts: the cost of tourism in the Caribbean 48
Pham, Hue 1, 3–4
Pham, Son Michael 3–4, 5, 14, 15, 16–17, 81
piracy 91, 95–103
political unrest 156–7, 169
pollution 32–40, 51–1
popularity of cruises 192–4
pornographic films 142
Prescott, John 161
Preussen 168
Pride of Aloha 35
Primetime 5, 6
Princess Cruise Line 23, 25, 37, 43, 106, 134, 165, 173, 175
prison ships 168–9
private islands 49

Queen Elizabeth 169
Queen Elizabeth 2 23, 35, 37, 90, 101, 111, 121, 159, 170, 172
Queen Mary 2 101, 104, 121, 145–50, 152, 154, 164, 167, 180, 189
Queen Victoria 107, 151

Rantzen, Esther 139
rape *see* sexual assault
Reagan, Ronald 175
Reef Explorer 182–4
Regal Princess 22, 26, 106
religious cults 189
Reno, Janet 33
Ristev, Nicole (nee Blaser) 176–8
Rivkind, Brett 8, 17, 76, 82
robbery 5
Rogers, Mike 98
rogue waves 171–3
romance 134–43
Romm, Dr Stuart 145–50
Rosenthal, Dr Wolfgang 173
Royal Caribbean International 8, 9, 11–12, 13–14, 27, 33, 37, 38, 39, 49, 87, 91, 102, 103, 104, 105, 109, 132, 169, 189, 192
  Project *Genesis* 105
Royal Olympic Cruises 142, 143
rubella 29
Ruby 24
Russell, Llew 100, 102

safety *see also* security
  Cruise Line Accurate Safety Statistics (CLASS) Act 82
  emergency procedures 108
  International Cruise Victims 80–1, 83–4
  Pacific Sky 2003 56–8
  ports of call, in 156–9
Saga 24, 139
San Diego 27
San Diego Union-Tribune, The 27
Sansonetti, Tom 34
Savitz, Jackie 37, 39–40
Scholar Ship 189–90
schoolies cruises 56–8
Schwarzenegger, Arnold 34
Sea 87
Sea Diamond 91
Sea Princess 25, 26
Seabourn Cruises 141
Seabourn Spirit 95–9, 100, 101
Seafarers' International Research Centre (SIRC) 129–30
Sears, Tim 117–18
Seattle Times, The 27, 108
security 15–16, 71–2, 80–2
  anti-terrorism measures 94–5
  congressional hearings 4, 7, 11, 16, 73, 76

piracy, against 100–3
sewage 32, 34
sexual assault 3, 5, 10, 58, 71, 73–5, 76, 78–9, 128
   Kelly, Janet 77
   Natalie W, rape victim 73–5
   Smith, April 76
sexual behaviour 58–9, 61, 70–1, 136–43
sexually transmitted diseases 28, 136
sharks 116
Shays, Congressman Christopher 4, 13–14, 16, 73, 82
Shepherd, Cybill 162
Shepherd-Irwin, Kathryn 158
Shipping Australia 100
Shore, Teri 38, 39
sickness *see* illness
Simmonds, Gavin 100
Sky Princess 136
Smith, Bree 10
Smith, Gavin 84
Smith, George Allen IV 8–11, 13, 103
Smith, Jennifer Hagel 8–10, 12
Smith, Margaret 154
Smith, Neville 150
smuggling 86–9
Soames, Nicholas 161
SOLAS Convention 100
Somalia 96, 99
Southampton 18, 21, 25, 26, 88, 145, 152, 153
Sparkman, Shelley 142–3
Speight, George 157

staff 77, 124–33 *see also* working conditions
   Anita, nurse 122–3, 128
   Bev, former steward 120
   Katie, former steward 121
   Sandy, former steward 124, 137
   Stephen, former crew member 137, 156
Star Princess 108, 180
Stephanis, Costas 20
Strathaird xii, 44
Straw, Jack 21
Suez Canal 61, 90, 153
Summit 37, 87, 150
Sunday Mirror, The 129, 136
Sunday Telegraph 59
Supple, Dr Charles 95–6, 99
Sweeney, Claire 162
swingers' cruises 140–1
Sydney 29, 52, 61, 104
Sydney Morning Herald, The vii, viii, 56, 58, 62, 65

Tarbuck, Jimmy 154
taxes 49
Taylor, Ann 71
Temple, Tracey 161
terrorism 90–5
Thompson, Mary Anne 55
Tiger Lily 186
Times, The 27, 109, 112, 153, 155, 162
toolies 57–8
tourism, effect of 41–3, 63
Tran, Hue 1, 3–4
tuberculosis 29

typhoid 30

MV *Van Gogh* 24–5
Vanuatu 2, 59
Veitch, Colin 109
Verrender, Ian 44, 63
Vigliotto, Giovanni 140
violence *see* assault
viruses *see* illness

Wanless, Mr 30
Ward, Douglas 164
   Berlitz *Complete Guide to Cruising & Cruise Ships 2006* 66, 136
Warwick, Ronald 147, 172
Washington Post, The 49, 50
Watkins, Graham 43
waves, rogue *see* rogue waves
weddings 25–6, 134–5
Welsh, Alan 115, 116
whales, protection of 37
Which? 24
Wilhelm Gustloff 168
Williams, Andrew 19
Wilson, Harold 169, 170
Wisdom, Sir Norman 163
Wood, Alma 69
Woodcock, Joshua 26
working conditions 124–33
Working Vacation Inc 138
The World 190
Wright, Captain Bill 11, 39

Zenith 87